THE PEGASUS DIARIES

THE PEGASUS DIARIES

John Howard

and

Penny Howard Bates

Pen & Sword
MILITARY

First published in Great Britain in 2006 by
PEN & SWORD MILITARY
an imprint of
Pen & Sword Books Ltd
47 Church Street
Barnsley
South Yorkshire
S70 2AS

Typeset in 10/12 Baskerville by Concept, Huddersfield, West Yorkshire
Printed and bound in England by Biddles Ltd

Pen & Sword Books Ltd incorporates the Imprints of
Pen & Sword Aviation, Pen & Sword Maritime, Pen & Sword Military,
Wharncliffe Local History, Pen & Sword Select,
Pen & Sword Military Classics and Leo Cooper

For a complete list of Pen & Sword titles please contact
PEN & SWORD BOOKS LIMITED
47 Church Street, Barnsley, South Yorkshire, S70 2AS, England
E-mail: enquiries@pen-and-sword.co.uk
Website: www.pen-and-sword.co.uk

Contents

Foreword

by

Lieutenant General Sir Michael Gray
KCB OBE DL

Chairman Airborne Assault Normandy Trust

T he story of Major John Howard's D-Day, glider borne, assault to capture the bridges over the Caen Canal and River Orne, has become one of the legends of the Normandy landings. Later, the canal bridge was renamed 'Pegasus Bridge' in honour of 6 Airborne Division. The name of the winged horse, Pegasus, ridden by Bellerophon, was chosen because it was the battle emblem, or flash, which all Airborne Forces wore so proudly on their uniforms.

The spectacularly successful nature of the night glider landings, the surprise they achieved, and the clinical effectiveness in which the operation was carried through with absolute precision, created immediate early interest. The long awaited return into Europe had started and the press had urgent need to relay good tidings to a public anxiously awaiting news, and this they did with gusto. The film *The Longest Day* later highlighted the story.

This book draws on John Howard's personal diaries, and gives a very private insight into the man who was selected to command and train a company group of raw young soldiers and then lead them to their destiny. On its own, the *coup de main* onto the bridges had no great strategic importance to the overall success of the Allied Operation OVERLORD. It was one of many crucial, sub-unit operations, executed by 6 Airborne Division, in a patchwork of events that sealed the critical eastern flank of the Allied landings on that longest of days.

What is significant to the story of the man and about which I have personal knowledge, is that, after the war, John Howard volunteered as one of a small group of veterans who were able to give of their time, to return to France to be guest speakers on the annual Army Staff College battlefield tours. He did this twenty-seven times!

Students from the College were able for three days, to listen to the stories of what occurred on 6 June 1944 and afterwards, on the actual ground in Normandy where it happened. They were able to study the detail of the battles through the eyes of those who fought them. For the generations of officers who sat at John Howard's feet, his story was exceptionally popular because it had glamour and he told it with such enormous enthusiasm.

Years later, when the Caen Canal had to be widened and a new bridge installed, the old bridge had become a symbol of the Airborne landings and was retained as a battlefield monument. It is now preserved in the grounds of the Airborne museum Memorial Pegasus alongside that same canal. A sculpted bronze bust of John Howard stands where his gliders landed. It has become a very popular tourist site.

John Howard's character and experience were ideally suited to the meticulously thorough planning and training required of such an operation. The narrative describes graphically, in his words, how committed he was to ensuring success, and shows his sensitivity to the well-being of his officers and men. Miraculously only one officer and one of his soldiers were killed in this attack but even this hurt him deeply.

The awards of a Distinguished Service Order and a *Croix de Guerre* for his leadership and bravery, were of enormous personal significance. John was always extremely conscious, as he puts it, '. . . of being a ranker promoted to the officers' mess'. Before the Second World War this was not a common occurrence and to be a major and achieve such awards was a vindication of all that he had set himself.

The success of capturing the bridges was surely the high point of John Howard's military life. It is sad that this elation was soon crushed by a patch of very bad luck. A few days later in a fierce fire-fight, in the village of Escoville, he was shot through his helmet, wounded and stunned, and had to hand the company over to his second in command. In this battle fifty-eight of his men were 'massacred' (his words). This was a 'body-blow' to John's compassion and, as if that was not sufficient, he was later wounded again with shrapnel in his back, during a mortar attack. He returned to England where, two months later, he had a catastrophic road accident from which he never fully recovered. He left the Army in September 1945.

This book adds significantly to the depth of the Pegasus Bridge story. As a young man John Howard had to 'pull himself up by his bootstraps' in order to achieve personal ambitions. It also shows just how complicated life was in wartime for a married soldier and dedicated family man. No matter how caring and sensitive his nature, he had to be aggressively determined to survive. What comes across very clearly is his disciplined approach to life and a single mindedness which enabled him to focus on priorities and to lead such a meticulously planned and successful operation on D-Day.

Later it took him a long time to come to terms with life as a disabled civilian, but, once he was settled, his luck began to change, mainly, I suspect, because of his own perseverance. He was appointed to a new and worthwhile civilian job, based in Oxford, which restored his confidence. This permanence also presented an opportunity, in his spare time, to be of immense value, telling his wartime story to the Army Staff College and to the Airborne Assault Normandy Trust, with the status this brought him.

These were later stages in his life and are not recorded in the book. A new career combined with the stability of a happy family life, raised his morale and understandably, he was a very proud man. He thereafter made a pilgrimage to Pegasus Bridge almost every year until his death in 1999. He enjoyed sharing the anniversary with his Norman friends and with the small band of his company veterans whom he loved so much.

'Ham and Jam'.

Introduction

T here was a leather-bound book in my father's green iron chest. I noticed it when I was helping him to get his medals ready for Normandy and I asked him what it was.

'It's a Five-Year Diary from the war years' he had replied. When I asked if I might look at it, he said, 'No. It's too personal. You'll see it one day.' The tone in his voice was one I was programmed to react to since childhood and I knew his answer was final.

My father, Major John Howard DSO, *Croix de Guerre avec Palme*, died aged eighty-six on 5 May 1999. Eventually, going through his papers I came across the diary again. It consisted of short daily notes made from January 1942 when he'd joined the Airborne Forces, and ended early in 1946, when he was beginning his career as a civil servant. His writing was legendarily difficult to decipher and I decided to transcribe the diary onto my computer. I found that it was indeed very personal in parts, and uncompromising in his opinions and prejudices. It was as I typed his words that the inspiration came for this book.

Of course, that was only the beginning, because I was to draw from my father's archive of original planning documents, maps, photographs, and the first accounts he began encouraging others to make, in the years after the war ended. There were also the more detailed notes he made while in hospital recovering from a road accident in 1945, although they were incomplete, and the tapes and videos he made, as well as the official Army records.

My first visit to Normandy with my family was in 1947 when I was three years old. I have returned to Bénouville many times since then, both with my father when he was alive, and now with my husband, George, when we go back every 6 June for the anniversary of D-Day. We go with the *coup de main* group, as we are known, which consists of the few surviving veterans of that assault team, relations and friends. We are like an extended family group now and have made many French friends there, and are treated with kindness and hospitality by the communities of Bénouville, Ranville, Escoville and Hérouvillette.

When the American historian, Stephen Ambrose, made such an excellent job of writing *Pegasus Bridge*, I really thought that the story of the bridges had been told. But my father's diary goes behind the scenes, giving a unique and honest account of a boy from a large London family who rose through the ranks to become an army officer in the 1940s, the class barrier he faced and his own reactions to this situation. It is also the story of a young married couple starting a family and searching for a home against the backdrop of the Second World War and is a revealing insight into the discrimination and unfairness of those times.

I owe my father's platoon commander Colonel David Wood MBE a debt of gratitude for tirelessly interpreting the military abbreviations and jargon for me. Also Colonel John Tillett for adding his personal recollections about the battle for Escoville. I would like to thank with great affection, the remaining veterans of 'D' Company who regaled me with their memories, especially Tom Packwood. My own family recollections were added to by my father's surviving brothers, Leslie, Bill and Roy Howard and his sister Wyn. And I must not forget my aunt, Lorna Kelly – more a big sister than an aunt to my brother Terry and me.

My gratitude must also be extended to General Sir Robert Pascoe KCB MBE of the Royal Green Jackets for his encouragement and assistance in finding me a publisher.

My final and most important acknowledgement is to my father, John Howard. He was sometimes a stern parent to my brother and me. Having such exacting standards for himself, his ambitions for his children were much greater than most. But he was always fair and loving, even if we sometimes felt that we could never satisfy his expectations of us! He mellowed into the best and most affectionate of grandfathers to my brother's two sons, Nicholas and Simon and my own two daughters, Suzanne and Kerry and, after my mother's death in 1986, I became immeasurably closer to him in his old age. I think of him many times every day and remain immensely proud to be his daughter. His gravestone reads, 'A man of great heart, strength and courage'.

He was ever that.

Penny Howard Bates
June 2006

Chapter 1

January & February 1942: Camden Town to the Airborne

I turned up the collar of my khaki service dress uniform against the softly drifting snow and the icy fingers of the wind that stole around my neck and face. Bracing myself against the cold wind, I reflected somewhat bitterly that later on in life, I would probably look back on this experience as a defining moment but, in the cold January of 1942, standing outside Basingstoke station in Hampshire, waiting for the Army vehicle that would take me to my new posting, and temporarily demoted to lieutenant in the British Army, I felt only the loneliness left from the recent parting from my young wife and the emptiness of an uncertain future.

My wife Joy was just twenty-two years old, a very pretty girl with pale green eyes, slender figure and light brown hair, and she was expecting our first child. We had been living in Oxford, sharing the house of a kindly, middle-aged couple, when Joy became pregnant in the late autumn of 1941. Joy's first pregnancy had coincided with my decision to join the new Airborne Division of the British Army. I had been serving as a captain with the Infantry Training Centre of the Oxfordshire & Buckinghamshire Light Infantry, stationed at Slade barracks in Oxford, and I had decided that being a training instructor was far too mundane for an energetic chap like me – I wanted to see some action and make a real contribution to fighting the war. The formation of the Airborne Forces seemed just the opportunity I'd been looking for.

Joy and I had been married in October 1939, and she had joined me in Oxford when a billet had been found for us in Headington with Kingsley and Jemima Belsten, a childless couple who seemed to take to us, the young newly-weds that war-time laws had obliged them to find room for in their home. In fact we were to become life-long friends. We had all settled into an amicable routine, and it had been a sad realization that this arrangement would have to end when I was accepted by the Airborne Division and posted to Basingstoke. There would be

1

little point in Joy remaining in Oxford without me there, and with a baby due the following summer, she had decided to return to live with her mother in the village where she had grown up – Church Stretton in Shropshire.

Joy was not entirely happy at this prospect, for her mother, Betty had re-married a few years before when Joy was about fifteen, and she was uncertain how she felt about her stepfather, Tom Caine, who was younger than her mother by about nine years. This meant that he was the same age as me for I was eight years older than Joy.

Tom and Betty Caine had a small daughter, Lorna, of whom we were both very fond. Betty ran the telephone exchange for Church Stretton and the family lived in the apartment over the exchange on the main street of Church Stretton. Tom Caine worked with his father and brother in their family business, an abattoir, a few miles away. Tom Caine was a countryman who had grown up in the Shropshire countryside with a profound knowledge and respect for the animals, the weather and seasons and the folklore of country life. It would have been hard to find a man with a more different way of life and experience from me than Tom Caine.

Joy's father had died when she was twelve and, not adapting well to her mother's second marriage, she had gone to live in New Brighton just over the Mersey from Liverpool, with her maternal grandmother and her Aunt Mollie, who owned and operated a chain of five florist shops in the Wirral area before the war. Joy adored her aunt and was closer to her than to her own mother. But at the outbreak of war, I had been nervous of Joy living near the large port of Liverpool which was bound to become a target for the expected bombing raids and although Joy was only nineteen, we had decided to get married.

I was a particular favourite of her mother and always had an excellent relationship with her, calling her 'Mommy' like everyone else in the family. But it was wartime and I would be unable to continue living with my wife now that I was being posted to Basingstoke to join the 1st Airborne Division. Joy longed for a home of our own and the security of peacetime, especially now that she was to become a mother. I knew that sharing her mother's few rooms over the Tele-phone Exchange with her stepfather and little Lorna was not what she wanted, although she was very grateful to them for giving her a home again. She was very sad as she bade a tearful farewell to the lady she had come to call Auntie Jim, for Jemima Belsten had become a very dear friend to her.

I had been born Reginald John Howard in Camden Town, in London, in early December 1912. I was the eldest of nine children born to Ethel and Jack Howard. My father went to fight as a foot soldier in the First World War when I was just an infant and he did not return until I was already at school. Seven more children had followed in quick succession. First came my sister Edna, known always as 'Queenie', and then another son, Frederick, known for some inexplicable

Howard reason as 'Bill'. Our family had a long tradition of nicknames which must have perplexed outsiders, especially since they sometimes changed over the years. The next child was another boy, Leslie, known as 'Tick', then a brother Stanley, and then Percy, and after him came Ernest Edward who was nicknamed 'Johnny' or 'Gin', and last, for at least a time, another sister, Winnie.

My father went to work for Courage Brewery where he earned a meagre wage as a barrel maker. If it hadn't been for the strict management of my indomitable mother, Ethel, our family might have sunk into poverty in the two-up, two-down house we lived in for some years in Camden Town. But somehow she managed to clothe and feed us all on what my father earned and keep our heads above water. I had been christened Reginald John after my father, and was always known in the family as Reg. But I always hated this name and could not wait to change it and be known by my second name, John, the moment I left home. Probably my parents were hurt by this and never quite understood my need to adopt this new persona, but it was part of my strong determination to succeed in life and not be subjected to the hardships and financial anxieties that had made our parents' lives so difficult.

The sound of an Army pickup truck rumbling into the station yard interrupted my thoughts, and the driver leaned through the open window and said, 'Lieutenant Howard, sir?' saluting as he did so. 'Yes, that's right' I replied, wincing slightly at this confirmation of my demotion from captain and, picking up my kit bag, I climbed into the passenger seat at the front of the truck. As we made our way through Basingstoke on the snowy roads, I felt my mood darkening. I began to have serious doubts about my decision to join the Airborne Forces. When I'd joined the Oxfordshire & Buckinghamshire Light Infantry straight from OCTU (Officer Cadet Training Unit) in the summer of 1940, I'd chosen it mainly because it was an infantry regiment and that was the kind of soldiering I understood, and also because it was the home regiment for the city of Oxford where I had been serving in the Oxford City Police Force, before the outbreak of the war.

But in late October 1941, a decision had been made for the 2nd Battalion of the Ox & Bucks, or the 52nd as they were commonly known, to be one of the three battalions that would eventually form 1 Airlanding Brigade, the glider-borne brigade of the 1st Airborne Division.

Ever since a famous memo sent by the wartime Prime Minister, Winston Churchill, in June 1940, to his Chiefs of Staff stating the need for forces that were specifically airborne, these forces had been assembled, mainly consisting of parachute brigades. However, trained troops were also needed to be transported in gliders to carry out attacks which depended on surprise landings of soldiers ready for action where parachutists, who were dropped over a large area and took time to muster and be ready to attack, would not be appropriate.

From the first there would be rivalry between the paratroopers and the glider-borne soldiers, but I had found myself attracted by the new force, which was apparently to be trained as a 'crack force'; elite brigades in the Army representing the latest kind of warfare.

After OCTU, I'd been commissioned into the Oxfordshire & Buckinghamshire Light Infantry and posted to the Infantry Training Centre at Slade barracks in Headington, Oxford as a Training Officer but, for a variety of reasons, I had not enjoyed this job at all, despite it meaning that I could live with my young wife at our friendly billet with the Belstens. I craved active service, and failing that, the feeling that I was training for a specific purpose. I wanted a job that would take me out of doors, doing hard, physical training out on the ranges, commanding a company. I honestly could not see myself getting that opportunity very easily in No. 1 Company, 16 Infantry Training Centre. I had learned the hard way that as a British Army Officer who had 'come up from the ranks' I just did not have the right background to be considered for promotion. At that time, I was a young man of extraordinary energy and enthusiasm and without an outlet for these qualities, I felt like a caged lion.

Late in 1941, the Regiment was asking for volunteers to join the Airborne Forces and for me, this opportunity had seemed like just the chance I'd been waiting for. When Joy told me that she was pregnant, it had seemed as if everything was falling into place. But I was ready for a new challenge and for the first time in her married life, Joy had to come to terms with what it meant to be an Army wife and have her own life dictated by the exigencies of my posting. Basingstoke was not a garrison town, there were no barracks there and the Regiment was awkwardly billeted and distributed around the town. The HQ Company was housed in a factory, the officers were in a variety of civilian houses and the rest of the Regiment shared a former chicken farm outside the town. There was certainly no provision for even the officers' wives to be given quarters close to their husbands. Joy accepted that she must ask her mother if she could live with the family in Church Stretton and Tom and Betty Caine recognized that Joy had no alternative and welcomed her into their home. Tom knew that he was fortunate to have escaped military duty since he was in a reserved occupation. Unable to import much food, Britain desperately needed people at home to make Britain self-sufficient in food. So Joy accepted her fate and packed up to return home to Shropshire and we faced our parting with resignation.

On this bleak day at the end of January 1942 , I found myself staring gloomily out of the window of the small truck taking me through to Basingstoke where it was already beginning to snow in earnest. The Army pickup slithered and rocked as the driver made his way through the furrows of snow where previous vehicles had made their way through the town. 'Soon be there, sir!' said the driver cheerfully to me, but I felt at that moment as if I didn't care if we ever arrived or not. I had accepted a demotion to join the Airborne Forces, from captain to lieutenant and losing those hard won pips was beginning to feel like the worse deal I had ever made. Finally, the pickup came to a grinding halt outside a large Victorian building. Certainly, it was the most dispiriting of arrivals and in the mood I was in on that day, I took an instant and violent dislike to the place, always referring to it as a 'bloody awful camp'. I went through the process of checking in with the Adjutant, and afterwards went to eat dinner in the officers' mess, which was in a public house, The Wheatsheaf, in the middle of the town. They all sat at tables of four and I was recognized and acknowledged by only one fellow officer there, Gilbert Rahr, who I'd known at OCTU.

I found myself billeted in one of the accommodation huts. To my complete disgust there was no mattress on the bed, only a folded blanket and, worse still, no fire in the hut either. I thought back to the warm and comfortable guest room where I had slept the previous night, when I had called at the Slade barracks in Oxford to collect my transfer paperwork. My warrant officer and other NCOs had made a presentation to me when I'd gone on leave in mid-January. I had found myself lost for words at that time and even when I'd stayed there so briefly overnight the previous evening, I had been among people I knew, and my loneliness at leaving Joy had been alleviated by a drink in the officers' mess with friends.

Now here I was, cold and miserable, reduced in rank and with no knowledge of what lay ahead of me. Pulling the rough Army blankets around me, I fell to thinking about my own family background for I'd started my recent fourteen days' leave by spending the first three days back in London, staying at my parents' house.

My father and mother had rented a three-bed semi-detached house on Buck Lane, a pleasant suburban road in the Colindale area. It had been my mother's idea of heaven when they first moved there and with most of her older sons in the Army, the house on Buck Lane with pleasant gardens back and front, made a spacious and comfortable home for the family now that there were only the two youngest children still at home. They were Winnie, a cheeky-faced girl just entering her teens and the 'baby', Roy, cherubic as a toddler and still angelic-looking at nine years old. There were frequent visitors to the Howard family home as all their sons, and daughter Queenie, now married and living close by, returned to see their Mom and Pop as my parents were affectionately known, and to be with one another, reaffirming the close family bonds that had been forged in our childhood.

In the silent and chilly hut in Basingstoke my thoughts returned to those early days. Despite the lack of material possessions in the overcrowded Howard household in the Camden Town years, there was much love and joy to be found in our large family. I never felt that I'd had a deprived childhood, despite the lack of privacy in the small rooms occupied by our ever-increasing family. As a boy, I can recall often finding myself in charge of my younger brothers and sister, the small ones squeezed together in a battered old pram, others hanging on to my short trousers, as I took them out into the streets around our neighbourhood, to get them from under Mum's feet for a while.

I found schoolwork easy and did well, gaining a scholarship to attend a good secondary school. But my parents could not afford the cost of sending me and besides, the money that I would earn when I left school at the normal age in those days, which was fourteen, was eagerly anticipated by my hard-pressed mother. Therefore, I continued my studies at night-school several nights a week whilst my school-mates were out at play. The studies continued when I left school at fourteen and took a job as a clerk with a broker's firm in the city of London. I was good at mathematics and English and was fascinated by the financial world that I now had the opportunity to see at close quarters. I saw the way successful business people lived, talked and behaved and I was influenced by this and was hungry for a good position in life and financial security for myself.

But my life was not all work and no play, for I was also discovering new experiences and pleasures in another area of my life. I had joined the local Boy Scouts troop, along with my brothers when they became old enough. It was run by the local church and led by the vicar, a man known to all as Father Walker, a caring but stern and sometimes cantankerous man, of whom I was much in awe. I never did lose that initial respect for Father Walker and he became a major influence on me, in religion and with the Scouting movement. It had been Father Walker who had first encouraged me to work hard and succeed in life. I had grown up in London but I now discovered the countryside of England when I went on the Scout camps, and the joys of swimming and boxing, running and doing exercises. As I breathed in the fresh country air I became an addict of the outdoor life. I saved up and bought my first camera and faithfully recorded the many camping expeditions, the snaps showing flushed young boys, tousled hair and happy, smiling faces. I continued going to the Scout camps, turning from Scout leader to teacher and instructor as I grew up and went out to work.

In our large and boisterous family, I perhaps stood out as the quiet one, the more serious of all my brothers, but I was unlikely to get away with any pompous or boorish behaviour, for the leg-pulling and banter that surrounded me at home would have knocked any such tendencies out of me very quickly! The Howard family had its own version of cockney humour, which took the form of quick and witty comments, fired from one to the other around the room, and ranging from gentle teasing to withering sarcasm. This family behaviour would last us all our lives and although we could be apart for years on end, we would all revert to it immediately once we were back in the family again. Pretentious behaviour of any kind was likely to be blasted on the spot. Any unusual activity from a new hat to an affected turn of phrase was likely to be made the centre of attention immediately and subjected to the rigours of the family scrutiny and ridicule. Any corners were thus rubbed off all of our personalities without mercy.

However, I suffered a setback when, in the wake of the financial collapse at the end of the 1920s, the broker's company I was working for went under, and I was thrown out of work. Just at that time my mother announced that, several years after my sister Winnie was born, she found herself pregnant again. She accepted this prospect with her usual sensible and capable attitude to all that life sent her. I reacted very badly for I felt scandalized that my parents had been so careless. Feeling wretched and helpless because I was out of work, I lashed out verbally at my mother. We were at the kitchen table and I'd been reading a newspaper. My younger brother Billy was there and he remembered the row. I threw the paper onto the table and shouted angrily at her. For some reason I simply couldn't face the thought of another baby in the house.

Afterwards I felt a deep sense of shame and regretted losing my temper with my mother, with whom I had a deep bond. But that incident changed my life forever because I took the decision to join the Army. This would mean that I would be able to leave home, making more room for the rest of my siblings, and I would be able to hold my head high with a job and be earning money again. At that time, it did not occur to me that the other benefit I would receive from entering the Army would be the chance to further my education and experiences. It was to prove an inspirational decision, and one my brothers would follow in due course.

I lay on the hard bed and stared into the darkness of the room in the freezing cold hut at Basingstoke, recalling the warmth and joking I'd enjoyed in my parents' home only two weeks before. Most of my brothers had been at home on leave from their Army units – all except Percy, who was our mother's favourite son and serving in the Far East. The family had fallen easily back into our habitual leg-pulling and lively, affectionate humour. My sister Queenie had been there too and mentioned running into an old friend, Rose. She had been teasing me, for I had once been engaged to this girl and everyone had joined in with the general mocking banter thereafter.

I had become engaged to Rose Bowyer when I was working at the Stock Exchange. She was the daughter of another of Mom's close friends and, despite our youth, the union had made the family very happy. It had just seemed the natural thing to do at the time and Rosie became a familiar face in our house-hold, even after I'd left home and enlisted in the Army. I can remember considering the vacancy list down at the Army Enlistment Office, weighing up the possibilities of the various regiments that were recruiting in 1931. Somehow the King's Shropshire Light Infantry had a nice ring to it to me at nineteen years old and when I saw the uniform they wore, my mind was made up instantly. It was navy blue, with buttoned epaulettes, a row of silver buttons down the front and, best of all, a very smart peaked cap. What a dash I would cut in that uniform!

7

After training in Colchester, I ended up at the barracks in the pleasant county town of Shrewsbury and quickly adapted to Army life. All the physical exercise from my Scout camp days came into good use as I entered into the sporting life of the Regiment, becoming a prominent member of several teams for boxing and running and representing the Regiment at gymnastics. I realized that I excelled at single, competitive sports rather than team sports like soccer. I was able to further my education in the Army and I passed the exams and became a tutor for mathematics and PT. After several years with the KSLI, I had been made up to corporal and it was suggested that I should try for a commission. There was already talk of another war with the rise of Adolf Hitler and the Nazi party and Germany re-arming, and it was felt that the Army would need more officer material. However, my hopes in that direction were to be crushed when I was told that with my humble background, I was not considered suitable for pro-motion, and that was that. My commanding officer didn't use those exact words but I knew exactly what he meant.

One day, early in 1936, I was persuaded to go on a blind date with a friend, Billy Busby. Billy had met a beautiful girl called Joy who could only be talked into meeting him at a teashop in Shrewsbury if she could bring along her friend Joan, and if Billy brought along a friend to keep Joan company. I agreed reluctantly for I was still engaged to the patient Rosie Bowyer. But at the tea shop, I took one look into the pale green eyes of the young Joy Bromley, and neither Billy nor Rosie stood a chance! Bill was left to chat to Joan while Joy and I talked endlessly, completely wrapped up in one another from the start. I was twenty-four years old and Joy told me that she was eighteen, which I readily believed for she looked eighteen and was very mature in her outlook. In fact, she was only sixteen years old and her mother had no idea that Joy was out in Shrewsbury, meeting soldiers like me in the afternoon! Joy might well have been sharply reprimanded had Betty Caine known but, after several weeks, she decided to tell her mother that she had met 'a very nice young man, who was serving in the Army and was twenty-four years old'. Having very recently taken a man of that same age as her second husband, perhaps Betty Caine felt obliged to let Joy have her way, but she insisted on meeting me. From that first meeting, Betty took a strong liking to me.

I realized that my feelings for Joy were very intense and I decided to confess to her one day that I was, in fact, still engaged to a girl in London. Whatever I might have imagined Joy's reaction to this revelation to be, I had had a frightful shock when, young as she was, Joy reacted quietly and in a very mature way. She took two steps away from me, let go of my hand which had hitherto been clasped warmly in her own and told me that she would not see me again until I had 'released myself from the engagement'. She was as good as her word and Betty Caine must have wondered what had happened to Joy, tight lipped and self-possessed, stayed home and refused to discuss the matter.

I was obliged to take the train to London the next weekend and tell my fiancée that I must break off our engagement. How Rose really took this news I can only imagine for she had been engaged to me for the best part of six or seven years. It cannot have helped much to learn that the reason was a sixteen year old girl whom I'd met only recently. I then went home and broke the news to my parents. They were very angry with me for letting Rose down so badly – they felt that I had brought shame on the Howard family. They were not kindly disposed therefore to show much interest in this other young lady who had stolen their Reg's heart, and it would be some time before I dared to bring Joy down to London to meet them. It was an inauspicious beginning for Joy's relationship with my family and was to have lasting repercussions.

I returned to my unit in Shrewsbury, free to pursue my relationship with Joy but very chastened indeed to have caused so much hurt and heartbreak back in London.

But by the summer of 1937, I'd taken my beloved 'Joybells' – my nickname for her – to stay with my parents in London. My father fell under her spell at once and forever, but Mom saw another determined female who now had a higher place in my heart than she had, and the two women were polite but cool with one another. I think my mother judged Joy to be a snob and saw that she was influencing me already and, with the intuitive knowledge of a mother, she realized that Joy would gradually draw me away from my family. When a son is called by a different name by his new girlfriend, from the name he is known by in his family, it immediately sets up a frisson of resentment each time she uses that name in front of them. This was not deliberate on Joy's part and neither was it her fault, for it had been me who had changed my name the minute that I'd left home. I was known as John Howard to all my Army friends. But this must have been the first time that Mom and Pop had heard me constantly called John by someone in their family home, and I can see now that it must have jarred.

Joy spoke with what the family thought of as a posh accent, and privately I think she must have judged the cheerful cockney slang used by the Howards and thought them all rather common. When my brothers and sisters teased one another and referred to past happenings and private family jokes, Joy must have felt left out. I used to find myself reverting to the dialect of my childhood and Joy was probably a little shocked and disappointed in me. This would have been a side of 'her John' that she did not recognize. But we were in love and determined to be together for the rest of our lives and Joy realized that she must learn to make an effort to get on with my family. My mother knew that Joy was going to be part of my life, like it or lump it. But in truth, my mother was nothing if not pragmatic, and her natural kindness would overcome her initial doubts about Joy. She had a big heart and it was large enough to include this diffident young stranger who came from such a different background. It was with these thoughts filling my head, I fell asleep at last in the cold bed in Basingstoke and dreamed I was back walking in the Shopshire hills with Joy.

The following morning, despite another fall of snow, I was ready for breakfast in the officers' mess, finding my way to The Wheatsheaf bright and early and was glad to see Gilbert Rahr. He was a friendly, amiable sort and, like myself, recently married. He took me back to the factory that Company HQ was occupying, for an appointment with the Adjutant. The Adjutant informed me that I would be seeing the Colonel the following day and that I should report for the start of a three-inch mortar course meanwhile. Somewhat confused about what was in store, I duly reported for the course but found to my delight the next morning that, after the interview with Colonel Giles, my captaincy was restored with immediate effect. I was removed from the course and instructed to take over 'C' Company of the 52nd Ox & Bucks from another officer, Digby Tatham-Warter. Tatham-Warter was to take my place on the course instead.

I was all too familiar with young officers like Digby Tatham-Warter, a likeable enough fellow but a typical 'top-drawer' officer, with a Sandhurst background. Doubtless his father and likely his grandfather too, had also served as officers in the Ox & Bucks and young Digby would have been schooled from birth to leave his public school as an Army cadet, enter Sandhurst, the prestigious training college for Army officers in Camberley, Surrey, and graduate from there as part of the elite band of young British Army officers; clean-cut, 'jolly good chaps' and confident of their status in life. Back in 1940, I had found many, but certainly not all, of these young men arrogant in the extreme and deliberately encouraged to be that way by their upbringing and privileged background. Being promoted from the ranks had made me a target for certain of these officers when I gained my commission. I had been ignored by a section of fellow officers completely. 'Cut' they used to call it and it had felt as if they had indeed taken a razor to my injured pride and cruelly slashed me. There had always been other officers in the mess, some of whom I knew from OCTU, like Gilbert Rahr, who would stand by me, and order me a beer and start talking loudly and telling jokes to cover the silence, placing themselves in between me and the deliberately turned backs. But I never forgot those times and never forgave. It had made me determined to show those bastards that I would be a better officer than they could ever be in their wildest dreams. While they were off at weekends invited to shooting parties or playing golf, I would be planning my training routines and drilling the men. Damn them all to hell with their double-barrelled names and their county family forebears. It made me more aggressive and, unfortunately, inclined to be prejudiced against anyone with an upper-class name or manner – that is until such times as I had proved myself and could meet such men on equal terms. But that was to be some years later, and in the first days of February 1942, I saw the restoration of my captaincy and being instructed to take the place of, what I then perceived to be a 'blue-nosed' young officer, as a decided upturn in my fortunes.

It cheered me up no end and I found myself whistling merrily as I walked briskly back to my quarters.

However, in the days that followed, I had a chance to get to know Digby Tatham-Warter better and realized, not for the first time, that I had been wrong in my initial assessment of him as a typical 'upper class pongo'. He was, in fact, an easy-going chap with an attractive manner and to my surprise, I found myself liking him. So when Digby suggested that we meet up and go to the 'flicks', I readily agreed.

I could not wait to use the telephone in the officers' mess to place an evening call to Joy and give her the good news. She was down at heart, missing me dreadfully and feeling unsettled in her mother's home in Church Stretton. But my news and the enthusiasm in my voice seemed to cheer her up and we talked about my recent leave when I had taken the train up to Church Stretton after my few days in London, and we'd enjoyed our time together, despite the lack of privacy in the flat over the telephone exchange.

I particularly liked the company of Joy's uncle, Walter, who was one of Betty Caine's younger brothers. Walter and his wife, Barbara, were much younger than Joy's mother, seeming to be nearer to our generation. We had gone to their house, charmingly called Windyways, and played pontoon for small bets. Barbara gave us supper and as we'd walked back through the small town, Joy had said wistfully to me, 'I wonder how long it will be before we can afford a nice home like Windyways, John'.

'We'll have to wait for a bit, darling,' I had told her. 'After the babe is born, maybe we could ask Tommy and Mommy for a loan?'

'I'm not at all sure about that,' Joy had said doubtfully. But for the time being, we just had to be content with our lot as Joy knew that my priorities lay in furthering my Army career and above all, having a real chance to do a bit for the war effort. I found myself forever writing things in my diary like, 'Let's just get on with it!' or 'Roll on!' for I was so desperate for some real action.

But in Basingstoke I found that 'C' Company, was in disarray. The men lacked discipline and encouragement, and their morale was low. Despite this, they seemed fit enough. I would have expected conscripts to have that kind of attitude, not regular soldiers. I was surprised but determined to lick the company into shape as soon as possible. I started immediately by taking them for a run, despite the winter weather. Then we went out onto the ranges for shooting practice but it was too cold for classification – that is for testing each man and determining his capability. We were taken out of Basingstoke in transport lorries onto the Army training ranges some distance away. Being out in the snow and wind was an endurance test but I was no stranger to physical hardship. This is what I felt made officers like me stand out from some of the others I had observed who, on such a day, might leave their NCOs to bundle along with the training while the officer himself sat at a desk in the company office in front of an electric fire. But I enjoyed being out there in the field among the men, shouting encouragement and occasionally bawling out the shirkers and, in my opinion, the men seemed to respond to this personal contact and my example.

The following week, I was sent up to London for a street fighting demonstration. The threat of a German invasion was very real at that time, especially down on the south coast. The soldiers had to be trained in street fighting – that is the art of fighting in urban conditions, from house to house, using the buildings for cover but also to be aware of their vulnerability to snipers. They might need these skills either to defend their own country from invading forces or to be ready to fight on the Continent. 'God knows,' the Colonel said to me, 'there's enough bombed out areas now for the men to practise on.' The plan was to use the bombed areas of Southampton which was closer to Basingstoke and more practical than London. The officers discussed tactics as we all stood amongst the rubble of the East End, and I thought about my own family not so far away, and was glad that they'd moved out to Colindale in the north-west of the capital.

Evidently the Colonel must have decided he wanted to get to know me a little better, probably because I was not the usual officer material. It might have been mentioned to him that I was a bit of a rough diamond but hopefully damn good at motivating the men. Whatever the reason, I can remember that he took me for a slap-up lunch at the Comedy Restaurant in Piccadilly, possibly to see how I behaved in a social situation. Despite my lack of experience in these matters, I had already found that I took naturally, and with a good deal of pleasure, to eating out when the opportunity arose. Colonel Giles paid the bill and I admired the easy grace with which he chose a bottle of wine and tipped the waiter.

An official 'warning' had been given to me of changes that were about to take place in my life. This may sound like a reprimand, but it was nothing of the kind. In the Army, an officer is officially warned by his Commanding Officer when he has a change of duties or is going to be promoted. In this instance, I was told that I was to take command of another Company, 'D' Company, with which my name was forever to be associated. I handed over 'C' Company to a fellow officer on 16 February, but hadn't any time to think too much about it since we were planning a 'raid' against a force from the Scots Guards, and starting a motor cycle course during the evening. Well, I'd hoped for plenty of action and now I was getting it.

On 17 February 1942 I took over command of 'D' Company and met many of the men I was to train and command for D-Day. Of course, I had no knowledge of what lay ahead and was concerned only with the men's accommodation and the stores problems. My new Company Sergeant Major was named McGovern and I liked the man and felt that we would work well together. I attended a company commanders' conference and felt, for the first time, the power of command and being, in some small measure, a member of the 'top brass' who could influence decision-making and strategy.

I also met some of my junior officers at this time and got to know them better. One of them was Brian Priday and I forged a special bond with this dependable and trustworthy man, which was to carry us both through D-Day. I also got to know Tod Sweeney, another of the junior officers in the 52nd who had volunteered to join the new Airborne Forces. Sweeney was an unusual man and so quiet that it took me a little time to realize his true worth. It was an Army practice to call all men who had the surname Sweeney, 'Tod' after the well-known East End murdering barber of legend, Sweeny Todd. Likewise all men named Todd, were nicknamed 'Sweeney', just as all Clarkes were 'Nobby', all Whites 'Chalky' and so on. These simple rules pulled the men together and enriched their camaraderie. You knew where you were in a trench, if good old Nobby Clarke was next to you!

This Tod Sweeney was a sensitive and deeply spiritual man who had nearly entered the priesthood, but chose a secular calling instead and brought his beliefs and morality into his everyday life. But he was also a private man and his convictions showed only in his consideration for his fellows. He was also capable of much humour and would fool about with the other young officers. He married, as so many of us did, as war became inevitable and had left his young wife Geraldine, just like I had left Joy, to make a life for herself. Tod Sweeney was destined to become one of my platoon commanders on D-Day and a lifelong friend. I was only too aware that if I was to succeed I would need men I could totally trust as junior officers and I began to look out for others that I could ask to join my team. Little did I know then that I was building the company that would one day spearhead the Allied invasion of Europe.

Chapter 2

February to April 1942: Background, Oxford and Marriage

I n the last week of February 1942 I found myself a very cushy billet. I was given accommodation at Ashley Lodge, just outside Basingstoke, with the friendly family of Dr Williams and his wife. It was a lovely old house and my bedroom there was quite the grandest that I had ever slept in. The Williams family took to me and I was treated as one of the family. I considered myself fortunate indeed to be billeted on such charming people and within days they had suggested that I might prefer to join them at their family meals as well, which would mean that I would certainly fare better than eating at The Wheatsheaf in Basingstoke. I was pleased to accept their kind offer and decided to ask the Quartermaster for a bicycle so that I could get to and from Ashley Lodge easily without waiting for Army transport.

It was at this time that I embarked on a period of company training to get to know the men and their capabilities, but I was also learning all the time myself. For the planned raid on the Scots Guards force, my Divisional HQ had decided to use a new idea of 'dummy paratroopers' to be dropped as a diversion. I gave the men a lecture about this innovation and they seemed very intrigued by it. I hoped their interest was due in some part to my skills as a lecturer!

During the planned raid on the Scots Guards the men acquitted themselves well and entered fully into the spirit of the raid in man-to-man combat. There was nothing the men liked better than a good rough house; it got rid of so much pent-up aggression and frustration. It was cold and windy out on the ranges watching the 52nd contingent slogging it out with the Scots Guards. Nobody understood better than me why the infantrymen of the 52nd could rise so magnificently to the occasion, given the opportunity to beat the living daylights out of a bunch of 'Jocks' without the fear of intervention by the military police! I came down with a heavy head cold after this event but it did not prevent me from being out on the ranges the following day for field firing practice and managing a decent score myself.

Two days later and the company was out on a night-time operation, after a cross-country run during the day when they managed five and a quarter miles in fifty minutes, with me running with them. 'Night Ops' as they all called them were to become a frequent part of the training programme. It was known by this time that an invasion of Europe was in the early stages of being planned, and it was rightly assumed that the infantry would have to fight both day and night. Stealthy attack under the cover of darkness was a very useful strategy and, as a former policeman, I had long been quite at home during the hours of darkness. They had done the occasional night exercise when I had been a corporal in the KSLI – never popular with the men because, as they graphically put it, 'it buggered up' their sleep and eating patterns. I felt thoroughly at home with the men out on the ranges and reflected that my career hitherto had just been leading up to this.

When I had finished the seven-year service with the King's Shropshire Light Infantry that I'd signed up for in 1931, I had seen the end of my life as a regular soldier approaching and thought long and hard about what I wanted to do next. I had become engaged to Joy in spring 1938, just as the end of my stint with the KSLI approached. Joy and I had discussed what we both wanted from our future life together, and had decided that we would like to settle down eventually to a married life in Oxford. I liked the city myself – it wasn't too far from my roots in London, and I could return there to visit my family quite easily, only about an hour on the train. Also, I had realized that I liked a life in uniform and the discipline and *esprit de corps* of belonging to a force of men. I therefore decided to become a police officer. To this end I went for an interview with the Oxford City Police and was accepted for the Police Training College which I entered in mid-1938. Out of 200 who started at the same time, I managed to come top of the course and was starred for promotion.

The close friends I made at Police Training College would last me for life, and the colleagues and contacts I made there in my relatively short time with the Oxford City Police, were to have far-reaching effects on my subsequent life and be of very great use to me in ways that could have hardly been foreseen in 1938. It was well-known that Germany was re-arming in 1938, but there was a profound conviction in England that there could be no possibility of another war – not a bare twenty years after the Great War. England was hopelessly unprepared and both politicians and people clung to the belief that, at best, the Germans were just sabre-rattling and, at worst, that they would content themselves with marching into a few small countries and re-adjust their borders to their pre-Treaty of Versailles positions. Young people like Joy and me got on with their lives and hoped the threat of war would go away. We planned for our futures as if there was no possibility of another war; it was all we could do at the time. If war came – well, that was another matter and we would have to think again and adjust to the circumstances. So I left Police Training College as PC 109 of the Oxford City Police and began 'pounding the beat'.

Like many young police constables, I was often given night duty and I found that I came to enjoy the quiet of the night, being the only one walking the empty streets for the police did not work in pairs in those days. A policeman had only his truncheon and a whistle and was expected to be able to deal with any situation that might arise. While I was beginning what I hoped would be a long career with the Oxford City Force, living a bachelor life in police quarters, Joy was in New Brighton with her maternal grandmother and her Aunt Mollie. She had first gone to live with them in May 1936, not long after we had first met. She wanted to learn floristry by working in one of her aunt's shops, and being naturally artistic showed real talent at it. I can remember the desolation I felt the night she left, returning to the Copthorne barracks in Shrewsbury after seeing her off to her new life. I wrote the first of many letters in what I described as 'a morbid tone, terribly depressed and unhappy'. I acknowledged Joy's wish 'to make a success of life' in going to New Brighton and it had the effect of stirring renewed feelings of ambition in me. I wrote that 'the fact that I have to wait over two years for an opportunity to put this ambition to the test (until I'd finished my seven years with the KSLI) positively appals me'. I signed this carefully typed seven page letter, 'Ever thine, John' which was to be my personal dedication to Joy all of our lives.

After we became engaged in the spring of 1938, when Joy was once again living back at Church Stretton with her mother, Tom Caine and three year old Lorna, her grandmother wrote a wonderful letter to me, congratulating me on being accepted by the Oxford City Police as well as on my engagement to Joy, which I would keep all my life. An esteemed and much loved lady with a calm, benign face, Sarah Sagar had a broken marriage behind her. She had left her husband and young family back in Church Stretton, for heaven only knows what reason, to go to Wallasey, Cheshire to live with her eldest daughter, Marie, known always as 'Mollie'. It was rumoured in the family that George Sagar, a very hard man, was impossible to live with. Their fourteen year old second daughter, Elizabeth, called Betty, was obliged to take over the care of the smaller children and to try to handle her stern and difficult father, known to all and sundry as 'The Governor'. Divorce was almost unknown in those days and Sarah must have gone through a very great deal of distress herself over the failure of her marriage and loss of her children. Thus, I can imagine she must have been more overjoyed than most grandmothers would have been, that her beloved Joy was to marry someone she felt was worthy of her, and to whom she was 'so well suited'.

The declaration of war in September 1939 changed everything. All unmarried women were required for war work, which could have meant a munitions factory, being a Land Girl or perhaps nursing but sadly not floristry. I certainly did not relish the idea of Joy working in a factory or being trained as a bus driver. We had planned to marry the following year anyway, and so we decided to bring our plans forward and were married on 28 October 1939, at All Saints Church in Church Stretton by my old childhood mentor Father Walker. Then Joy and I caught the train down to London, still wearing our wedding clothes for a brief honeymoon spent at my parents' house on Buck Lane. A photograph was taken with my parents, on the steps leading down from the windows of the back living room and Joy looked radiant. She wore a dainty dress in pale lilac, with a generous corsage of real orchids pinned across the front. On her head was a very flattering little navy-blue hat in the latest 'Air Force' style, set at a rakish angle. She looked so pretty but best of all was her smile, which lit the dull October day, making it seem like mid-summer.

As newly-weds, we had hardly a chance to settle to married life together before more changes rocked our world. Being so recently a regular soldier meant that I was among the first to be called back into the Army as a 'reservist'. My job with the Oxford City Police would remain open for me to return to when the war was over, providing that I was fit to carry it out. As a reservist I was obliged to rejoin my old regiment, the King's Shropshire Light Infantry, at Copthorne barracks in Shrewsbury, and Joy once again went to live with her mother. I re-enlisted as a full corporal. Within two weeks I was a sergeant; a month later in early February 1940, I became a company sergeant major. In April 1940 I was promoted to a regimental sergeant major. It seemed that in a time of national need, my leadership qualities and officer potential were immediately spotted – suddenly my background was no longer important, and my undoubted success, however brief, in the police force had been recognized. In May 1940, my brigadier offered me a chance of a commission. It seems odd to me now, but frankly at that time, I had serious doubts about being the right material. But my new wife persuaded me that I should definitely give it a try. Thus in June, I went off to OCTU and graduated as a second lieutenant. I hardly had time to draw a breath from re-entering the Army as a corporal in January 1940, to becoming a commissioned officer. It was time to take stock of the situation I found myself in, and Joy and I decided that we really preferred to return to Oxford and make that our future base. For that reason, I applied for a commission in Oxford's home regiment, the Oxfordshire and Buckinghamshire Light Infantry.

At first, back in Oxford with my new regiment, I feared that I had made the most frightful mistake. The Ox & Bucks was a fine old county regiment and had not long returned from duty in India. The officers were nearly all the same 'county types', and some of them at least, did not regard an upstart from the ranks as the right kind of fellow to uphold their long and distinguished history. I was to learn later that it was well known at Sandhurst that a new officer would be ignored in the officers' mess for the first six weeks of his service as a matter of course in the Ox & Bucks, no matter who he was. But unfortunately I did not realize this and so took this treatment very personally. So began my miserable first months at Slade barracks, being 'cut' in the officers' mess and shunned as I went about my duties as a training officer. The Ox & Bucks did not have many officers from the ranks at that time so I daresay I received the brunt of their prejudices – but it left me feeling very sore and quick to take umbrage. The Regiment had a mass of small protocols and regulations that just had to be learned and taken on board. It was a minefield of petty 'dos and don'ts'. Some of the customs from the years in India still remained, with the occasional use of Hindi expressions, all guaranteed to make a newcomer like me feel wrong-footed and excluded. Each regiment has its own peculiarities – the Ox & Bucks only saluted their colonels the first time they met them in the day and they didn't ever drink a 'loyal toast' because they felt their unswerving loyalty to the King should be taken for granted. They never used abbreviations referring to fellow officer's position – the medical officer, always the MO anywhere else, was the medical officer in the Ox & Bucks. Slips of the tongue would inevitably cause a curled lip and loss of face. I found myself obliged to watch every word and move, until the rules became second nature to me. My CO was a sensitive man and he called me into his office and suggested that I should arrange for a decent billet and get Joy to come down to join me in Oxford as soon as possible. I was keen to act on this advice and within a month, Joy had joined me and we were both installed with Kingsley and 'Jim' Belsten in Headington. I gritted my teeth and learned to ignore the more offensive of my fellow officers until such time as they got so used to seeing me around, that they grew bored and treated me the same as everyone else. I felt as if I had won a battle but realized that my war was still to come.

By the end of February 1942, I had started the training schedule for 'D' Company of the 52nd Ox & Bucks, now part of the Airborne Forces, that would take my company right up to D-Day. I was increasing my men all the time, on 28 February seeing another eleven men arrive, all to be found civilian billets in Basingstoke. The men in 'D' Company had done an anti-tank rifle course and this had revealed that they were unable to hit a moving target. The other officers and I had been engaged in a number of TEWTs, which stood for Tactical Exercise Without Troops. The point of this kind of exercise was that the officers could decide upon their strategy for carrying out an objective without having the men standing around. It was essentially a problem solving exercise and thus, when the soldiers were involved at a later stage, the officers could give them ready formulated instructions. There were evening courses going on as well for much of the time. I did a field radio course on how to operate the Army radios used for communications out in the field and the codes and procedures that went with them. I really quite enjoyed that course, but I never took to the German lessons, finding it an impenetrable language.

The weather turned to heavy rain at the beginning of March but that didn't stop me ordering 'D' Company out on a forced march; eight and three-quarter miles in two hours five minutes. I was apparently already getting a reputation for being a hard taskmaster and perhaps this was true, for I did not consider this to be a very good effort and wrote 'Must do better' in my diary entry for that day. I also noted that Joybells had sent a rabbit down, shot by Tom Caine on the Stretton hills and the housekeeper at Ashley Lodge made an excellent pie with this windfall.

The weather turned frosty again when the company went out onto the thirty-yard range for training for firing from the hip with LMGs (Light Machine Guns – Bren guns). It was called 'zeroing the sights', which was testing all the sights on the guns and we discovered that all of them needed smaller ones. The soldiers were to find many shortcomings with the weapons that were issued to them, both the Bren light machine guns and the Sten sub-machine guns – upon which, ultimately, their lives depended. They were manufactured hastily in the panic to arm for war, and the Sten gun in particular, although popular with the men because of its weight – just seven pounds – could nevertheless be unreliable; its mechanism could stick or indeed, it could fire unexpectedly. The Bren could be deadly in close combat, if it worked as it should have done, but it was the cause of many accidents in training and, doubtless, just as many fatalities in battle. Once on the battlefield, it became common practice to get hold of a dead German's gun and anything else one could lay one's hands on. The German Schmeisser sub-machine gun was found to be a much more reliable weapon.

My afternoons might often be spent in the company office because I was trying to sort out the paperwork and to re-design the company platoons and sections. By D-Day my company would consist of four platoons, and each platoon had twenty-four men, reckoned to be a Horsa glider load. Each platoon had three sections – five men forming a Scout Section and two Rifle Sections of seven men each, two two-inch mortar-men, an orderly and the platoon sergeant and platoon commander making up the twenty-four soldiers. There were in general, six companies to a battalion, being four rifle companies, a support company of heavy guns and mortars, and the HQ Company consisting of the Quartermaster and other staff. The 1 Air Landing Brigade (of glider-borne troops) comprised the HQ staff plus rifle battalions of the 52nd Ox & Bucks, The Royal Ulster Rifles, The Borders and The South Staffs. Later on, when the 1st Division was split up into the 1st and 6th Divisions, (6th chosen to confuse the enemy into thinking there were more divisions than there actually were), they were joined by the 12th Battalion of the Devonshire Regiment, but in early 1942, the 1st Division consisted of one air landing brigade plus two paratroop brigades. This was the structure in simple terms.

1st Airborne Division was under the command of Major General F. A. M. 'Boy' Browning, a dashing officer, famous for being married to the novelist Daphne du Maurier. Indeed it was she who suggested the legendary red beret in 1942 and having a pale blue Bellerophon astride the winged Pegasus on a maroon background as a shoulder patch. A second airborne division, formed in 1943, became known as the 6th Airborne and was under the command of General Richard 'Windy' Gale.

At this time I was helped by a man I had a lot of respect for called 'Chalky' White as second in command, always called a 2 I/C in the Army. One of my other junior officers, David Wood, thought Chalky White was 'elderly', but then David was just nineteen himself at the time and this comment was made after Chalky had chewed him off a strip. There was a cross-country run and I managed to come in first – it never hurt to show the men that I could hold my own. Whatever they did, I took a pride in doing it as well, right alongside them, and would do my damnedest to do it better. I studied the results from this run and put together a company team to compete in the Regimental Inter-Company Competition, and left the men in no doubt that they were expected to win. I walked the selected team around the cross-country course; it was hilly and very rough in parts, but I was absolutely determined that our team would do well. In the event, the favourites, 'B' Company, won the race but our team did well, and I came eleventh myself. Each man on the team received twenty cigarettes as a reward for a good performance. Cigarettes were a basic currency in the Forces in both the First and Second World Wars, useful for both bartering and reward, but I did not smoke.

Still 'empire-building', I had my eye on a young man called Denham Brotheridge, known to all as 'Den', whom I'd met at Slade barracks where we'd taken an instant liking to one another, both being promoted from the ranks. Den was a Midland man, from Smethwick, near Birmingham, and a superb sports-man. It was felt that he would almost certainly have been offered a career as a professional footballer when the war was over. Thus Den played what they then called 'soccer' which was the sport the soldiers knew and loved, and not cricket or rugby like most of the other officers in 52nd Ox & Bucks. Soccer was the sport of the ordinary man, then as now, and Den Brotheridge was to become an immensely popular platoon leader, able to talk easily to the men under his command and earn their undying allegiance. Brotheridge was at that time on an OCTU course at Sandhurst and I scrounged a motorbike one afternoon and rode over to see him. Unfortunately, Brotheridge had gone out and I found myself obliged to write to him instead but I made the effort because I very much wanted Den to join 'D' Company. We met at a conference in Bournemouth and Den confirmed that he would like to come to 'D' Company, but only after he had completed his OCTU course.

On 19 March the battalion held Exercise YORKER and I briefed the com-pany thoroughly the day before in Basingstoke. They were on parade at 07.00 hours and were to be out for the two days following, billeted rather uncom-fortably in an air raid shelter which was the best we could arrange at the time.

However, I made a mental note to be at the front of the queue from then on to grab favourable billets for the men when out on exercise.

The battalion fared badly during this exercise and 'D' Company were the only ones to hold their area as instructed. But the men enjoyed the mock battles to secure a pillbox and used their two-inch mortars to great effect, producing a most satisfactory amount of noise and smoke. On the third day of the exercise, 'D' Company bungled an attack to re-take a bridge, but all the time they were learning tactical lessons even when they failed to pull it off. I had arranged for them to breakfast in a quarry and they were back in the barracks by 14.00 hours, thoroughly tired and up to their eyeballs in mud. My diary recorded, somewhat ruefully, that I had a stye on my eye – a sure sign that I was overdoing things and needed to slow down a bit. But 'bull-at-a-gate' was the only method of operating I was familiar with, as Joy was wont to remark fairly often in the years to come.

On 22 March Second Lieutenant David Wood reported to me for duty at Basingstoke with 'D' Company, straight from 164 OCTU. He was a fresh-faced, sandy-haired lad with a very agreeable disposition, even-tempered and ready for a bit of fun. Coming from good middle-class stock, he had been on holiday with his family in Dunster, Devon when war had broken out. The lazy days of a golden holiday in late summer, suddenly changing into the charged atmosphere of a country at war, anticipating air-raids any night. He had taken to his officer training in his typical good-natured way, and he showed great enthusiasm for joining the Airborne. Wood told me later that he had heard that I was a zealot – the actual words used were unrepeatable – and he had therefore faced his new OC with a certain amount of trepidation. His manner appeared hesitant and unsure and typically, I gave him one of my quick, 'up and down' assessments, judged young Lieutenant David Wood and found him wanting. I wrote of him in my diary that day, 'Isn't of much use to me, but may shape up in time'. However, I was to change my mind completely in my estimation of David Wood when got to know him.

I'd been given a five-year, leather-bound diary, and the entries were made year by year on a single page for any given date, each being written beneath the one for the year before. Thus, a year later, obviously glancing up to my previous entry and noting the deprecating remarks I'd made about Wood, I wrote in 1943, 'Ref. above – David Wood is a rattling good Officer!! … wouldn't lose him for the world'. David Wood was destined to become part of the 'D' Company legend alongside the other officers and men.

During March, I was informed that 'D' Company was to be moved into accommodation at Bulford camp on Salisbury Plain, which meant that all the messes and the soldiers' and officers' accommodation would be in the barracks there and I would have to make the move with all the others. I was certainly very glad to be leaving the scattered regimental arrangements at Basingstoke behind for a proper barracks again, however, it also inevitably meant that my time at

Ashley Lodge would come to an end, for which I felt regret for I had thoroughly appreciated my time there being an honorary member of the Williams' family.

In the meantime, the training schedule continued unabated with 'night ops' spent on tank hunting, field firing practice and a soccer match – 'D' Company versus the local police force. Of course I was missing seeing Joy dreadfully, but my days were so full of physical exercise and mentally planning for training schedules to keep the men constructively occupied, that I really did not have much time to dwell on our separation.

Back into training with my company, I noticed that seven men had dropped out of a forced march. It was my habit to have each one of them in front of me separately, to give the reason for what I perceived as their weakness, and they had to give a damn good explanation. In 'D' Company you were guilty until proved innocent! I only noted grimly in my diary that such interviews gave 'good results'. The men were also instructed how to use the new rations that were being introduced ready for when they were in battlefield conditions. These were tinned and dried rations that could be heated or reconstituted in each soldier's mess-tin, heated over a fire or in some cases, a small gas heater. 'D' Company managed to produce a sample of these gourmet delights for their dinners out in the field, and then I saw to it that they participated in a seven-a-side rugby competition to finish off the day.

On Good Friday, at the beginning of April 1942, I was working normally and joining the men for a cross-country practice run ready for the brigade run. I finished work at just after 16.00 and went back to Ashley Lodge where I helped out by laying a path in the garden. On Easter Sunday I went to early Communion with Mrs Williams. There was an officers' motorcycle trial in the afternoon, for which I was a little over-enthusiastic, coming off the bike and wrenching my knee badly. I blamed bad organization of the trials for this mishap and was furious because it meant that I was out of the brigade cross-country run the following day. I was so competitive at that time in my life and entered all sports with a total lack of caution, bordering on recklessness, but on that occasion, I recall that I comforted my sad heart with a long telephone call to my beloved Joy.

On Easter Monday I went to see the brigade run with a 'Scott's Dressing' on my bad knee. 'D' Company's team did well, coming third. But on the next day, I was to receive the dreadful news that my brother Percy had been killed by the Japanese. He'd been serving in the Far East with his unit. I wrote bitterly in my diary, 'Pray God I'll have the chance to avenge his death!' and added 'Poor Mom'. Percy was the favourite of my mother's six sons and the only one lost in the war. She was devastated by the news of his death. A lone photograph of Percy's grave, marked by a wooden cross, was sent to me and I kept it all my life.

But there was no time to grieve, as the company move into our new quarters in Bulford camp was scheduled for the next day, 9 April. We had been given a

'Spider' block, so-called because the blocks radiated out from a central area. It was part of Wing barracks and was to remain the home of 'D' Company for the best part of the next three years. I was miserable about leaving the comfortable billet at Ashley Lodge and the home comforts provided by the Williams' family. It did not help that the day appointed for the move was pouring with rain, but the lads worked well and it all went smoothly. I was pleased with 'Spider' block, the mess area was large and I gave orders for the new block to be scrubbed out. A few days later 'Spider' block was officially inspected and found to be in good order. I was pleased to be able to drill the men on the parade ground that was situated conveniently close by with the Company HQ building at one end of the drill square.

13 April was nearly a very unlucky thirteenth for me. I was attending a demonstration of the new fighter aircraft at Imber, when a Hurricane mistakenly strafed the ground in an area where the spectators were standing. I'd been standing with a group of men I'd known from my old regiment, the King's Shropshire Light Infantry, and I described the incident later as 'an appalling mistake! I was lucky to get away with it!' It shook me up at the time even though we all accepted that accidents happened when training for war. Mistakes were made and soldiers were killed or maimed.

The following day, I made a flight in a Tiger Moth aircraft and declared that 'the stunting made me feel bad', which was somewhat of an understatement. The Airborne Forces chaps were considered fair game for the daredevil young pilots to try out a few flips and spirals, and my 'dodgy tummy', which was to become a legend with 'D' Company, would have certainly rebelled at being flown upside-down or in a dive. The glider trip we made the following day would therefore have felt much more comfortable and I noted that it was 'a perfect trip, everyone enthusiastic', and nobody was sick. This would have been unusual, because the gliders in use at that time were probably Hotspurs, which held only six or seven men with two pilots, and were infamous for 'pitching and yawing' on their tug-ropes, causing nearly everyone who ever flew in them to be sick. So our good experience upon that occasion was a lucky one.

It was a good time for me to be notified that I could go off on ten days' leave and I was overjoyed for I hadn't seen Joy for three months. I telephoned her to give the good news and it took her by surprise. It seems that it resulted in a flurry of bed-linen and moving furniture in the flat over the Church Stretton Telephone Exchange, but Joy was thrilled. On 16 April 1942, I began my leave by getting a lift with the Quartermaster, Jimmy James, and another officer, Harry Styles, who were going into Oxford on company business. This saved me a lot of time as I didn't have to go into London and out again by train. I'd managed to obtain some wine by bartering a few of my store of cigarettes. Wine was in very short supply and Joy was pleased with this special treat when she met me on

Shrewsbury station. We took the train back to Church Stretton together. Joy was in her sixth month of pregnancy and looked blooming, especially to me. We walked hand in hand the short distance from the railway station in Church Stretton to the post office, above which Joy was living. Her half-sister Lorna and her mother were away visiting her grandmother and aunt in New Brighton but returned the following day. I found Tom Caine gruff and unfriendly at first, but he always gave that impression to start with until he got used to visitors.

The weather was very good on the first day of my leave and I walked in the hills behind the little town and did some climbing which was something I loved to do and gave me a bit of exercise. Due to her condition, Joy could not accompany me on the more strenuous walks but I managed to take her to the cinema several times during my leave, and on one occasion we even took my mother-in-law, Betty, too for we got on well together. On the next day I was once more keeping my fitness levels up by climbing one of the steep hills that rose up behind the town. Little Lorna watched by the window of the flat over the post office, waiting for me to come into sight far away across the valley as I scaled the hill. Reaching a certain point I would turn and wave a white handkerchief vigorously at the distant houses, knowing that Lorna was waiting and would see me and jump up and down, waving back and calling out for Joy, 'Jee-Jee! Come and see Johnny!'

Lorna had no garden to play in, but there was a large, flat roof over an extension that had been built onto the post office beneath, and it was railed off for safety so that she could play out there. Her father Tom, who was handy at making things, had made a play-house for her and Lorna would remember all her life, sitting out there on her roof space and hearing the life of the little town all around her, as the sounds rose up to her level. She recalled especially hearing the soldiers singing as they boarded the train close by at Church Stretton station, taking them away on active service.

Church Stretton was, in fact, bustling with military life. The hills that surrounded the small town and which had given it the nickname 'Little Switzerland', were an excellent cover for storing military vehicles, fresh from the factories and being stockpiled ready for the invasion of Europe. Enemy aircraft were not likely to bother with this rural part of England, too hilly and dangerous for low reconnaissance flights. Church Stretton had a new bypass, opened just before the war, and it was decided that this wide road would be closed off again and used as a massive storage park for the stockpiled military vehicles, with camouflage netting thrown over them so that they could not be detected from above. It was argued that the local farming community hadn't had the road long enough to get used to it and besides, they could go back to using the old road, through All Stretton to get to Shrewsbury. It was wartime and sacrifices had to be made but that didn't stop the farmers and townsfolk from complaining about having to go all the way round the old road again. The small town was considered strategically important therefore, and this warranted military guards on the front and back doors to the post office/telephone exchange. Lorna was a friendly child and she chattered to the guards, making a great friend of one of them in particular, crying miserably when 'Harry' was posted elsewhere.

Betty Caine was issued with a certain amount of explosive with stern instructions to blow up the post office and telephone exchange, in the event of a German invasion of the British Isles. This conjures up a wonderful picture, even now, of this rather stout lady in her early forties at that time, laying the fuse and setting light to it while the townspeople stood well back, gawping! It poses the question of just how many post offices in England might have been reduced to smoking rubble had there been a false alarm about the Germans landing at Dover or the Isle of Wight.

I passed my leave enjoyably, playing pontoon again with Walter and Barbara on a couple of evenings. And then my spirits sank as the end of my leave approached. On the last day Joy and I walked up the Carding Mill valley, the almost vertical sides of the hills, dotted with sheep, rising steeply away from the valley floor on each side, but neither of us could relax and enjoy the beauty of the hills and the babbling stream running alongside the stony lane which wound up through the bottom of the valley, because of the heaviness in our hearts at our imminent parting. 'Blast the ruddy war!' I said and meant it.

Chapter 3

April to October 1942: Coastal Training and the Long March

I arrived back at the railway sidings by Bulford camp mid-evening on 25 April, after an extremely tiresome journey with many delays. I had returned to face bad news and several problems. One of my junior officers, Liutenant Nick Nicholson was on a parachuting course, and a friend of his had been killed when his jump went badly wrong. Nick himself was slightly injured and would not be available for an intensive training schedule that I was planning. I was very frustrated by this misfortune, as I had come to rely on Nick, finding him one of my most dependable officers. I also had to have an inoculation that we all received from time to time, and this always made us all feel very ill for a day or two. But I forced myself to keep going, however, putting my mind to the continual problem of planning the training schedule for the men in my company. Airborne troops needed to be highly trained. It presented an enormous worry to all OCs to think up new ideas to camouflage the same old training without it becoming too repetitive, despite the advantage that the airborne role in battle was a new one at that time and their training held experiences that were not to be found in other branches of the Army. It was vital to hold the men's interest and to challenge them.

I had made a study of the skills required of an infantryman. I knew that the men needed to be physically very fit but above all to have stamina – bags of it. They should be able to march ten miles in full kit in two hours and shoot straight immediately afterwards; cover twenty-two miles in full kit in six hours; stay out of doors for days in all weather with no extra clothing; scale a cliff with or without ropes; attack a man without the use of weapons, just physical combat; and they should all be able to jump ditches and streams over eight feet wide. Maintaining men at that level of fitness without them becoming stale, took some careful planning to vary their training and keep them eager and competitive. Then there were the technical skills that the trained modern infantryman needed, even in 1942. I made a list of them and carefully built these required elements into the men's programme. They needed to be first-class marksmen, have a knowledge of rifles, light machine guns, machine carbines and pistols, use small mortars, know about PIAT guns (Projection Infantry Anti-Tank Gun), throw and use many types of grenades, lay and take up mines, have a working knowledge of explosives, be ready to guard against poisonous gases, know how to use natural and artificial camouflage and use the ground for cover; apply elementary first aid and know about rations and how to cook in a mess-tin. On top of that the soldier needed to understand the complexities of tactics in the field, working with a section, a platoon or sub-unit for movement and operations. Many of the infantrymen should be able to ride a motorcycle or drive a military vehicle and know how to use a field wireless set and telephone.

This was an immense variety of skills, even accepting that the men who volunteered for the Airborne were likely to be motivated and above usual intelligence. I always held the view that my men were top-class soldiers and if they weren't, then I would bloody well see to it that they were turned into them. I fully realized the importance of excellent training and was absolutely determined that 'D' Company would be the best company in the Regiment.

Another of our problems was the uninspiring nature of the country around Bulford for training purposes. I'd tried to find more interesting terrain along the few river valleys but every time we came across a suitable place on one of our recces, we would find that the local farmers, fed-up with their crops being trampled by Army boots, had plastered the area with large signs saying 'Private Land' and 'Out of Bounds to Troops'. Thus I was obliged to carry out reconnaissance trips, usually on motorbikes with a fellow officer, to find more suitable training areas and, if possible, talk to the local farmers and gain their cooperation. I felt that it was immensely worthwhile doing this because the change of country benefited the company a great deal. Despite having to organize transport for the men, a few days away from the barracks freshened everyone up and I was to find that much of their most valuable tactical training was carried out on what I used to call 'these jaunts'. It was on one of these recces that I first met a man I always remembered with affection as Farmer Young. The Youngs lived at The Grange, Titchbourne and they were most cooperative with my necessity to train the men in the kind of farmland that combined fields and lanes with wooded copses, hills and streams – the sort of country they might well be fighting for in France. The Youngs were happy to provide barns and clean straw for the men's billets and good rooms in the farmhouse for the officers, with even a hearty cooked breakfast.

I always went to a great deal of trouble to locate such training areas and to diplomatically approach the local farmers, so that no feathers were ruffled in the process. I placed enormous emphasis on the men training in realistic conditions, both by day and night. In early May 1942, I would find a new training area at Normanton Court and only a few days later, organized the men to go there for the final day of my intensive training, which had been cut short by three days because of an inspection by Divisional Command. I was absolutely furious when officialdom got in the way of my training schemes. Nothing annoyed me more. I said, 'It's monstrous!' to the sympathetic Tod Sweeney, 'Bang goes my bloody scheme!'

On 21 May the King and Queen visited Airborne Division. The day began with heavy rain and I could see many of the top brass glancing anxiously at the sky. But by 16.00 hours when their Majesties were due, the skies had cleared and all went well. The visit was deliberately casual and the King and Queen watched a demonstration by the troops and then after gracious waves to everyone, they departed in an open-topped vehicle that was completely new to me. It was love at first sight! We referred to the vehicle then as a 'Blitz Bug', which was one of the original nicknames for what was to become universally known as a Jeep. Naturally, I could not wait to get my hands on one, and just two days later managed to obtain use of one for one of our recces. Unfortunately it was raining and we got very wet indeed, but this did not dim our enthusiasm for this new toy and I observed that although there was no cover, the 'Blitz Bug' or BB as we shortened it to, could go anywhere cross-country.

In the early 1940s, the US Army had requested all automobile manufacturers to come up with some kind of a light reconnaissance vehicle to replace the motorbike/sidecar combination, which had been used until then for reconnaissance work and sending messages. They were reasonably specific about the weight and size of such a vehicle as well as the necessary engine-power and payload. One company came up with the design for what was famously to become the Jeep. The name is believed to have derived from a slurring of the abbreviation for 'general purpose' vehicle – GP. I found this new form of transport irresistible, but it would be some time before I came to refer to it as a Jeep in my diaries. However, I began to get a reputation for being a very fast driver and somewhat wild on occasions, resulting in my junior officers in particular, becoming rather wary of travelling with me at the wheel. It came to my ears that, following me on the road one day, the driver of the lorry behind me carrying the troops remarked to his mate, 'Blimey! Did you see the way the Major took that corner?' and the other soldier said, 'Yeah – it's a good job he ain't a Glider Pilot or we wouldn't stand a bleedin' chance!'

At the end of May, another twenty-six men arrived to join 'D' Company, from the King's Rifle Regiment. We'd been down in Southampton all day on a TEWT, preparing for the company to do a three-day street fighting exercise down there. It had been a very wet month and we had all endured another day of being soaked to the skin as they planned the training exercise.

'One thing we *won't* need to train for, is ruddy wet weather' I had remarked, shaking out my heavy cape. I then went over to the troop's mess, as they sat down for their dinner, to have a look over the new contingent and noted in my diary, 'New men seem OK – all cockneys' which certainly found favour with me.

As the month of June arrived, my telephone calls to Joy were full of anticipation for the birth of our first child, which we had both hoped would be at the end of the month. Whether it was this added frustration of waiting upon events that were beyond my control, I felt even more tense and ready to fly off the handle than usual. Colonel Giles was being posted and Colonel Guy Rowley was taking over with Peter Young as his 2 I/C. A route march was cancelled as the men were engaged elsewhere and, infuriated by this setback, I decided to organize and set-up a sand table ready to lecture the men. This simple device was exactly what it sounded like – a children's sand-box, in table form. It was used for planning exercises and tactics, and was intended for group participation. As a visual aid for a lecture on battle tactics, when the men's interest could easily stray, I would find it a most useful tool. This was the first time I'd utilized it and I was keen to get the men's input.

The weather had now turned very hot, and when a glider exercise was suddenly cancelled, I blew my stack, putting in my diary 'What a bloody Army this is! Roll on! Roll on!' in total exasperation. I marched over to the company office to see the Colonel and got the glider exercise rescheduled for two days' time. In the meantime, I was able to brief a platoon on the sand table and was pleased with the result. The glider exercise on 9 June proved successful and brought up quite a few new points for consideration. So it was that I returned to the officers' mess in the evening feeling more cheerful. I remember the sun was setting behind the curve of the plains beyond Bulford camp, and somewhere not too far away a farmer was mowing his fields and the sweet country smell of haymaking filled the air. The telephone shrilled in the mess and I was called to speak to the Adjutant. 'What now?' I wondered irritably, as I picked up the receiver. The Adjutant was brief and to the point. I should instruct an orderly to 'put up your Crown', for I was promoted to major!

As June 1942 progressed, I found myself becoming even more jumpy and irritable than ever as I waited for news of the birth of our first child. Everyone I came into contact with felt the sting of my short temper, especially my junior officers. I overheard Chalky White saying to Tod Sweeney 'Lord! I wish to God that the OC's wife would have that ruddy baby!' when they returned from yet another route march on 19 June, when White had felt the rough edge of my tongue for not putting enough effort into it. Sweeney had answered, 'Yes, little does she know that we are all as desperate for it all to be over as she is!'

But Joy was certainly suffering more than any of them. Maternity clothes in 1942 consisted of thigh-length home-made smocks in heavy cotton, worn over a straight skirt with a laced waistband for expansion. Joy was saving her clothing coupons to buy cottons to make summer dresses for after the baby was born, so as the hot days of June dragged by for her, she sweltered, bulky and uncomfortable in heavy clothes; my normally eye-catching wife of twenty-two, for the first time in her life feeling bloated and unattractive. I realize now that she felt depressed and sometimes frightened. Above all, she said that she wished that I could have been beside her for support and comfort.

Joy's mother and her husband, Tom Caine, were busy packing up at the flat over the post office in Church Stretton, for they were about to move. Tom had decided that with Lorna growing and the prospect of Joy living with them for a while at least, the time had come for the family to move to a house of their own. Tom and Betty Caine liked to play their cards close to their chests in respect of money matters. The prospect of any speculation about their plans or what their financial position might be, was anathema to them both. Secrets and hushed conversations were the order of the day and Joy knew better than to ask questions. So it wasn't until Lorna mentioned that she was 'going to have a real garden to play in' in front of Joy and her mother, that Joy found out about the move and Betty was obliged to expand further on the subject. At such a late stage in her pregnancy, Joy had mixed feelings but dutifully helped them to pack up as best she could.

Worrying about Joy so far away from me increased my irritability and I was like a primed grenade ready to explode. I had become particularly irritated by the new Battalion 2 I/C, Major Peter Young, who was a stickler for keeping correct records, one of the more superior of the officers and definitely not my type at all. I recorded one day in late June that Peter Young had made a lot of what we called 'bumph' for training that was extra and, in my view, unnecessary paperwork. On the following day, I noted in my diary that I'd '. . . spent late evening typing ruddy schemes for the benefit of "Sour-Puss" Young'. I happened to be several officers short at the time, with some on leave and others on various courses, and this had made me feel more pressured than ever. A night operation exercise with the men when they did a river crossing in the dark went well but, on returning to the barracks the next morning feeling understandably sluggish, I had another verbal spat with Young. I found Nick Nicholson in the officers' mess and said furiously to him, 'I've just had another bloody row with "Sour-Puss" Young! He's giving me hell because I let Tod and Woody go on leave at the same time. I tried to make light of it but he can be such an arrogant bastard!' Nick was aware that I had a bee in my bonnet about Young and he'd replied, 'Yes, he's a bit of a know-all, John. I call him Peter Wise', alluding to a popular wireless programme of the time. But I was not mollified and continued to feel immensely pressured and irritable and felt that Young was too haughty to approach with any of my problems, leaving me feeling vulnerable and put-upon.

By 3 July the Caines had made the move to their new home, Hill Crest. It was a house on the outskirts of Church Stretton, on what was actually a continuation of Sandford Avenue. This wide, tree-lined road was always known to the family as the 'New Road' and Hill Crest lay about one third of the way up on the right-hand side. It was a substantial, three storey family house set in a pleasant garden, fringed by mature pines and deciduous trees. This was to be the Caines' home, bar the odd hiccough, for the rest of the decade and was enshrined in Lorna's memory as her favourite family home for the rest of her life. It was also to be the first home for our son Terence John Bromley Howard, born on 12 July 1942 at College Hill Nursing Home in Shrewsbury. I wrote in my diary for that day, 'A Son!!! God Bless my Joy, how I long to see them.' I did not drink much at that time but was persuaded to make an exception on this occasion. It must be imagined that my junior officers celebrated my son's arrival almost as much as I did.

The news of the baby's arrival had reached me after a particularly unpleasant couple of days. For one thing I had lost my 2 I/C Chalky White to another company and was told that Brian Priday was to replace him. I particularly liked Priday so this was not a problem but it meant that I would have to train him, and it would take time for him to be up to speed and as useful as Chalky had been. Also, I had been out for two rainy nights with the platoons on Cranbourne Chase ranges for field firing and had given Tod Sweeney a bad time when his 25 Platoon made mistakes. 24 Platoon were out with me the following night and David Wood made sure they performed much better and, abrasive as I was feeling, I was able to comment that they'd stayed alert all night. Woody must have breathed a sigh of relief as I marched grumpily away towards the pickup truck.

On 20 July my feet fairly flew as I ran to catch the train. I arrived in Shrewsbury by 15.00 and went straight up the road to the College Hill Nursing Home to see Joy and Terry. I truly felt as if I had never been so happy in my life as I hugged Joy to me and gazed upon my little son's face for the first time. I had arranged to spend the night in Shrewsbury with Joy's aunt, Ina Barnwell, so that I could go into the hospital again the following morning to see Joy and the baby. Then I had Terry's birth registered and caught the train to Church Stretton, walking from the station up the sloping road to Hill Crest, which I was seeing for the first time. The house impressed me enormously and as I was welcomed into the spacious hallway by Joy's mother, Tom Caine stood behind her with a smile that was a greeting in one eye and a 'See what a splendid house I've got, soldier!' in the other. But I didn't care for I was over the moon. Writing in my diary that night, I put 'To Hill Crest for the first time – preparing for my family. Grand!'

The next day, I fetched Joy and baby Terry home to Hill Crest where Lorna was so excited with her new baby cousin that she thought it was Christmas in July.

The next few days were happily spent settling Joy into her new routine with the baby. Three days later, Betty's two sisters, Ina and Mollie, arrived to welcome this new member of the family. On 25 July, the 'churching' took place. This was an old custom in which the new baby and mother go to church as a thanksgiving for the safe arrival of a healthy child. It was a very happy occasion, with all the family going to church together and then returning to Hill Crest for tea. Tom Caine produced a bottle of Scotch and he and I shared a glass or two, content in each other's company and happily watching the women fussing over the new baby and spoiling little Lorna. I just couldn't bear to think that my leave was coming to an end so soon and I would be returning to 'bloody Bulford'.

Next afternoon I was back to the reality of the war and my job with 'D' Company but I found that Nick had done a good job in my absence and 'D' Company had managed to win a 'Know Your Enemy' competition. Even Peter Young seemed more civil, but I couldn't overcome my dislike of the fellow. The Company was buzzing with the news that arrangements had been made for the Regiment to go down to Ilfracombe in Devon for three weeks' coastal training in a few days time, and I immediately began to make plans for this.

Just as I was packing up to go to Ilfracombe, I had a surprising telephone call from Joy one evening, suggesting that she ask my mother if she would like to go up to Church Stretton for a week or so. I was delighted with this kind offer, for several reasons. I had been in touch with the family in London and learned that Mom had been profoundly down and depressed ever since she had heard of my brother Percy's death. She had gone on brooding about it and the family all felt that what she really needed was a change of air and 'a bit of a holiday'. I had told Joy about this and she had evidently talked about it with her mother and they had decided that now they had so much more room at Hill Crest, it would be a kindness to ask my mother to visit. I telephoned my parents and the visit was quickly arranged and Mom took the train up to Shropshire a few days later, on 5 August. She was made very welcome there – it was the only time she visited Joy's family but by all accounts the visit was a success. I was very grateful for this thoughtful gesture from Joy's family and rather hoped that it would herald a new era of understanding between Joy and my mother.

The Regiment set off for Ilfracombe and 'D' Company was billeted in a hotel overlooking the sea. I felt that it was a bit cramped, but the view and sea air more than made up for any inconvenience. Many of the men had rarely seen the sea, and at least a couple of them had never been to the coast before in their lives! They were excited and very enthusiastic about training under these new conditions. For myself, I could hardly wait to go swimming in the Lido overlooking the beach. Ever since I was a boy, I could never resist the opportunity to strip off, don a bathing suit and dive into the water. It was one of my favourite pastimes. Unfortunately for the three weeks we were there the weather was unkind and there was rain and mist instead of the sunshine we had all hoped for. The men did platoon training on the beach, firing live ammunition over each other's heads into the sea. They were all most amused to find that the crowd of holiday-makers and locals who had gathered to watch, were pretty shaken by the bullets flying around and scampered back up the beach into the dunes to take cover.

I had all the men in the swimming pool to select a team for the Regimental Gala. During the practice swims I managed to come first in both breast and backstroke. I took it as a personal affront when 'B' Company just managed to beat 'D' Company during the actual Gala, but succeeded in performing well myself. The weather continued to be fairly dismal and as a result of all the swimming practice I caught a bad cold and felt pretty fed-up, specially when my post seemed to have been snarled-up somewhere and I didn't get any letters from Joy for nearly a week.

The assault course at Woolacombe was legendarily difficult and included a section of cliff-climbing which got the better of many of the men. David Wood would remember forever that there was also a confidence test they all had to go through, in which the platoons advanced along the beach in extended order while coming under machine-gun fire from the sand dunes. Live ammunition was used, in theory above their heads and in front and behind them, but Wood recalled it as all too realistic and very dangerous. There was a special technique for handling this situation, which was basically to run like hell. To add further realism to this scenario, the instructors threw home-made grenades at their feet as they ran. These grenades were supposed to be all noise and no impact but Wood had his eardrum blown in by one nevertheless, and was hospitalized for six weeks thereby missing the best bit of all, which was the 128 mile march back to Bulford.

At the end of three weeks the company spent the last day cleaning their billet and packing up. We set off for Bulford bright and early on the morning of 27 August in full kit, marching over the hills of Devon in blazing hot sunshine. In those days I had a stick that I habitually marched with; it had a brass cap that made a noise as it struck the road with each stride. The men sweated and cursed in their heavy serge battledress. Even I remember it as absolute hell. Men were falling by the wayside left, right and centre from the ranks of the Regiment, even from 'D' Company. I decided to act swiftly by pulling the men aside that I knew were stirring up the unrest and giving them a sharp lecture on discipline, example and *esprit de corps*. We camped by a stream for the night and the men asked if they could wear lighter clothes the next day. Permission was granted to march in their shirt-sleeves. They marched almost thirty miles to St Andrews Bay the following day, where they again camped for the night. Some of the men were so dehydrated and exhausted that we didn't set off until lunchtime the next day but managed to march fourteen miles during the afternoon. The men were still marching in their shirt-sleeves when the temperature suddenly dropped and a cold, hard rain fell, soaking every man to the skin. Still, I noted optimistically in my diary that 'D' company were marching much better and their spirits were high. We spent the third night jammed into a Salvation Army Hall and none of us slept well. The Regiment was off early next morning. During the day one of 'D' Company collapsed and, having lost another one to heat exhaustion on the first day, we were now two men down. But we spent the third night in a village school and, because we were not so cramped, all managed to sleep better.

On the fourth day, the men were put onto hard rations and Tod Sweeney in particular was suffering from badly blistered feet. His feet actually ran with blood that seeped into his boots but he went on marching. My brass-capped walking stick was beginning to look battered and worn. The fourth night was passed in a hutted camp which I thought at the time was very cushy but possibly anything with a roof was looking good by that time. At last the end was in sight and 'D' Company's excellent marching meant that we were placed at the head of the Regiment.

I later learned that one of the men, Tom Packwood, had said to his mate that he reckoned that I had a bet on with a couple of other officers that 'D' Company would 'win' the place at the head of the Regiment and I didn't care if the poor buggers crawled back into Spider block just as long as they marched in first. I believe Wally Parr had quipped, 'I know where I'd like to ram that bleedin' walkin' stick'. But, despite the grumbles, they marched better than ever, because nobody wanted to let 'D' Company down. They covered twenty-five miles on the last day and for the final five miles, had to march at full regimental pace with 'rifles trailing' just for good measure. Major Peter Young took the salute as 'D' Company swept into Bulford camp in record time and I can truthfully say that it was one of my proudest moments. 'D' Company's feat was the talk of the Regiment. Poor Tod Sweeney only just made it and it was later said he marched on courage alone for the last two days. The brass cap on my walking-stick was worn almost entirely away and I had to discard it.

In the afternoon of the next day, 'D' Company were granted forty-eight hours' leave with immediate effect and I lost no time in catching the train and travelling all night. I reached Church Stretton at 07.00 and ran up the road to Hill Crest. Finding nobody yet up, I climbed in through a window and surprised Joy with a cup of tea. My son Terry had grown enormously and the family was on standby in case I could make it home for Terry's christening. So it was all arranged for the following day, 4 September, and Terry was christened at a private chapel at a large house just down the road from Hill Crest. Joy had made herself a very pretty frock of floral cotton and looked wonderful as she stood proudly by my side in my service dress uniform with my brand-new Airborne red beret pulled to the right over my hair.

The leave was over all too soon and I was on my way back to Bulford. Having a drink in the Mess that evening, Nick Nicholson said with a grin, 'I say, John, have you heard that Peter Young's been recommended for a Staff Officer's Course?'

'Really?' I said, trying to feign interest.

'Yes' said Nick, 'They're long courses, you know, he should be away for two months!'

'Well, in that case' I replied, brightening considerably, 'I think he really should go, don't you?'

'Absolutely, old man' replied Nick, raising his glass, 'Chin-chin!'

There was another glider exercise the next day. I was irritated by the lack of coordination between the Army and RAF, which I naturally put down to inefficiency on the part of the RAF. I can recall that the glider landed with a very jarring bump and I reflected that we were lucky that the only casualty had been Brotheridge who suffered a stiff neck. I was back into full training mode with the men, out on the thirty-yard firing range, where I noted with satisfaction that they were improving their shooting skills. That afternoon I began to put a boxing team together, weighing in myself at eleven and a half stones.

A very quick twenty-four hour visit to London to see the family, brought swift retribution on my head from Joy. She didn't telephone me for two days after I got back to Bulford and I began to worry that something was really wrong. 'D' Company were all going around in shirt-sleeves despite the chilly days at the end of September, the idea being that it would toughen us up, and I found myself feeling bleak both inside and out after Joy finally rang me late in the evening. I rather wished that she hadn't bothered for she was both angry and spiteful about me going to London without her. Joy had never forgotten that I been engaged to the daughter of one of my mother's friends for several years before I met her. Perhaps Mom had said something to her when she'd been up in Shropshire that had stirred Joy's feelings up again. I really didn't understand why my wife, who was normally sweet-tempered and loving, could so suddenly flare up at the thought of me being 'at large' in London on my own. 'What she thinks I can get up to in just twenty-four hours, I can't imagine,' I thought ruefully to myself. The odd pint in the Green Man with Pop was hardly living dangerously. But the next day, Joy was on the phone to me again, full of remorse for her bad temper. She said that baby Terry was waking in the night and yelling loudly, 'He's got a voice like a sergeant major!' she said, causing me to smile broadly. Joy went on, 'I simply dare not let him cry for long as it disturbs everyone else in the house.' She'd just been tired and feeling a bit low, she said and she missed 'her John' more than I would ever know. After that, I went around with a spring in my step again.

By early October 1942, I was ready for a break from the routine at Bulford. Arrangements had been made for me to attend a battle drill course in Derbyshire, but before that I was off on a week's leave in Shropshire. I travelled up there overnight and was knocking on the door of Hill Crest by 07.10. Joy was used to my ways by then, and was already up and with breakfast ready for me. Terry, full of noise and smiles, was in the kitchen with her. I discovered that Joy's grandmother, Gram, was at Hill Crest as well, and we all made a happy family gathering. Lorna would remember her grandmother's visits to them from New Brighton with affection, and was surprised to find that whenever Gram stayed with them, they never ran into her grandfather, the Governor, and yet they usually saw him every week. The estranged couple evidently gave each other a wide berth.

Next day we called in at Windyways to see Walter and Barbara, but we found Walter up in arms over a letter he had received. 'Look John,' he said, waving the letter in the air. 'They say that I'm eligible for the Army – at my age! Don't they know I work in agriculture?' Walter was plainly rather worried. He was, in fact, in his early forties at that time. But I found it difficult to be sympathetic – I had been in the Army almost from the beginning of the war myself, and there was a growing resentment between the men who were serving in the Forces and some of those who had been exempted from military duty. It was perceived that there was a section of society at least who were thought to be getting away with it and furthermore, profiting by doing so, in safe, well-paid civilian jobs. Much as I liked Walter Sagar as a person, it seemed to me that here was a fit man, in his prime, still living and working in safety at home. These feelings were to come to a head soon enough, but faced with the indignant Walter, I tried hard to be non-committal on the subject. In the event, Walter Sagar appealed against his call-up and his occupation was deemed important enough to national food production to exempt him.

Next day my leave was over and it was time once again to return to Bulford.

Chapter 4

October 1942 to June 1943: Christmas at Bulford and Return to Ilfracombe

My week's leave had been over all too soon and on 18 October I made my way to Chesterfield by train via Crewe. The course was useful and after the exigencies and boredom of training, I felt sometimes as if I was on a holiday. On the first day we found ourselves 'crawling under fire' and I was pleased to note that at the end of it there were no casualties. The skies seemed to me to be full of paratroopers being trained and I realized that much emphasis was going to be placed on the Airborne Forces when the invasion of Europe came. I got on well with a fellow officer on the course, Dick Bartlett, and we took advantage of the excellent entertainment laid on for us with ENSA concerts and films. It was quite a hard course physically, with assault courses and cross-country runs, but I thrived on all of that. The 'storming pillbox with flame thrower' day on the course went down especially well. But on the next day, I found myself out on the Derbyshire moors, crawling up the bed of a stream with live ammunition whipping around me, and decided that it wasn't quite so much fun. However, a good grouse dinner at The Shoulder of Mutton with Dick Bartlett restored my humour. My long letters from Joy also cheered me and the promise of another night at Church Stretton that could be squeezed in when the course finished, on the way back to Bulford, made it all seem worthwhile. Even a night 'op' hurriedly digging-in amidst a heavy wet November fog before dusk, failed to dampen my spirits. I found myself staring up into the under-belly of a great Churchill tank the next day as it rumbled over our trenches during a mock dawn attack. I could see that this kind of experience was excellent preparation for what was to come and would enable me to pass on this knowledge to 'D' Company during training.

It was back to Bulford the following day, to find that despite me being away for a whole month, Brian Priday and Nick Nicholson had kept things running smoothly.

I was crossing the barrack square when I saw Peter Young walking towards me. I had completely forgotten that Young would have returned from his SO course. I thought, 'Hell! – Sour-Puss Young is back to drive us all barmy!' when, to my surprise, Young greeted me in a friendly manner and asked if I wanted to go for a run with him. I was too taken aback to do anything but agree. We met up half an hour later and set off at a steady pace along the lanes around Bulford and chatted as we went along. I was genuinely astonished to find that we had very similar views on many of the subjects that we discussed. On a one to one basis, I found that I could get on well with Peter Young, but somehow, in the working environment Young's manner irritated me profoundly. He came from an upper-class background and his attitudes and interests were alien to someone with my history. The officers usually had Saturday afternoons and Sundays to follow their own activities and at such times, Peter Young and other officers of a similar type would be invited to go shooting or fishing, and I could be extremely scathing then about such pursuits. My goodwill towards Peter Young proved to be only a temporary lapse and I was soon back to cursing under my breath every time Young came into view carrying files of instructions and directives.

At the end of November 1942 during glider training, one of the gliders crashed and six of the 'S' Company lads were killed. This accident brought home very forcibly to all the glider-borne troops how dangerous it could be. On the same day, news reached me of another friend who had been killed on active service overseas and someone else broke his leg during training. It was no wonder that after grenade throwing training, I was relieved to note that there had been no casualties. Although the men enjoyed throwing grenades and seeing the explosions that followed, accidents were frequent and often disastrous. David Wood regaled us in the mess with tales of how one or other of the men had pulled the grenade pin and then dropped the ruddy thing in the bay from which they were throwing them. All hell would break loose with wild yells from both the man concerned and the instructor, to get out of the bay immediately and take cover. Occasionally someone would move too slowly and be caught in the blast. Such things happened when soldiers trained with live grenades. It was inevitable that accidents occurred from time to time.

'D' Company did well in the Inter-Company cross-country run at the beginning of December. I had been absolutely determined to do well in this event and my training schedule had been unrelenting. News had reached me that there was discontent among the men, mainly caused by a fifteen mile march with the warrant officers, which had been followed by a soccer match against the Royal Ulster Rifles. This would have been acceptable but for the fact that the organization had forgotten to lay on food for the men – usually considered to be a major feature of such an event. The cross-country run took place a few days later, with me also taking part as usual. To my delight, 'D' Company won easily, coming in at what I later described as a canter and I came in sixth. Capitalizing on success, I gathered the men of 'D' Company together and gave them a pep-talk which seemed to go down well with them all and I felt it had settled the men's grievances.

In the officers' mess that evening, I found that 'D' Company winning the Inter-Company cross-country was the main topic of conversation and many a toast was drunk to their success in the Brigade cross-country which was to be a few days later. I walked the course with the team, my usual practice, and said later that it was a 'pukka brute of a course'. Even I was falling into the Indian phrases of the Ox & Bucks. Nevertheless, our team won the Brigade cross-country and I was full of pride writing in my diary 'Am on top of the world'. Christmas was coming and three days afterwards I would once more be on leave for nine days. I even found myself wishing Peter Young the compliments of the season in the officers' mess.

Christmas 1942 was a light-hearted time for me. I was aware, as everyone was, that the Regiment was likely to be mobilized in the early part of the following year, but rather than dreading this eventuality, it was in my nature to eagerly await the opportunity at long last to play a part in the real action of the war. I was full of energy and enthusiasm. Knowing that the Oxford City Police dance was being held on the evening of 21 December, it did not take long for me to persuade Brian Priday to scrounge a 'Blitz Bug' with me and slip off to Oxford for the dance. We had a great time there, the ladies admiring our dress uniforms and generally making us feel like regular heroes. I was pleased to see all my old friends there and they all wanted news about Joy and Terence John Howard. I found myself handing around snapshots to admiring comments. Brian and I could hardly tear ourselves away to make the journey in the open-topped Blitz Bug back to Bulford.

'D' Company were organizing a stag party to be held in the gym on Christmas Eve. It would be a chance for the men to let their hair down and they were preparing a couple of 'sketches' in which they could poke fun at the officers. This was the one time of year that they could get away with this. The party was a great success and I found myself laughing until my tummy ached. In this warm glow I went to Midnight Mass, wishing that my beloved Joy was beside me, holding my hand. Christmas Day on camp was spent attending early church parade and then a football match. Christmas dinner was served and afterwards it was traditional for the officers to make hospital visits to any of the men unfortunate enough to be laid up over Christmas. My idea of a jolly Boxing Day was a seven mile cross-country run which naturally 'D' Company won, and then the officers went off to the 'flicks' together.

I was on leave in Church Stretton for New Year 1943. I remember that it snowed heavily and we were confined to the house much of the time, but I loved every moment with my family. I did manage to get into Shrewsbury to be fitted for a new service dress uniform at the tailor there. My diary entry for New Year's

Day read 'Wonder where I'll be this time next year? – we're sure to be needed in the spring. Roll on and lets get it over!' Still on leave in Church Stretton, a situation arose that made me aware of the difficulties Joy faced living in her mother's home. She was a very tidy and organized person; what might almost be called 'an obsessive cleaner' in today's terminology. Betty Caine however was much more casual about her household and Joy had become increasingly irritated by what she saw as muddle and dust around her. Matters were not improved by the necessity for the Caines to find room at Hill Crest for a family who had been evacuated to Shropshire with St Dunstans, a charity for the blind, and they occupied half of the two upper floors of the house. This naturally made the living conditions more restricted there and Joy felt confined and lacking in privacy. Two days into the New Year, Joy decided to turn out the Caines' sitting room and set about it with zeal, using me to help her move furniture and carpets. I was disappointed at missing an opportunity of a fine day to take Terry for a walk in his pram and found that I wasn't the only one to be put out. Betty was confined to the kitchen with the children and she finally became so impatient that she went into the sitting room to demand that Joy bring this premature spring-clean to an end. Joy was at the end of her tether too and the two had a furious argument ending in Betty erupting into the hall shouting, 'Well Joy, if you don't like the way we live perhaps you'd better find somewhere else to go!' Betty Caine had a mighty temper when she lost it and the phrase 'Mommy's in one of her moods' could strike terror into other members of the family down the years and clear the house quicker than an air-raid siren in London. Joy was in tears by that time and I helped her clear up and we eventually did take Terry out for a walk.

By the time we got back to Hill Crest Betty had calmed down and made tea for us all. She realized that somehow she and Joy must get on living with one another at close quarters and she made the suggestion that Joy could use the small morning room just as her own sitting room where she could be alone at times. It was a very thoughtful gesture and Joy was delighted to accept this offer. We set about buying some furniture and turning the room into a comfortable retreat for Joy and Terry. I was immensely relieved by this compromise because the prospect of them without a home did not bear thinking about.

All too soon my leave was at an end and I was back into the thick of it at Bulford, irritated by the Battalion 2 I/C, Major Peter Young and the inevitable pile of 'bumph' that emanated from him. There was a battle drill demonstration and our Divisional Commander, the dashing General 'Windy' Gale, set all the young officers' tongues wagging by turning up clad in what was known as a 'flying smock'. This was a loose-fitting jacket, worn over a battledress, and made out of a thick, camouflage-patterned material. It was versatile and extremely warm and it was the first time that any of us had seen one. Since they were to be standard issue, all of the young officers immediately applied for these 'flying smocks' and within a couple of weeks, most of us were similarly attired. I took a great liking to mine, finding it both comfortable and very warm, wearing it long after the war was over when I was gardening.

In contrast, my new service dress uniform had been dispatched to me from the tailor in Church Stretton, arriving at the end of January and I wore it to dinner in the mess and was much gratified by the compliments received from my fellow officers. These things mattered to us all and were a great boost to our morale. Everyone was on tenterhooks about the Regiment being sent on active service very soon.

I was up to my eyes planning a whole week of night training, scheduled for the end of January. At that time Peter Young was usually invited away to a house-party at weekends as many officers in the old county regiments like the Ox & Bucks were. If they were near enough to London and the home counties many such officers from privileged backgrounds would continue to go away for week-ends, visiting friends and to carry on enjoying shooting parties, hunting or other such activities. This was guaranteed to bring out all of my prejudices against upper-class pursuits, but my disparaging remarks were quelled on this occasion by Brian Priday saying, 'Well John, Young's off on leave this week, so at least we'll get some peace for the night training!' to which I had replied, 'Thank God for that!'

The first night training was to be a 'UT' exercise; that is for the platoons to be taken in a covered truck some distance and dropped off at night in unknown territory, and it was up to them to work out where they were and find their way to a chosen rendezvous within a time limit. Such was my desire for this exercise to be as challenging as possible, I had cursed the fact that a full moon would mean that the men would be able to see much more clearly at night and that would make their task easier. David Wood's platoon arrived at the rendezvous in admirably quick time and I was very impressed with their orienteering abilities, until Wood let slip that his Corporal, in a fine display of initiative, had spotted a nearby farmhouse and knocked up the inhabitants to find out where they were. It had honestly not occurred to me that anyone would take such a simple short-cut. I had envisaged the men studying their maps and compasses for some time, then having furious disagreements trying to pinpoint their exact location, before taking the wrong direction several times until they finally found their way to the rendezvous.

In general the men hated this prolonged night training. Reveille was at 18.30 in the evening and lunch at 01.00 and it played havoc with their digestions as well as their sleep patterns. But the more they did it, the more they found that their bodies became used to adapting to the new regime. The cold winter weather did not help, and most nights we all got soaked to the skin. By the end of the week there was a hard frost to add to our discomfort and I was glad when our final exercise finished by 06.45 and I could get my head down for four hours' sleep before dragging myself off again to do yet another recce for more training locations.

Glad of a week's peace from Peter Young, I was on my way to meet my fellow officers in the bar of the mess when I noticed him entering the Battalion HQ.

'Peter Young's back almost a day early from leave!' I said to Nick Nicholson, absolutely infuriated. 'The man's a menace!' Coming back early from leave was simply unheard of.

'Actually' said Nick, 'The word is that Young is being posted.'

'Is that so?' I said, my interest immediately taken by this uplifting piece of news.

I was using a bicycle one night to get across the camp, pedalling furiously in double quick time as was my wont when, in the impenetrable darkness of the blackout, I ran into the end of a building I hadn't expected to be there. I hit my knee hard as I came off the bike and it had to be plastered up and I was unable to take part in the brigade cross-country run the following day. I was frustrated enough with myself, without incurring Peter Young's wrath again and a sneering remark about my 'crazy bull-at-a-gate attitude letting the Company down'. The cool, calculating and aristocratic Young was never likely to understand the impetuous energy of a man like me. We were creatures from different worlds. However, it came to pass, that within a fortnight, Young was posted, and eventually commanded a parachute brigade, which landed in Sicily. Thus, I was able to comment privately in my diary that I felt relieved to be rid of this man who had been a constant thorn in my side. I also felt at that time that many of the other officers were equally pleased to see the back of Young. He seemed to be the kind of man who rubbed a lot of people up the wrong way. Therefore, I felt a pang of remorse and not a little shame, on receiving a letter from Peter Young a few days later saying generously that in his opinion, 'D' Company was the best damn company in the Regiment!

On 12 February 1943, while out on the ranges doing a field firing exercise, David Wood accidentally shot Den Brotheridge in the calf, when his notoriously unreliable Sten gun went off unexpectedly. Wood felt absolutely dreadful about this as he saw Den taken off on a field gate which they improvised as a stretcher to Shaftesbury Hospital, but as his OC I could see immediately that it was a complete accident and supported Wood at the Court of Inquiry, which was held two days later at the hospital. Later that same month a man in 'B' Company was shot through the stomach by a Sten gun in a similar mishap. Sadly it was an all too frequent occurrence. Wood was cleared of all blame, but he was the kind of chap who went on feeling very bad about the accident in any event. On visiting Den with me, Wood stood awkwardly by Brotheridge's bed, proffering his chocolate ration, some apples and several magazines and promised they'd have 'a damn good night out' when Den was up and fit again. Den was a good looking chap and winked at a pretty nurse as she swept by the end of his bed in her starched uniform. 'I was ready for a rest, old man,' he told David Wood, smiling,

'The scenery in here is jolly good, anyway!' We both followed his glance and smiled appreciatively. Both Wood and I got the impression that Brotheridge would not be short of visitors.

Although I was very understanding and supportive of David Wood, with the benefit of hindsight I can see that I did not always read situations right and could at times appear very hard with some of the men. On the very same day that I stood up for Wood, I had my Company Sergeant Major, McGovern, in front of me and delivered a lecture on malingering. McGovern had been off sick a couple of times with what he had said were 'headaches'. I considered headaches to be 'a women's complaint' and had no time at all for that kind of nonsense. I was pleased therefore to note that McGovern returned to duty forthwith. A week or so later he was once again on sick leave and at the beginning of March he was admitted to hospital with a suspected tumour in the head. Sadly that was the end of him and I wrote in my diary 'Damn bad luck!' But whether I meant this remark for 'D' Company or the unfortunate McGovern, was never made clear at the time.

Mobilization was very much in the air in early 1943, and it was important that all the men were kept up to date with their inoculations. Brian Priday was in bed for nearly a week after he reacted badly to his vaccinations and with Den Brotheridge still in hospital, I missed him badly. I had a very bad night myself after my own inoculations with what I described as 'delirium and bad dreams' and I recall being very shaky for a couple of days. But this did not prevent me from taking the company on an eighteen mile route march that every man completed in five hours and twenty minutes. The new Battalion 2 I/C, Mark Darrell-Brown who had replaced Peter Young, met us halfway and was pleased at our performance and attitude. I liked Darrell-Brown at first and thought he was a 'good chap' and was gratified to find that he did not interfere like Young had done.

On 7 March, with Brian Priday and Tod Sweeney I went to visit Den Brotheridge in hospital and found him in great form. I felt sure that he would soon be out. A few days after that, Priday's medical inspection revealed kidney trouble and he found himself taken into Shaftesbury Hospital as well! I was now missing two of my officers and was obliged to take on Priday's office work myself. I hoped very much that both Brotheridge and Priday would soon be back with 'D' Company, but on 20 March, I received the news from the doctor that neither man would be leaving the hospital for some time to come.

The Regiment was to be mobilized very soon to fight overseas. In fact, it was originally intended that it would be joining the Airborne Forces that were going to invade Sicily. This meant that neither Priday nor Brotheridge would be with the company when we left for active service. I was privately devastated by this news but in public it was necessary to keep morale high and I took it on the chin. Nick Nicholson had assumed the duties of 2 I/C for 'D' Company temporarily. I went in to Shaftesbury to see my two friends in hospital and took in a box of food for them. On the following day, 21 March, I received the official warning that we would all be given embarkation leave. It was typical of my attitude then that my reaction was of pure jubilation, writing in my diary, 'At last!! Let's get going!' Three days later, I was catching the train to Church Stretton.

Joy was very disturbed at my news that the war was about to start for me and 'D' Company very soon. It seemed at times to be happening somewhere else and to other people but now this was all to change. I was thrilled and excited at the prospect of finally getting a chance to prove my leadership skills and carry out whatever task 'D' Company was given. For Joy, however, it was very different. All she could think of was that I might not come back or, if I did, that I might be badly wounded. These could be our last days together and Terry might have to grow up without a father. She went very quiet and I could see that it was an effort for her to put on a brave face and behave normally. Terry was teething and had disturbed nights, refusing to be left in anyone else's care. One night we were asked to Walter and Barbara's house to play cards and decided to take him with us wrapped in a blanket. It wasn't considered 'the done thing' to take babies out at night in those days and there were no facilities for doing so, but Walter and Barbara smiled indulgently and suggested we put him to sleep on their bed. We kept checking him but he slept quite peacefully there and at the end of the evening we walked back from Windyways with me carrying him snug in his blanket in my arms. Joy linked her arm through mine and both of us wished that it could always be that way, the three of us together. I even felt like we had our own home when we got back late after Betty, Tom and Lorna were all in bed, and we could go into Joy's little room and be alone together.

My brother, Leslie, was stationed fairly near to Shropshire, at St Athan in Wales with the RAF and was invited over to Church Stretton that weekend to join us all at Hill Crest. The weather was very good and we had a splendid time. I was like a dog with two tails to show my brother the beauties of the Church Stretton countryside and the fine family home at Hill Crest, to say nothing of my lovely wife and wonderful son! I was also proud for the Caines to see my brother looking very dashing in his RAF uniform. Joy's family made Les very welcome and Les made a great fuss of little Terry. He thought that Terry favoured the Howard side of the family in his features, but he had Betty Caine's brown eyes that could twinkle when she was in a good mood. I took Leslie down to the station on the Sunday evening to catch the train back to his Squadron, and as I retraced my steps up the hill towards Hill Crest, that familiar sinking feeling came over me as I realized that my leave was over as well, and the dreaded goodbyes would soon have to be made.

The next morning it was time to go. I held Terry in my arms and kissed him goodbye, feeling dead inside. Joy went with me to Shrewsbury to see me off on the train south. She was wearing a new suit and looked so pretty and I didn't know how I could bear to leave her. She tried so hard to be brave, but the tears overcame her as I stepped up onto the train and it pulled out of the station, I leaned from the window and watched her growing smaller and smaller, still waving from the platform and looking very alone.

I made the changes of train from Northampton to Waterloo and thence to Andover like an automaton, finally reaching Andover at 18.30. David Wood was waiting for me in a Blitz Bug. David must have taken one look at my face and decided to leave well alone.

Back at Bulford, I found out that the embarkation was not after all, imminent. Whatever was happening had been deferred until mid-summer, so I was able to ring Joy and tell her that I would be certain to get another leave in before we went off. All the companies were hard at work perfecting their drill ready for a big parade with the 43rd and 52nd Ox & Bucks on 10 April. The parade went off very well and we were inspected by the colonel of the Regiment and other top brass including General Paget, GOC Home Forces. We officers celebrated the success of this grand military occasion in our messes and the subsequent hang-overs were equally impressive! We were all full of enthusiasm and ready to go. Therefore, it was a really profound disappointment for the whole regiment when, on 12 April 1943, we were informed that a decision had been taken that the 52nd were not to go abroad after all. Our time had not yet come. It was the 1st Airborne and not the 6th who were to be mobilized, the lads from the South Staffs. and the Borders. I felt completely depressed about this piece of news and so did the rest of 'D' Company. But we had to come to terms with it and carry on training. My immediate thought was that I must try to get the men out of the barracks and vary their training so that they did not dwell on their disappoint-ment and lose the enthusiasm that had marked their progress so far. It was to turn out later that we were all very fortunate not to be chosen for that particular mission. There would be much to learn from the mistakes that were made in Sicily and the 6th Airborne would benefit from being much better prepared for our own action the following year in Normandy.

'D' Company was immersed in exercises and I organized a night out under canvas. The weather was fine and dry for the end of April and I was pleased to note that everyone enjoyed a night under the stars. The local farmer, named Bright, was a good fellow and I managed to get my hands on quite a few eggs, which went down very well back at the officers' mess. After handing the eggs in to the kitchens at one end of the dining hall block, I decided to ring Joy as I'd missed my call the previous night, being out with the men. I was unable to speak to her but Betty Caine told me that Joy was in bed, very poorly with the measles. It was still a serious illness in 1943, especially if you caught it as an adult. So I said I'd ring again the next day, but I was really worried about Joy's condition, and whether the children were already incubating measles. Lorna was old enough to cope with it but if baby Terry caught it, things could be much more serious. In fact, Joy did not pass the measles on to Lorna or to the baby. Terry didn't catch the measles until he was about five and then, he handed it on to his little sister, who was left with her eyesight permanently damaged by it. But I realized well enough what problems could arise from measles, having seen two of my siblings very seriously ill in our childhood. I was very concerned about Joy but I went off for a dinner at the officers' mess of the 43rd Ox & Bucks where we had been cordially invited to dine. Despite my anxieties I enjoyed the occasion, being the only one sober when we got back at 03.00 hours. It was the Easter weekend and I felt lonely and depressed. But on Easter Monday, I was amazed to receive a lovely letter from Joy, who was feeling a little better. She sent an excellent portrait photograph of Terry that had been taken at a local studio in Church Stretton on my last leave.

I had a weekend pass, not long enough to go back to Church Stretton unfortunately; but I could dash up to London to see my parents. I was very glad indeed that I had done so, for it turned out that by some rare good fortune I found almost all my brothers home for the weekend as well. All the Howard men went down to our father's local pub, the Green Man, where we practically filled the public bar with loud chatter and raucous family joking; causing the other locals to say to one another, 'Blimey, all of them 'owards are like a ruddy invasion!' Mom stayed home to get the dinner ready in time-honoured tradition, probably giving a silent, grieving thought for the one son who would now never return home again, her Percy.

By the beginning of May 1943, I had a new platoon commander, Second Lieutenant Tony Hooper. Brian Priday was back with 'D' Company but we were still waiting for Den Brotheridge to be fit enough to return. There were more accidents with grenades. In 'B' Company three men were killed and one badly injured during training. Then on Cranbourne Chase ranges, a man in 23 Platoon was hit by a 68 Grenade and sadly died of his wounds early the following morning. It was a fact of life at that time and they carried on with the field firing training, having a competition between the platoons. I wrote in my diary, 'What bad luck' referring to the accident and then that the 'Falling Plate Competition' was 'great fun'. I awarded twenty cigarettes each to 24 Platoon for winning the shooting competition.

Later in May, I heard that my Junior Officer Nick Nicholson was to become a weapons training officer and would be leaving 'D' Company. Nick had been a most reliable NCO as well as a good friend and I was very sorry indeed to be losing him. But the good news was that Den Brotheridge was back, on light duties at any rate. The Regiment was to go to Ilfracombe at the end of May again and I was preparing for it. I had a weekend pass again and had arranged for Joy to travel down to London to stay with my family on Buck Lane, hoping sincerely that she would get on well with them and overcome some of her prejudices. However, 'D' Company was down at Studland Bay carrying out a field firing exercise in very bad weather for late May. I found myself driving back to Bulford in the pouring rain on a motorcycle to catch the train to London to see my family. My feet can hardly have touched the ground, as I didn't reach Buck Lane until 22.00 on Saturday evening and was back in Bulford on the Monday morning. But it had been wonderful to see Joy and my baby son and to find that they seemed settled and relaxed at my parents' home and that Terry was being 'spoiled rotten'.

I had left Lieutenant David Wood in charge of 'D' Company for the weekend and was very pleased to see how well he'd coped. I found everyone busy packing up to go to Ilfracombe. The battalion went down there by train and the officers went by road. We were billeted in a small hotel and I made sure that I had a sea-view. The weather took a turn for the better and we began a regime of regular sea bathing, cricket and bowls for relaxation. I felt on top of the world but my good mood did not last long, as June blew in with rain and cold winds and I found myself having to impress my senior officers with 'D' Company's achievements. The Colonel went with us on a sixteen mile route march around the Devon hills that we accomplished in only four and a quarter hours, which certainly impressed him.

I had decided that I would start concentrating on teaching the many non-swimmers among the men, how to swim. To someone like me, it was basic common sense that all soldiers should know how to swim, and within a month or so my instinct was to be proved correct during the Airborne landings in Sicily that were so nearly a complete disaster. On 3 June, the Divisional Commander of the 6th Airborne, General 'Windy' Gale came down to Ilfracombe and seemed to pay 'D' Company quite a lot of attention, and said that he was most impressed by their fitness. It was at this time that the men of 'D' Company adopted the name of 'Don' Company amongst themselves. This nickname was taken from the phonetic alphabet code that was used in wireless transmissions, 'Don' being the word used for the letter 'D'. It was just a passing phase that we all adopted to intensify our feelings of *esprit de corps*, which was a vital part of the training. That way each man rated his performance not as an individual but as part of the team. 'Don' Company would be the best and fittest company in the Regiment, and not to put in maximum effort on the sports field or on a training exercise was to let 'Don' Company down. 'Don' Company was more than a title or an emblem, it had an intrinsic identity of its own, a well-oiled machine of which each of the officers and men was a working part.

I had spoken on the telephone to Joy, still in London at my parents' home and getting on well there. This made me very happy indeed that she and Terry had enjoyed their time at Buck Lane. I had told her how wonderful Ilfracome could be when the weather was good.

47

'Surely this rain won't last much longer – we're certainly due for a fine spell,' I told her during one of our evening calls.

Joy had replied, 'Well, we're going back to Church Stretton tomorrow, John, now there's no chance of you coming to London again, and we mustn't outstay our welcome here – gosh! I wish we could come down to Ilfracombe just for a few days – it would be so lovely to show Terry the sea and sand!'

This conversation took place on 6 June. Little did I know what an important date that would be, one year later in 1944. In June 1943 my thoughts were taken up with how I could organize somewhere in Ilfracombe for my wife and son to stay so they could come down on holiday. I discussed it in the officers' club with Gilbert Rahr. I said, 'I've told Joy that she simply must come here.'

'Crikey John!' Gilbert had answered, 'You'd be taking a bit of risk if the Top Brass decide to object and carpet you over it! Do you really think there's a chance they'd let it go?'

'Just so long as the training schedule remains unaffected and I put in the hours and effort they expect of me, I can't see why they'd object to my wife and son turning up in Ilfracombe for a summer holiday. I know it's wartime but people do still go on holiday!' I had replied.

My enthusiasm rubbed off on Gil Rahr who had a wife and two young daughters and who, he suddenly realized, would really benefit from some sea air.

I made a few enquiries and found a very pleasant lady, Miss Harris, in Ilfracombe who had paying guests on occasions, and she agreed to borrow a cot for Terry as well. I couldn't wait to tell Joy on the telephone that night, and we began to get very excited about planning a seaside holiday. For her part, Joy got a knitting pattern for a swimsuit and managed to get the coupons for the wool and began to knit furiously. Knitted swimsuits were becoming fashionable in 1943 since no others were generally available.

In the meantime, to avert any criticism, I threw myself into the training schedule, taking the men cliff-climbing on the downs. There was a 200 foot drop in one place and the cliffs were chalky shale and dangerous, and another day of wind and rain made it even more difficult, but I was glad that at the end of it, there had been no casualties. I found that my good friend Nick Nicholson was to be transferred to 'S' Company as weapons training officer and despite voicing my annoyance, Nick had to go. We were all too busy with a forced march to Woolacombe and tackling the now infamous assault course that had so daunted the men and their platoon commanders the previous year, to dwell on his going. The weather had turned fine but there was a cold wind for more cliff-climbing training and I found myself being stung by the flying sand out on the downs. I had started a tug-of war competition to keep the men's interest and competitive spirits up.

That afternoon I travelled to Salisbury with the Colonel and my fellow company commanders in the 52nd, Digby Tatham-Warter, 'Flaps' Edmunds and

Gordon Temple. We were to attend a company commanders' lecture on the following day back at Bulford, but because the Colonel was with us, we were all staying overnight at The County Hotel in Salisbury. This was a rare treat for me for there was a part of me that was beginning to really appreciate the good things in life. So we all enjoyed a tea in Taunton and then went out to dinner at a local fishing club that 'Flaps' and Digby were members of just outside Salisbury. I described the dinner as 'slap up' in comic-book terms in my diary. However I felt that the lecture the next day that was the main reason for the visit, was a failure and a total waste of time. Bored by the lecture and anxious to get back to Ilfracombe as soon as possible, we left the Colonel in Bulford and the four of us hurried out to our transport. The Blitz Bug was revved-up and I remember how we all drove back to Ilfracombe through the balmy evening light of early summer, at 80 mph to arrive in time for dinner in the officers' club down there. I was full of anticipation at the prospect of seeing my wife and son again and in high spirits at driving madly around the countryside with my gallant fellow officers. I felt that for an evening at least, I could lay aside the burdens of training a company of men for war, and pretend to be suave and carefree, just like they were.

Chapter 5

Mid-June to September 1943: Family Life and Waiting for War

On 16 June 1943 I went to Exeter to meet Joy and Terry off the train, ready for their holiday in Ilfracombe. Terry was eleven months old and full of fun. Joy had managed to bring his large pram that had been a present from Betty and Tommy Caine at Terry's christening, and it had travelled in the guard's van of the train. I handed it over to my orderly one night and he emblazoned the front panel of the pram with a pale-blue 'Pegasus', the Airborne emblem. Now there would be no mistaking the Major's son when out on his walks.

Conscious that Joy's & Terry's presence in Ilfracombe was slightly controversial, I applied myself to my job with 'D' Company while Joy settled into Miss Harris' house and took Terry out onto the sands for some seaside air. That first evening I took Joy to the officers' club where she was able to meet my fellow officers in 'D' Company for the first time. She did not let me down and I was so proud of her. It was Waterloo Day the following day and this was marked with an all ranks' dance that evening and an officers' dance the night after. Taking this rare opportunity to socialize, we left Terry with Miss Harris as babysitter and, probably because of the sea air, he slept soundly.

I kept up the non-stop training schedule and activities during the day with more cliff-climbing and tug of war competitions, swimming and running. At the officers' dance in the evening, Digby Tatham-Warter, always known to appreciate 'a good filly' rather hung his nose over Joy at the dance and caused me an unwarranted attack of jealousy. But fortunately Joy was introduced to Gil Rahr's wife, Susan, and the two young women took an instant liking to each other and fell into a lively conversation. Digby sauntered away to find more responsive company. To show that I was not slacking with my wife and child around, the next day I led the men on a seventeen and a half mile route march in four and three-quarter hours and was very pleased at 'D' Company's performance. David

Wood came to dinner with Joy and me at Miss Harris' house and we went to the flicks afterwards to see *The Immortal Serpent*. As we walked back to Joy's lodgings, I felt that the wind had dropped and the air felt much warmer. The following day was indeed much better weather and I took my small son into the swimming pool for the first time, after a walk with Joy. The days passed pleasantly enough with Joy spending time with Susan Rahr and her two small daughters, and evenings at the officers' club sometimes playing bridge.

On our day off, the weather dawned sunny and clear and both the Rahr family and Joy, Terry and I set off for a day on the beach at Woolacombe. It was a gloriously hot day and we all had a wonderful time as recorded on my camera. But unfortunately we underestimated the strength of the sun by the sea and all the adults and the two Rahr children suffered sunburn and some sunstroke. The only mercy was that Joy's natural instincts had prevented Terry from being sunburned too because she had made sure he wore a hat and put him to sleep in the shade of some rocks.

However, I dared not succumb to my painful sunburn and it was work as usual the following day, and Joy was obliged to put on a brave face to attend another dance that evening. The hot sunshine continued but we tried to keep in the shade as the effects of our sunburn continued for several days, preventing me from taking part in a planned route march and keeping Joy to a sedate routine of morning walks and afternoon rests. Terry was as good as gold all the time, relishing the change of air and sleeping like a top. The social whirl of the evenings continued unabated and Joy and I would look back on this pleasant fortnight as one of our happiest and most normal times during my Army life. This happy and relaxing time together would, in fact have far-reaching consequences for us in the shape of a baby daughter born the following March, but neither of us had any idea about this souvenir of our time in Ilfracombe for a month or two.

Whether it was because of my divided interests and the debilitating effects of my sunburn, the men seemed listless and to lose interest in the coastal training. They did not do at all well in the heats of a swimming competition and I was not happy to see them failing. I gave them all an encouraging lecture which I hoped would revive their interests and was pleased to see 'D' Company winning an Inter-Company route march carried out under an unrelenting sun. All too soon, it was Joy's and Terry's final day in Ilfracombe and we were feeling very blue about our imminent parting. There was another dance at the officers' club that last evening, but we were both quiet and rather subdued.

The next day, I took my wife and son to Exeter to catch the train for Church Stretton. I returned disconsolately to Ilfracombe feeling lost without them both. I returned the cot Terry had used to its owner and then dined at Miss Harris' where her gentle and understanding conversation cheered me a little. The swimming finals were held on the following day, and 'D' Company lifted their performance to come in third and to win the diving competition. Joy called me in the evening to say that she and Terry were back safely at Hill Crest, where everyone was amazed at how well they looked and how Terry had grown.

It was time to pack up and leave Ilfracombe. That year it had been decided not to march the Regiment all the way back to Bulford as on the previous year, causing many a sigh of thankfulness amongst the men. Tod Sweeney and David Wood did a special celebratory dance during one of their crazier moments in the officers' club. However, they were all to take the train to Taunton and march back to Bulford from there! I was once more focussed on our training programme and remarked to my junior officers, 'This exercise on the way back should be fun, don't you think?' causing Brian Priday to make the comment that he thought that I had a very warped idea of fun.

I spent my last evening in Ilfracombe once more eating my meal with Miss Harris who was reckoned to be a very good cook. Her speciality was duck and she had prepared it as our final meal. I found myself regretting this meal for I suffered a very bad bilious attack within twenty-four hours of eating it but was not put off duck, since it was now one of my favourite meals. This illness was unfortunate since we were all obliged to do a twenty-eight mile march from Taunton to Yeovil through the following night. I felt ghastly and couldn't sleep during the day when I wanted to. The next night we set off at 22.00 hours again to march at what I euphemistically described as a 'lope' to the Cranbourne area, where the Colonel had arranged a kind of 'Dunkirk' evacuation procedure. He had laid on every available means of Army transport and trailers which took us all up to Fordingbridge, where the exercise ended. From Fordingbridge the next day, the Regiment marched back to Bulford camp. I noted with disgust in my diary that the pace was 'too cushy' owing to the bad feet in the leading column which consisted of the regimental headquarters staff. But I was uplifted to find a fat letter from Joy waiting for me back at Bulford. I was already impatient for my leave to start in a few days' time and was counting the hours.

On 10 July 1943 the news came through about Sicily being invaded and we realized that the 1st Airborne Division was involved in the landings and waited to hear how things had turned out for the Airlanding Brigade. In fact, the Sicily landings were disastrous for the Airborne Forces and the invasion itself only succeeded by a hair's breadth. The gliders were released late in the evening of the 9–10 July, with the men of the South Staffs Regiment, Ist Airborne Division, thirty-two men to a glider, packed with ammunition . The Halifax tugs were told not to approach the coast too close because of the enemy's anti-aircraft fire and were forced to take a circuitous run-in to Sicily via Malta because of enemy radio location. Upon reaching Sicily, the Halifax pilots, inexperienced in tugging gliders and unaware of the dangers of releasing them too soon, were instructed to approach the coast to within not less than 3,000 yards and the gliders were released two and a half miles short of the promontory they were aiming for, the

Maddalena Peninsular. There was a strong off-shore wind that night, which considerably reduced the gliders' speed and gliding distances. All these problems resulted in some gliders crashing into the sea, and some falling short of their landing zones and landing right by enemy gun emplacements, being instantly fired upon or having grenades thrown into them, and the ammunition on board causing the gliders to explode. Some exploded on landing anyway with inexpertly loaded ammunition. In the gliders that crashed into the sea, many of the men were unable to swim the short distance to the beach and drowned. Of 108 gliders, fifty fell into the sea and twenty-five were never seen or heard from again, some being sent forty miles off-course. These problems and miscalculations nearly resulted in the failure of the action.

Those who landed fought with extreme bravery. One all-important bridge, Ponte Grande, was taken, then lost again and finally re-taken. This bridge was near the town of Syracuse and vital to the advance north into Italy. The para-troopers landed on the 13–14 July and took Primosole Bridge, despite a third of them being killed or wounded. But the push into Italy was achieved, although the difference between success and failure was very slight. General Montgomery said of this action, 'Had it not been for the skill and gallantry of the Airlanding Brigade, the port of Syracuse would not have fallen until very much later.'

The Airlanding Brigade had succeeded in their mission but at a dreadful cost in men, gliders and equipment, and many lessons had been excruciatingly learned for their comrades in the 6th Airborne to add to their store of knowledge. This information was learned gradually over the next weeks and months. I recall discussing the news of the invasion of Sicily with Digby Tatham-Warter, as I put the company's paperwork in order, waiting to go on leave. 'Do you think this is the beginning of the end, Digby?' I said, 'I hope not, John!' said Digby spiritedly, 'I'm transferring to the paratroops, and I want a chance to see some action!'

I was genuinely surprised at this news for I could imagine few worse situations myself than jumping out of an aircraft, first praying that your parachute would open, and second having no idea where you would touch down. Much preferable to arrive by glider with a pilot in charge of the destination. But I had observed that the 'para-boys' as they were known, declared that they wouldn't 'prang' into action for all the tea in China. And the glider troops felt as strongly as I did about parachuting into action. Evidently Digby had decided to 'cross over'. There was a definite rivalry between the two aspects of the Airborne Forces – for one thing the para-boys received more 'risk money' than the glider lads; they got two shillings a day extra pay, where the glider troops only received one shilling, with sixpence of that taken back for income tax. It was the cause of much ill feeling on the part of the glider-borne soldiers.

'So you're off on leave,' Digby had said, winking at me, 'Be sure to give my best wishes to your delightful wife!'

'Eh?' I had replied somewhat sharply, 'You keep your best wishes to yourself, you cheeky bugger!' But I was smiling at him.

I slipped off to catch the night train up to Shropshire on the night before our son's first birthday. Thus, at 07.00 on 12 July 1943, I arrived at the station at Church Stretton and, leaving my case with the ticket-collector there, I hurried up to Hill Crest with a wooden horse on wheels under my arm to give to Terry. It was painted white with black spots dotted all over – Terry's first 'set of wheels', but by no means to be his last. I found the family all up early to greet me with breakfast ready, and Terry squealed with delight when I set him astride the horse and pushed him along. The day was sunny and hot, and we had tea in the pretty garden. Tommy Caine picked a large bowl of strawberries from his highly successful strawberry patch as a treat for us all. The following days were spent contentedly walking around Church Stretton with Terry in his pram and calling in on relations. The news about the invasion of Sicily had broken in the news-papers. I felt almost guilty when several people asked why I wasn't over there in Italy with the rest of the Airborne Forces and had to explain that I was as perplexed as they were that I was still waiting for orders to go off on active service. However, I couldn't explain to anyone, not even Joy, just how frustrated I was becoming at the pointlessness of the endless training with no action in sight.

The weather turned cooler, but I was making the most of my time with my family. One morning Betty Caine showed me a parcel she and Joy were wrapping up to send to my family in London. There was a selection of food items – butter, cheese, a couple of tins of fruit, a jar of home made jam and some garden-fresh vegetables from the Sagar greenhouses and nurseries, which Joy was bundling up into a parcel on the kitchen table.

'That's wonderful, Mommy' I said, most appreciative of the kind thought that had amassed this store of food in such times of rationing. I knew just how pleased my mother would be to receive the parcel and that my hungry family would relish every mouthful down in London. Joy and I set off for the post office, balancing the parcel on the coverlet of Terry's pram, eight year old Lorna skipping along-side us hoping that she would be permitted to have a go at pushing the pram in the park on the way home.

As we went along, Joy told me in a low voice so that Lorna wouldn't hear, that she thought she was pregnant again. Having a baby while living with her mother's family was one thing, but having two babies to care for with no home of our own, was quite another. If we were going to have another child, the need for us to find a home of our own would become essential. Men never know what to say to their wives and partners in such circumstances and I found myself at a loss then as to how to reassure Joy. It did seem rather soon for us to have another baby on the way. Half of me felt thrilled at the prospect of having another child –

Terry was such a wonderful little chap – but the problems another baby would bring were enormous.

It was Sunday the next day and Betty Caine had 'pushed the boat out' as we said then, by cooking duck and green peas for dinner. I was very pleased indeed and enjoyed my dinner immensely. We took Terry out in his pram for a walk in the afternoon, calling in on Joy's Uncle Arthur for a cup of tea and found the Governor, Joy's grandfather, there. I confess that I did not like the old man much for I found him cantankerous and manipulative; holding the family to ransom because he had money, property and power, and even his sons were in awe of him and would avoid incurring the old man's wrath at all costs. I tried hard to be polite for Joy's sake, but it was not in my nature to easily kow-tow to someone I disliked and possibly I let my feelings show. The Governor was sharp enough to have realized that here was one man who was not afraid of him. I was to find myself regretting that I hadn't 'buttered' the old boy up enough later in the year when I wanted a favour but it would be too late by then and perhaps, upon reflection, it was better that Joy and I were never to be in debt to George Sagar. On that day, the Governor had held court over the tea-table at Arthur's and Irene's house, covering all subjects, starting with the way his three sons' philandering was a drain on the family business of growing and distributing green grocery and flowers. Both Walter and Arthur had a weakness for fast cars and a good life-style, and Richard had disappeared off to America at the outset of the war. The old man then continued to criticize the way the war was being run, and that soldiers kept training at the country's expense when they should have all been out there fighting and bringing this ruddy war – that was also ruining his business with all the rationing and restrictions – to a hasty end. All this coming from a man who had never worn a uniform in his life despite living through two world wars, and had also kept his sons at home making a good living in civvy street while others less fortunate did their fighting for them. The Governor really rubbed salt into my wounds and I longed to tell the old man what I really thought of him and his sons. But I did not want to upset Joy for I knew that she had always been very fond of her grandfather. So I bit my tongue and fumed silently, only letting my feelings out as we walked home.

'The Governor is a ruddy old wind-bag!' I had exploded, as I guided the pram along Sandford Avenue. 'He drives me mad! I don't know why Arthur and Walter put up with the old goat!'

'Because they owe their good homes and livelihoods to him, John,' Joy had said sensibly. 'You know he owns lots of houses and flats, and he might even let us have one for a reasonable rent one day – it's no good falling out with him when he could do us a real favour and find a roof over our heads.'

'Yes, and doesn't he know it!' I said in exasperation, hating the thought of having to grovel to the Governor to beg him to find a home for my wife and our possibly growing family. Suddenly, I felt very low; my leave was almost over and there was the very real prospect that my wife was going to have another child, and I just did not know how we could possibly afford a house of our own, even if we could find one available. I was faced with returning to Bulford for more training, endless training, and I just did not know when and if I would ever be given the chance to prove myself as a commanding officer in battle.

I arrived back in Bulford camp on 22 July, feeling sour and under utilized. However, I found that I had been put down for three courses, one after the other, and the general feeling among my brother officers was that it was thought that this would give me something to think about and lessen my frustration, which my senior officers were obviously only too aware of. A highly motivated man who becomes irritated and bored is likely to be a destructive force, and the upper levels of Airborne command evidently had their eye on me and did not want to run the risk of me losing interest and enthusiasm. It had been decided that I needed some inspiration and therefore, since my junior officers were by that time trained and capable, I could be spared.

Word was received that the Regiment would be mobilized in three months' time although nobody knew any more than that. I was in the company offices going through the paperwork, and organizing the training schedules for Brian Priday to take over again.

'Do you think this three month warning is for real, Brian?' I'd said to him.

'I don't know, John. I think they're just trying to keep us quiet,' replied Priday.

'What, just as I'm being sent off on these courses to keep me quiet!' I said, pulling a face.

'Yes, something like that!' said Priday.

In truth, all of us, officers and men, were beginning to wonder if we would ever see action. On 26 July news came through that Mussolini had resigned in Italy, and it began to look as if it might all be over before 'D' Company had the chance to fire a shot.

I handed over the company to my 2 I/C, Brian Priday, and caught the afternoon train to London, on my way to Cheshunt College in Cambridgeshire to do a ground attack course. I was able to spend the night visiting my parents at Buck Lane, but despite hearing on the phone from Joy that she was still overdue, I decided to say nothing at home until we were really certain that Joy was definitely pregnant again. The next day I continued my journey on to Cambridgeshire. I found the course was a good one and mentally very stimulating, which was what I needed. I had telephoned Joy and given her the number of a local call box, and was delighted when she duly rang me there at the appointed hour. She told me that she would be going to the doctor in a few days for confirmation of her condition.

I was able to take daily swims in a local river, which reminded me of my days as a Boy Scout and helped to use up my boundless energy. I found that the course gave me lots of ideas and information to pass on to my company and I found myself grateful to my senior officers for the opportunity to mix with other officers on the course and exchange views and experiences with them. The course ended on 2 August and I was sorry to leave but I was able to spend another night at my family home on Buck Lane. I went down to the local swimming baths with my youngest brother, Roy, watched by brother Bill and sister Queenie, with a good deal of heckling from the sidelines.

I got back to Bulford again to find that it was all much the same there. I was pleased to resume my long telephone calls from Joy in the privacy of the officers' mess, and she told me the news that her second pregnancy had been confirmed. 'Roll on March '44!' I had said to her, little knowing that I would have more on my mind by then than a new baby. The next day, we all had a lecture from the General on the lessons learned from the Airborne action in Sicily and were very disturbed by what we were told. It shook our confidence badly in glider-borne invasions, although it was stressed that many of the losses were the direct result of mistakes by the 'tug' aeroplanes. 'And that's supposed to make us feel better about it!' I said.

In the days that followed, 'D' Company were involved in another exercise and I found myself in the field for a whole weekend, just when my absence had meant a load of paperwork needing to be done. On top of this, I was ordered by the Colonel to give a series of lectures and, in my irritation, felt that I was being singled out unfairly. In mid-August, Exercise GROUSE took place involving a glider flight after a day spent loading the glider at Thruxton. We landed at a place called Dumbell Copse and I'd grimly noted that there were, thankfully, no casualties, although I was sick as a dog myself. How I cursed the fact that I was so airsick in the glider but there seemed nothing I could do to prevent it, the only good thing being that after we landed, I felt fine again immediately.

I continued with the lectures that I had been instructed to give and was pleased that they were received well, both by the officers and the men. But I was still feeling frustrated by inactivity. I had a furious row with one of the Quartermaster staff over some rifles and was unapproachable for several hours as I fumed about the man's attitude, referring to him as 'A ruddy martinet!' The platoon commanders under me must have been relieved when I once again handed over 'D' Company to Brian Priday's charge on 22 August and took the afternoon train to London. This time I was attending a course at the Chelsea barracks on street fighting. I was supposed to be billeted at the barracks but had made elaborate arrangements for my genial and obliging batman, Evans, to cover my tracks, so that I could stay at my parents' home in Colindale and Joy could join me there with Terry. This involved an extremely early start each morning so that I could liaise with the faithful Evans, who met me each day with whatever clothing and equipment I would need. This worked well, and I was able to be with Joy each evening, even attending the theatre one night to see John Gielgud in *Love for Love*, which we much enjoyed. Naturally, Joy was able to tell my family our good news about another baby being on the way. It was no good trying to explain to my parents the fears we had about finding a home for ourselves. Mom and Pop had lived in a couple of rooms with a family that grew to nine children eventually. To them two small children seemed no bother at all! But we had begun to worry about finding a home, especially with the prospect of me being sent overseas to fight hanging over us. I felt a growing sense of urgency to find somewhere, especially since Joy had told me that unfortunately she was not getting on so well with Tom Caine. It seemed that Tommy had made some disparaging remarks about me. He seemed to be resentful about me as I was so obviously a great favourite with Betty, his wife. It was always going to be a tricky relationship, and Joy was now pretty fed-up with the situation.

'You know, John' she said to me, as we returned from seeing the film *Arsenic and Old Lace* at the picture-house, 'it would be really nice if we could find a flat somewhere near where Mom and Pop live. I mean, we could have our own place but you wouldn't be so worried about me being on my own if we were near to your family.' I was very pleased to hear her making this suggestion and readily agreed to explore this possibility. The course I was on at the Chelsea barracks was fortunately not very demanding and well within my capabilities but there was an assault course on the penultimate day and I had found that having to scramble over a plank quite high up, was certainly not my favourite pastime. I was asked to design an exercise on the last day of the course and in typical Howard-fashion, it was fairly wild stuff involving making an attack using flame-throwers on carriers. It was voted such a success that the course instructors told me they would incorporate it into future courses, calling it 'Exercise Howard'!

Cheered by this, I returned for my last couple of days at Buck Lane, bearing a case of apples from the kindly Evans for my family. On the following day, my final one before returning to Bulford, I chased after a flat I'd been told about nearby, and also some furniture, but to no avail. The war had made home making so difficult as to be almost impossible. Any available houses or flats were snapped up almost immediately, and furniture was becoming so scarce, since very little new furniture was manufactured at that time. In London especially, the effects of so many homes being lost, along with all furniture and possessions, from the bombing in the East End, was now being felt very seriously. The needs of one young couple to find a home, however modest, seemed doomed and I found myself dwelling on these problems and they began to eat away at me.

Back at Bulford, having said goodbye to my family again, I felt gloomy and despondent. I was once more exasperated by having to deliver lectures on ground attacks and also by changes to the regimental programmes. 'Bloody coats on – coats off!' I fumed to Tod Sweeney, who good-humouredly took on the task of smoothing down my feathers yet again.

'They don't know whether they're on foot or horseback, John!' said Tod smiling at me. 'Never mind! There's a band night this evening and I hear we've got a splendid dinner lined up.' Nothing could cheer me up quite like the prospect of a good feed. I had an enormous appetite that I put down to expending so much energy, both on playing sports and giving vent to my frustrations. Over the dinner, which was quite as good as promised, we all talked about Berlin being bombed heavily. At the outset of the war there was a tacit understanding at the highest levels of command that civilian areas were not to be deliberately bombed. However, the German *Luftwaffe* had ignored Hitler's express instruction to bomb only military targets and one night, had dropped bombs for the first time on the East End of London around the docks, causing immense damage and outrage. From then on it was gloves off and both air forces frequently bombed the civilian populations of the major cities, with the intention of destroying the morale of the population and undermining public opinion. This meant that the fighting soldiers at the battle fronts, for the first time in history, no longer had the security of knowing that their loved ones would be safe in their homeland. It was a frightful development in modern warfare.

On 3 September 1943 there was a National Day of Prayer to mark the fourth anniversary of the start of the war. The Regiment marked this with a Drumhead Service. I loved to hear the Regimental Band and found the service very moving. The news that the 8th Army were invading the mainland of Italy renewed my feelings of impatience to get going but a phone call from Joy in the evening took my mind off any military frustrations and replaced them with matters nearer to home. It had been decided that Joy and I would continue to look for a flat near to my parents' home in London and we had approached Tommy and Betty Caine about the possibility of a loan. I had written to them while I'd been on leave at Buck Lane and Joy had asked her mother whether they'd reached a decision. She had received a very non-committal reply which she relayed to me over the phone and I was very puzzled at their lack of interest. A few days later, Joy told me that there was trouble brewing at Hill Crest because the Caines claimed that there were financial problems with their business, the abattoir that was jointly run by Tom, his brother and father. Listening to my wife's voice on the telephone, I sighed deeply. For some unknown reason, Tom and Betty Caine kept their business affairs cloaked in mystery, as if there was a constant and imminent danger of some frightful revelation casting them down into ruin and insolvency. Joy and I found this attitude both perplexing and irritating in equal measures. Of course, there was a black market for fresh meat during wartime, but I honestly didn't imagine that Tom and his brother were any worse or any better than many another farmer or abattoir owner. It was unlikely, I felt, that they would be singled out and made an example of for any 'under the counter' dealings they may have practised. I wasn't naive enough to imagine that the chicken and ducks that appeared on the dinner table at Hill Crest, nor the occasional gift of meat that found its way to my large family in London, was the result of judicious hoarding of many meat coupons. Favours were done and repaid on the quiet, and goods exchanged all over the country. It was impossible to stamp out the people's natural urge 'to do a deal'. Most folk took the view that as long as the wartime restrictions were sensibly applied to prevent food shortages and starvation, a blind eye turned to a deal here and there was only to be expected.

But Tom and Betty Caine were unduly sensitive about what others knew about their business, and they carried this to the extreme. An innocent and careless comment could elicit black looks and stony silences from the pair of them and it was necessary to guard one's tongue for fear of causing offence. This did not make for a particularly easy atmosphere in their home and at times like this, when dark hints were voiced that money was 'disappearing' and they were 'feeling the pinch', Joy knew better than to ask any details. It meant that any prospect of them lending Joy and me money to help secure a home, was now out of the question.

'I bet this is just a smokescreen so they don't have to lend us any money!' I said, suspicious and forgetting in an instant the many kindnesses that Joy's family had shown me; immediately ready to think the worst.

'I really don't think so, John,' said Joy, 'Mommy told me that they may even have to sell Hill Crest!'

'What?' I shouted, causing a passing orderly to almost drop a pile of linen he was carrying. 'I can't believe they'd leave Hill Crest. It would break all their hearts!'

'I know,' said Joy miserably, 'but it's definitely on the cards.'

'What will you do?' I cried, running my hand through my hair in consternation.

'Well, Mommy says they'll make room for me and Terry somehow, but I rather think that they are hoping we'll find somewhere of our own before the new baby arrives.'

I put the telephone down, more worried than I had ever been in my life before. Hell! I must do something to find a roof over our heads. Now it was more important than ever.

Chapter 6

September to Christmas 1943: Searching for a Home

Early September 1943 found me out in the field with 'D' Company and once more trying to vary their training routines to keep them interested and keen. We did an attack exercise against the men of 'A' Company, and their enthusiasm using two-inch mortars set fire to a haystack and burned it to a cinder. I decided to send Tod Sweeney off to deal with the indignant farmer and to hand out the usual form that had to be filled in to claim compensation. Tod could smile so sympathetically and was better at placating angry civilians than any of the other officers. By the time he'd finished, their loud and infuriated grievances would have died down to a grumbled, 'Well, I suppose there is a war on' as they trailed away to attend to the broken window, burned out haystack, trampled cornfield or damaged roof. Of course, there was nothing the men liked better than a good fire, a lot of noise and much smoke. On that occasion I smiled indulgently, and then sobered up as my thoughts ran on to how we would cope when the gunfire, smoke and explosions were real and dangerous. Very often, the exercises we engaged in did manage to recreate the conditions of war only too realistically. Men were still frequently being maimed and killed in accidents and this did have the effect of keeping the soldiers and all of us officers on our toes.

The night exercises continued, often in the pouring rain, but the men seemed to have grown used to being out of doors in cold and wet conditions, and their spirits were surprisingly high as they would arrive back at the barracks at 03.00. It was the junior officers' duty to check that each man had a hot shower, something to eat and a hot drink and was dry and comfortable to go to bed for a few hours. Often, by the time the officers had their showers, all the hot water would have been used and they had to grit their teeth and put up with a cold one. But the boxing competitions were especially successful for 'D' Company at that time. I noted with real satisfaction that out of six champions, three were from 'D' Company.

I was once again due to go off for the final of my three courses at the Infantry Training School near Darlington in the north-east of England. I handed over command of 'D' Company to Tod Sweeney upon this occasion, as Brian Priday was himself on an Anti-Tank Mine course. Gilbert Rahr was also on the course with me, and we set off together to spend the night in London. Rahr went to see his wife and daughters and I took another opportunity to see the family at Buck Lane. I did not waste even these few precious hours, trying to follow up on possible accommodation for Joy and Terry and looking at furniture. But I was appalled by the price of the furniture – even for what I described as 'utility muck'. I just couldn't see a light at the end of the tunnel at that time, in respect of setting my family up in a home of our own.

The following day I continued the long train journey up to Darlington. The accommodation in the camp was poor, but the first evening there I was writing off about a vacant flat I'd been told about in London. There was little entertainment in the evenings and Gil Rahr and I passed the time playing bridge with a few of the other officers, when there were no lectures. To add to my feeling of despondency, the weather turned foul with heavy rain turning the outdoor sessions into mud-baths. But surprisingly, I once again found myself beginning to enjoy the course, especially some of the more compelling lectures which were given by senior officers who were very strong characters.

A phone call to Joy in Church Stretton was a mixture of good news and bad. On the one hand, Joy told me that the Caines were definitely moving from Hill Crest but were having no luck finding anywhere suitable. When they moved, however, it would be to somewhere smaller which would mean that Joy and I could have some of their furniture. But she was desperately worried about where she would go with Terry when the Caines moved. Well into her second pregnancy, Joy had little to take her mind off her problems, unlike me who found my days full of activities and new ideas. But I was determined to keep on trying to solve our housing problem, even when I received a reply from London telling me that the vacant flat that I had enquired about had been taken. However, I began to give up hope that we would ever find anywhere near my parents in London. Taking five minutes to read the newspaper, I came across a cutting in *The Times* for a cottage in Hampshire and immediately wrote off for it, my spirits rising as I wondered if this would be the answer to our problems – only to hear a week later that the cottage had been sold to someone else.

The course covered a lot of ground for me. There were demonstrations on advance guard, and house clearing and frontal attack, and lectures on preparations for battle and the importance of training junior commanders. Then we moved on to TEWTs, the problem solving exercises. We all did a reconnaissance of an area set up as a minefield and were required to de-activate some mines ourselves. I had begun to realize just how serious a problem mines were likely to be on the battlefield. The course ended with the charismatic Colonel Stewart giving a lecture on morale and I hung on his every word. Fine commanding officers were always to be a great inspiration to me and to reinforce my belief that a company would only be as good as the leadership they received. But COs that did not match up to my high standards and appeared lacklustre, would never elicit any respect from me and at that time in my life I could be most un-compromising in my opinions.

The three week course ended on 2 October and I caught the midnight express from Darlington to snatch a brief few hours with Joy in Church Stretton. Making my usual early morning arrival, I was delighted to find that Terry instantly recognized me, holding out his arms and making little cries of welcome. But there was little else to please me there. The Caines seemed engrossed in their own concerns about where to move, and Joy was evidently very downcast. Lorna had been sent off to a local boarding school, The Mount, and there was not even her cheery, childish prattle to enliven the general air of gloom. I felt wretched about leaving Joy somewhere she was evidently so unsettled, but I was helpless to do anything about it and my frustration with our situation grew even stronger. I was obliged to take the early train down to Waterloo again, and then on to Bulford. Immediately on arrival, I was taken by military transport to act as an umpire on Exercise COMPASS, with Den Brotheridge commanding 'D' Company and doing very well by my estimation. After attending an umpires' conference in the wake of the exercise, I had a paratroops' demonstration to attend and was so tired in the evening that I had no chance to write the letter of encouragement that I had intended to send to Joy.

The following day I had to organize another exercise for night attack field firing with only twenty-four hours' notice, briefing the company at 14.00 hours. That was how it was for me, with hardly a moment to dwell on my worries. Not so for Joy though, for at Hill Crest they were starting to pack up, having almost decided on where to move to. Therefore, Joy had also made a decision; for the time being she would go to London and stay with my parents at Buck Lane. The atmosphere in her mother's household was by no means as carefree and happy as it had once been, and making allowances for the Caines' anxieties and their impending move, Joy thought it would be best to leave them to it for a while. She was compelled therefore to pack up all our belongings, dismantling the little morning room, so lovingly assembled and enjoyed.

On 8 October Joy and Terry took the train down to London, their possessions piled into Terry's pram in the guard's van. She was glad to be met at the station by her brother-in-law, my brother Stanley home on leave, and he helped her back to Buck Lane where Mom and Pop had kindly made the front bedroom vacant for them. On the same day at Bulford camp, Brigadier Hugh Kindersley came to carry out an admin inspection of the Regiment and I stood for three hours out on the parade ground with 'D' Company. I played a sedate game of bridge during the evening with Gilbert, Gordon and 'Flaps' Edmunds, whilst down in London,

Joy tried to get used to the noisy hilarity of the Howard household after the quiet and preoccupied atmosphere that had marked the final weeks at Hill Crest.

That weekend, I had a thirty-six-hour pass and caught the 11.55 'Airborne Special' from the sidings near to Bulford camp. Airborne Command Initiative had taken the enlightened view that to keep morale high, the soldiers were all to have a thirty-six-hour pass every other weekend. The men who lived out of the London area were allowed to catch an earlier 'Airborne Special' train, which left Bulford at 10.55, so that they could make their onward connections to their homes. But the Cockneys, of whom there were many, all caught the 11.55 on the Saturday and it was often a fight to find space to climb aboard. As the train pulled into Waterloo, the doors would swing open even before the train came to a halt, and the men would pour out, hastening down the platform, a seething mass of soldiers, their red berets seen from slightly above like a rippling sea of bobbing red heads. The ticket collectors at the barriers braced themselves for the onslaught, supposed to check the men's rail passes and becoming overwhelmed as pieces of paper were shoved under their noses and then whipped away. Some of the bolder fellows, the 'scallywags' as I always liked to call them, like Wally Parr in 'D' Company, would sometimes be too impatient to wait in line at the barriers and would run to the side and shin up the railings, scaling them in an instant, just as they had been taught to do on assault courses, and with wild yells to their comrades, be off at a run disappearing into the crowds and down into the Underground, before the porters and Military Police could catch up with them. They would all have had passes – it was just devilment and high spirits and everybody understood that. I just loved this atmosphere and the excitement in the air, and it never failed to put me into a good mood for the weekend. I was immensely proud to be a member of the Airborne and every time I met another man in a red beret, the smart salute with pointed fingers up to the cap-badge, gave me a thrill I could not have put into words. It was an intense feeling of *esprit de corps* and being part of an elite band of men. As long as I live, I will never forget that feeling of pride and brotherhood. I was never to experience it again.

The drawback to these weekend leaves, was that in catching the late train back to Bulford, you didn't get back into camp until 01.00 or 02.00 hours. You still had to be up, dressed and on parade, usually doing PT by 07.00 on the Monday morning, most often wondering where the hell the weekend had gone.

I found that Joy and Terry had settled in well at Buck Lane and we were pleased with the comfortable double bed in the front bedroom, until Terry woke us at 05.30 ready to get up and play. We had a pleasant day visiting my brother Stan and his wife, Peggy, with whom Joy was becoming very friendly. Then it was back to Bulford for another week but by working like a demon all day the following Saturday, I managed to get a train that got me back to Buck Lane by 8.15 in the evening, so that I could spend another Sunday with my family. Joy had not expected me and was absolutely amazed when I put my head round the living room door, finding her sitting in the corner of the room knitting and listening to the wireless. Early on the Sunday morning, my brother Johnnie arrived home on leave as well, making quite a crowd at home. Joy and I went off to look over a house in Golders Green Rise but found it very dark and we both disliked it. I had approached the Housing Officer for the Army and even written a letter to our Member of Parliament, but despite receiving a very polite reply, it seemed there was no help to be had in finding somewhere to live. I had to rush to catch a train back to Bulford and arrived back at the camp by 23.30.

There was another night exercise that week and for the first time we were issued with the new sleeping bags that had just been introduced in the Army. I was most impressed and declared that they were 'really magnificent!' Also there was an Inter-Company boxing competition that I, fiercely competitive as ever, was most anxious for 'D' Company to win. They got through to the final but, I recorded in my diary, had 'hellish luck' and were just beaten by 'H' Company. I was beaten in my own match but was congratulated on 'showing guts' and received a heavy blow to my nose which re-arranged my features considerably. I looked into the mirror in my room and thought to myself, 'Oh God, how on earth will I face Joy looking like this?' Next morning I went along to see the medical officer and was immediately sent to Tidworth for an X-ray, to discover that the nose had been broken. By 14.00 I had been operated on and the nose straightened, being given a really wonderful anaesthetic to knock me out. I had sore ribs and sprained thumbs as well but was discharged from hospital the following day.

I decided that I would try to find somewhere to live in Oxford and contacted my old Police friends there to see if they could help. My contact there, a man called Bill Scarsbrook, told me that he had put out all the feelers possible but it really would be just a matter of luck if somewhere came up. I went to the 'flicks' with Brian Priday to pass the time, as I was off on seven days' leave the next day. I caught the evening train on 25 October arriving in London late, but Joy was on the platform to meet me. We went back to Buck Lane together; it gave us a chance for a quiet chat and Joy told me that my mother was having such problems with her leg ulcers that the family had clubbed together to find the money for her to go to see a private doctor, instead of her having to go 'down the 'ospital' which was the only way ordinary people could have their chronic complaints seen to in those days before there was a National Health Service.

I had a frustrating leave overall, despite spending precious time with my wife and son. I exhausted every avenue in an attempt to put a roof over our heads, even going to Wembley Town Hall and wasting hours waiting in a long queue, all to no avail. On 28 October it was our fourth wedding anniversary and I was very grateful that I could be with Joy, getting my sister Queenie to organize a lovely bunch of flowers for her which she arranged and put on the chest in the crowded bedroom. Mom's leg was improving with the doctor's treatment, but she was supposed to sit down with it on a chair. This wonderful lady who had raised nine children and kept house all her life, simply could not sit still and do nothing. Someone had only to mention 'havin' a cuppa' and she was heaving herself out of the chair saying, 'Here, let me use the best cups and there's a bit of marrow jam to 'hev on that bread,' despite shouts from all of us around telling her to 'sit down!'

One day I went to Wakeman's Hill, Burnt Oak, and Stag Lane calling in on people I knew from my days working in London. Joy was four and a half months pregnant and I had noticed that she seemed 'rather big' for half way through her time and felt very sorry for her. She couldn't keep up with me at the spanking pace I habitually walked, and caught the bus, meeting me along the route. Both of us felt the need to get out of the crowded house on Buck Lane to get some fresh air, as well as keeping the lively Terry entertained. On 1 November I gritted my teeth and wrote to Joy's grandfather, the Governor, about a flat. Joy had heard from her mother that he was converting one of the houses he owned on Sandford Avenue called 'Devon', into two flats, and I wrote to ask if Joy and I could rent one of them. It was fairly common at that time for houses to be split into two, so that two families could occupy the one house in reasonable privacy. This was because the wartime laws forced people with larger houses to let the extra rooms to other people who would be 'billeted' on them. Knowing that my letter would arrive the following day, since the postal service was very reliable then, and desperate to know whether there was any chance of our all-consuming worry of accommodation being solved, I rang the Governor. The old man said that unfortunately, both the flats were already spoken for, and I was forced to turn my desperate hopes back to the chance of a house being found for us by my contacts at the Oxford City Police. The next day my leave was at an end and I had to return to Bulford.

It was mid-November and Exercise TEST TUBE occupied most of the next week, 'D' Company being transported out to a training area in the middle of the night, as if we had arrived by glider. We proceeded to 'dig in' taking the role of 'advanced guard', and were visited by the Brigadier. Taking the company to Hays camp where they rested all day, I was nevertheless out on reconnaissance trips, moving out at 13.00 to act as the enemy for the Devonshires. A battle ensued before we were all able to return to barracks. I found a letter waiting for me from another contact in Oxford who told me not to hold out any hopes for a place there, and my spirits sank. I was unable to get back to London that weekend because of de-briefing for Exercise TEST TUBE but was somewhat mollified to find that the only company to be praised in the Regiment by the Brigadier, was 'D' Company for their expertise in 'digging in'. A company commanders' conference the next day contained a severe warning about apathy within the battalion, but I knew that the reprimand was not intended for 'D' Company. I darted off afterwards to catch the early afternoon train for a thirty-six hour pass and Joy met me at Waterloo. I just tried to be glad of the time together and we put our worries aside for the time being.

At Bulford again, I found a lot of the men going down with a flu bug. The next day, 'D' Company had a turn in the 'gas chamber' which every company did periodically for testing all their gas masks and drill. This was followed by medical grading where each man was tested for his fitness to fight. I tried to throw myself resolutely into my job training 'D' Company for action, and to forget the immense problems of trying to find somewhere to rent or buy for my family to live. I was, therefore, quite unprepared for a letter I received on 26 November from Joy's grandfather, the Governor, in Church Stretton. I had specifically asked the old man to bear Joy and me in mind if another of his properties were to become available, and yet here he was informing me, quite dispassionately, that the other half of the house that he himself lived in, called Colwyn, had been let to someone else. It was the last straw! I had never liked or trusted Joy's grandfather, and now the old swine had just gone over our heads to deny us a home, and was acting with an incredible lack of concern for his granddaughter and her family, by calmly writing to tell me about it. I saw red and sat down and penned one of the most angry and vitriolic letters of my life, part of which said:

> If we fellows in the Forces cannot get help from our friends in these trying times, what hopes have we got ? It's alright for the 'forces-shy' element, they have homes, see their families everyday and ... generally feather their nests for after the war with no war risks to worry them. [Here, I was referring to the Governor's sons, Arthur and Walter who, much as I liked them person-ally, I felt could well have been serving in the Forces.] ... While the likes of me ... have little or no security for the future, see our families without homes, and are compelled to suffer the indignities of asking our supposed friends for help ... In the near future we go into battle and seriously risk our lives, not only for our precious families, but also for the 'forces-shy' shirkers ... My own family are unfortunately not in a position to help us any more, though they have given us part of their own small house whilst we try to find somewhere else to go. At the same time, my wife's kith and kin, though in a position to help, will not do so – what a lop-sided world it is!

Sixty years after writing the letter, the outrage, resentment and contempt still crackled from the pages and, re-reading it, I only wish that it might have been possible to see the Governor's reaction when he received it. As I saw it, my wife came from a family that had remained peculiarly unaffected by the war. The Governor had seen to it that neither of his sons would have to go into the Forces, appealing on their behalves when necessary. Naturally, it was understood that certain men were needed to work in agriculture to provide the food that the nation desperately needed now that almost no food could be imported. Walter and Arthur were deemed to be such workers, and indeed, Tom Caine was as well.

But it was only too understandable that to me in those times, with a wife, child and another baby due in the spring, that I would regard such men with envious eyes. I did not complain about doing my duty for my country; indeed I was eager to serve in the best way I knew how. But I was furious to see this hard-hearted and callous old man letting his property go to whoever he thought would be able to pay him most rent, rather than helping his own granddaughter, for whom he was always supposed to have a soft spot. I can truthfully say that I never felt so bitter in my life about anything and this whole episode would colour my judgment and shape my attitudes about wealth, property and what I perceived as unfair treatment, for the rest of my days.

Joy telephoned on the evening I posted the letter and unfortunately I let my anger with her family show, cursing her grandfather and telling her just what I thought of Arthur and Walter. Joy was plainly upset and shaken. She was terribly hurt and surprised at the Governor's behaviour for she had pinned her hopes on him. My anger must have been like a physical blow to her, living in one bedroom with my large and boisterous family in London, without her husband most of the time, already heavily pregnant and with a very lively and mischievous toddler to look after. I was to learn later that she cried hot tears into her pillow that night, muffling them so as not to wake Terry. Her tears were shame for her family's behaviour and, above all, she was distressed at me being so angry with her. She told me it was a profoundly low time for her and I hadn't even gone off on active service yet. All that was still to come. Joy had wondered whatever was to become of her and her little son and the unborn baby already stirring within her. Back at Bulford, I'd bitterly regretted my quick temper and the angry words on the telephone to the wife I loved so dearly.

I was busy preparing for 'D' Company's trip to Yeovil, where we were being sent for swimming practice in the pool there. In the aftermath of the Sicily invasion, it was decided to put the Airborne Forces through intensive swimming training, so that in the event of gliders ever having to ditch into water again the men would at least have a chance of saving themselves by swimming to safety. This policy was in accordance with my own thinking and I was keen to put it into action. At the end of a wet November, the camp did not represent comfortable accommodation, but we made the best of it and at least the camp cinema was a good one. The men trudged through the mud to the swimming pool for tests and I had to send two men to what we referred to as 'the slammer' or 'in digger', for refusing to enter the pool. I was sharing accommodation with Den Brotheridge, 'slumming' I called it, for I had become used to a better billet by then.

Out of the blue, I received a letter from Oxford telling me there was the chance of a house and was so confident about securing it that I rang my friend Bill Scarsbrook and asked him to make arrangements for a bed at the Radcliffe Hospital in Oxford for Joy's confinement the following March. Joy was overjoyed at this news and had telephoned to her mother asking if there was any possibility of a cash loan to buy the house, just to tide us over until I could make arrangements for a mortgage. Tom and Betty Caine had finally found a new home themselves and had moved to a house called Stanford, much nearer to the family business at Longville-in-the-Dale, near Much Wenlock. Apparently Stanford was a smaller house and much easier to run than Hill Crest, but Tom Caine was most unhappy about leaving Hill Crest and so was Lorna. From what Joy was told, Hill Crest had not actually been sold but was due to be auctioned in due course. We still could not really understand what was going on. However, it did mean that they had more money to spend on Lorna's education, and her mother had also said that she and Tom would be agreeable to making a short-term loan to us. Unfortunately the agent I had been in touch with in Oxford, a Mr Weekes, was off work and possibly this was what led to the difficulties that followed. I had a thirty-six-hour weekend pass again and arrived in London on the Saturday afternoon and, thinking that our worries were at an end, we had a very pleasant weekend. I went back to Bulford via Andover and ran into my Colonel who offered me a lift in his Humber which I gladly accepted, not only for the convenience but also for the chance to have a ride in such a splendid car. I was always to be fascinated and enthralled by luxury cars, but it would be many years before I was able to afford one of my own.

'D' Company had returned to Bulford from Yeovil over the weekend and first thing next morning, I contacted Mr Weekes to secure the house in Oxford for us but a day later I received the sickening news that it had been sold by a private treaty for what was an enormous sum in those days – £1,275. It was my thirty-first birthday the following day, 8 December, and this was a most unwelcome birthday present. I received a parcel from the family at Buck Lane as well as Joy's family sending cards from Shropshire. Betty had also sent me a letter, asking that I write formally to her husband requesting the loan to secure a house. I had just gone through the ordeal of asking Joy's grandfather for a favour only to have it thrown back in my face, and I did not relish having to write a begging letter to Tom Caine as well. It irked me more than I could say, but I fetched a pen and paper and wrote the letter to Tom, despite being fully aware that it was Betty who held the purse strings in that household. It certainly looked as if they were just making me grovel.

On 13 December, the announcement was made that 'D' Company's Christmas leave was cancelled. We had all been hoping we would be able to spend a day or so at home with our families and it came as a great disappointment to the men, although to tell the truth, I had been expecting it. Things were not going well for me and I felt that Christmas at 'bloody Bulford' was the icing on the cake. It was decided, therefore, that Joy may as well return to Shropshire so that she and Terry could spend Christmas with her family although she had no idea until she got there just how restricted the accommodation would be. She

69

couldn't believe that they had left their fine family house for this small cottage, which was down a rutted lane in the countryside.

News came through that our Colonel, Guy Rowley was going to take a staff job in India, but nobody yet knew who would replace him. The company was given thirty-six hour passes for the weekend before Christmas and, unable to see Joy, I decided to go to Oxford to visit all my friends and contacts there. I spent a good day there seeing my old police friends and putting more impassioned pleas out for everyone to try to help us to find somewhere to live. I felt that this trip to Oxford had done some good, despite a dreadful journey back to Bulford on a very foggy night. I found a message waiting for me to ring Joy in Shropshire and rather worried, I placed the call. But Joy seemed unable to talk freely to me on the telephone and I could only gather that something was wrong and she was very unhappy with the situation with her mother's family and was thinking about returning with Terry to London before Christmas. She said she would telephone me again the following evening and rang off.

I worried all day about what was going on in Shropshire, but it was the Inter-Company cross-country and 'D' Company won it easily, with me coming in eighth. Afterwards, I had to have my TAB injection and it made me feel very faint and queasy and I had to excuse myself from the dinner table. But I hung around the officers' mess to receive Joy's call. She sounded distracted and unwell, having caught the flu from Lorna, and told me that she was definitely taking Terry back to London by train the following day.

The next day, 21 December, I was at a conference at Brigade HQ and so had to shake off the effects of the TAB injection and present an enthusiastic face to the world. It was a busy day and I was unable to find the opportunity to ring Joy at Buck Lane before 20.00. But she had already gone to bed, feeling exhausted after her journey and still suffering the effects of the flu. Little Terry was safely in his cot, sleeping soundly as well and Pop could throw no light on the reason why Joy had returned so suddenly but said that he and Mom would look after them for me. Relieved to know that my wife and son were safely at my parents' house, I was still concerned to know what had happened to make Joy leave her mother's house so suddenly.

In the days that followed, I gradually had the tale of woe from Joy over several telephone calls and a long letter. It transpired that Joy had arrived at Stanford and been appalled by the living conditions there after the space and comfort of Hill Crest. The house was in disarray and by Joy's high standards, most un-welcoming. The atmosphere was tense and it was evident to Joy that her mother thought that she would pitch into all the chaos and muddle, as she had done on occasions before, and clean up, sort out and wave some kind of domestic wand and turn everything into order and cleanliness by Christmas. When Joy asked Tommy why on earth they had left Hill Crest to move there, he would only shake his head and suck his teeth, disappearing off to the yard, as the family business was known, or down to the local pub, the Longville Arms. Betty Caine was in one of her moods. She'd made up her mind what would be best for her family and that was that. Joy was over six months' pregnant and very bulky this time and she found just looking after Terry, caring for themselves and doing a little cooking, was just about the limit of her capabilities. Sorting out her mother's disordered house was quite beyond her at that time. To add to this, Joy had let her feelings be known about the Governor's behaviour and had made a few sharp remarks about people in reserved occupations. Betty thought she was getting at Tommy, and the two women had words. All in all, Christmas spirit was pretty thin on the ground.

Tom and Betty were genuinely shocked when she said she was going back to London, and Lorna had burst into tears saying, 'Don't go, Jee Jee! I want you to stay!' But she had made her mind up to go and so Tommy loaded her belongings into his Standard Flying Nine car, to run her into Church Stretton to catch the train. Her mother was very defensive and had said to Joy, 'Oh well Joy, if you want to go – then go you must,' and watched them put their things into the car, stony faced. On the way to Church Stretton, Joy had said to Tommy, 'That place is awful Tommy. What on earth are you thinking about to give Hill Crest up for Stanford?'

Tom was very loyal to his wife, he just said, 'Well, there was more than one reason, Joy – you know how Mommy can be. There's things you don't know about. Anyhow, we might not stay there for long.'

He adored Joy's mother and had come to rely on her judgment, even when, deep down his instincts told him that she was wrong.

'Well, I hope not!' said Joy with feeling, 'Nonie doesn't like it there at all. What a good job she loves boarding at The Mount so much!'

Nonie was Lorna's nickname in the family. Tom's expression changed and he took his eye off the country lane ahead for a moment to glance meaningfully at Joy, 'It's not over yet. Hill Crest doesn't come up for auction for a month or two and you never know what may happen!'

He would say no more, but Joy was left feeling that despite the fact that hitherto, Tom always did whatever Betty wanted, maybe this time he would stand up to her.

Nobody ever did understand why Betty insisted on moving the family out of Hill Crest to the cottage in the late autumn of 1943. Lorna would say many years later that she didn't remember much about that time because she was boarding at The Mount school nearby, which she had really enjoyed and recalled with great affection. She thought that her mother just had a whim to live in a cottage over in Longville and near to the yard where Tommy worked. Perhaps Betty thought that the running expenses of Hill Crest were too high and keeping the large house clean and tidy was too much work on her own. In any event, the Stanford experience was not one the Caines wished to prolong. Without telling Betty, sometime in the New Year of 1944, Tom went to the auctioneer with whom they had placed the sale of Hill Crest and 'bought in' the house. That is, he took it off the market. It was chilly weather and the house had been empty two or three months, so Tommy went up there and lit fires in all the main rooms and made it look warm and cheerful again. Then he went back to Stanford and, brooking no arguments, made Betty pack their clothes and possessions. He'd arranged for a lorry to collect the furniture and Lorna was at home for the weekend from school. With no more ado, he drove his wife and Lorna, back to Church Stretton and Hill Crest. Lorna would always cherish the memory of returning to her favourite home, running in and finding fires burning in the grates and being able to unpack and feel as if they had all come home at last. Just for once, Betty meekly accepted Tom's decision, and they all settled down again and put the dreary memories of Stanford behind them.

Joy never did tell my family why she had returned to London so hastily, leaving them to assume that she had fallen out with her mother for some reason. She had learned to get on with my family and respected them for improving their way of life and moving out to the suburbs. And we were both very grateful for them letting Joy have one of their few bedrooms as a haven for herself and Terry, especially while her own family seemed to be going through a difficult time. But Joy and her mother soon made it up again and kept in close touch. We still needed Tom and Betty's help to secure a house when we found one.

Chapter 7

Christmas 1943 to March 1944: Home Making and Marking Time

Through the open door I could hear Brian Priday's wireless set in the next room; they were playing the carol *Good King Wenceslas*. It was Christmas Eve 1943 and I was at the table in my room in the officers' accommodation hut at Bulford camp. In my diary I wrote 'Pray God it will all be over by next year'. I had no way of knowing that the country would still be at war a year hence but that it would all be over for me. Earlier in the day, all of the men had posed for a Company photograph to be taken. That long horizontal photograph would hang in my dining-room throughout my family life and when my daughter, still a child, asked me why many of the young men had pencilled circles drawn around their heads, I would tell her quietly that they were the 'boys who didn't come back'. She would learn much later where they hadn't come back from.

On Christmas Day the new Colonel commanded the Church Parade. He was Colonel Mike Roberts and my first impression was that he was quiet but looked as if he'd be efficient. There was the usual Christmas meal served at lunchtime for all the troops, where traditionally, they were looked after by the officers, and we entertained ten American officers in the mess for the day. I enjoyed chatting to the Americans but in the evening, I was to be found letting my hair down in the sergeants' mess, where I still felt more relaxed. I became quickly bored hanging around the camp over Christmas and filled my time by talking several of the men of 'D' Company, Gooch, Barwick, Norton and Ferguson into joining the Regimental Boxing Team. I commented in my diary that it had been announced that the second front – that was the invasion of France, was to be commanded by General Dwight Eisenhower with General Bernard Montgomery. This news was received with mixed feelings because the British Forces recognized that they were no longer in charge of the military decision-making process. The sheer numbers and weaponry of the Americans now meant that they had the upper hand among the Allies.

The Prime Minister, Winston Churchill had been ill with pneumonia during December, and it was rumoured that he would never be fit again to run the country and spur the people on to victory. But the news came through on 29 December that Churchill was well on the road to recovery and this cheered me up as I was listening to the evening news, preparing to go off on a night exercise.

On 30 December Colonel Mike Roberts had lectured all the officers for the first time and we were all suitably impressed. I tested the section leaders on the last day of 1943 and decided that they needed more training in one or two areas. That evening I reflected that another year had passed without action, but I knew that 1944 was going to be very different. I was frustrated and restless to be off and into action, my diary entry for 1 January 1944 reading, 'Still at b. Bulford – waiting – waiting – is soul destroying'. But I was able to dash off on thirty-six hours leave to go to London to see Joy and Terry at my parents' home.

On 3 January 1944, I heard from one of my Oxford contacts that there was a house available in Cowley. I was very afraid of being let down once again and wrote to Joy about it in a fairly offhand manner, in a letter I was posting to reach her on her twenty-fourth birthday, having failed to get to the shops to buy her a birthday card. Joy was not so casual about it and leapt into action immediately. She left Terry with his grandmother and caught the train to Oxford to view the house, sending me a 'wire' to let me know where she was. I was intrigued to know more about the house but had to wait for our usual evening telephone call the next day.

The company was up at 04.00 hours doing Divisional Platoon Exercises at a place called Beaches Barn on 5 January 1944. This had been Colonel Roberts' idea and I had felt that it was a good one to test the platoon's performances. But it wasn't very popular with the men because they had scheduled the 'D' Company party for that same evening and all put in a great deal of work planning and rehearsing for it, especially Brian Priday. However, it says much for the standard they had reached in their training at that time, that 'D' Company triumphed during the demonstration attack. We were all anxious to get back to barracks to prepare for the party, and for that reason I was possibly not in a very receptive frame of mind when Joy rang me full of excitement about the house she'd been to see the day before. I had had such an early start that morning and had been busy all day. By that time I was keen to get off to the Company party, but Joy was full of the house. It was a semi-detached house on the Garsington Road in Oxford, which I knew was close to the Morris Motor Works and I must confess that I had aspired to finding a home in a better neighbourhood. This accounted for my lack of immediate enthusiasm for the place and also because, when Joy told me how much they were asking for it – in excess of £1,200 – I was horrified and told her that we couldn't afford it. After so many months of waiting for somewhere to come up, Joy was both exasperated and very disappointed with my attitude and we ended up having a row on the telephone about it. Of course, as ever, I regretted my words the minute I had put the phone down. Cursing silently to myself, I felt a hand on my shoulder, 'Come on, John!' shouted Tony Hooper, 'we've got a party to go to!'

Brian Priday and the company staff from HQ had organized an excellent evening's entertainment that I would remember as indicative of the spirit and unity of 'D' Company at that time. The men had laid on a series of little plays and scenes pulling the legs of the senior officers and using everyone's idiosyncrasies to hilarious effect. Selfishly, I soon forgot my disagreement with Joy over the house, roaring with laughter, clutching my sides and almost falling off my chair. It brought us all close to one another, this shared night of careless laughter, and we would remember it for a long time. I looked around at my 2 I/C Brian Priday, and the junior officers, Den Brotheridge, David Wood, Tod Sweeney and Tony Hooper and felt that I was indeed blessed to have such a fine team of men around me for whatever lay ahead. My feeling, by that time, was that we had all been through the training syllabus several times and we were complying with higher Training Instructions of carrying out, per week, one day's section training, one day's platoon and one day on a company exercise. I always regarded keeping fit as an undying code but I realized that occasionally some of my junior officers found it hard to have quite as much enthusiasm for it as I did. But I now felt that 'D' Company was ready for action and for carrying out whatever task would be required. We were just 'marking time' and I was finding it increasingly difficult to constantly think up new ways of presenting the continuous training and sporting endeavours to maintain that state of readiness. Therefore, I was glad when one of my senior officers came in with a scheme of his own and was keen for the men to do well.

The next morning, somewhat bleary eyed at first from our party the night before, 'D' Company were engaged on an advance and frontal attack exercise. Colonel Roberts came out to observe but was given the wrong map references and arrived a little late. However, he seemed very impressed to see the men in action. I was fully occupied for that day and the next, doing reconnaissance for an anti-tank exercise the following week, and officers' training all afternoon and evening. On returning to my room, I found a letter waiting for me from my mother. I eyed the envelope rather as one might a primed grenade, my mother's careful looped writing striking alarm, for she was not one for casual correspondence. Sure enough, I found a stern rebuke from Mom within the letter, telling me in no uncertain terms that I had a duty to my wife, son and expected baby to find a home for them, no matter what obstacles had to be overcome. Undoubtedly, Mom may have had a hidden agenda in writing to me this way, since it was they who were occupying her front bedroom. However, she had certainly witnessed Joy's anxiety and profound disappointment at having found a house to buy, rushing off to Oxford to view it and then encountering my refusal to face the economic truth that we must expect to have to pay over the odds for a property during war-time. I rang Joy straight away to make arrangements to meet her the next day, despite a training session on the Saturday morning making it a tremendous rush to catch the 11.55 train from the sidings at Bulford.

I met Joy in Oxford and we went to see the house. I was impressed with the property for it was close to shops for Joy and there was a small garden at the front and a larger, enclosed garden at the back where children could play in safety. Joy's green eyes held mine, appealing for me to buy the house, and I spoke to the agent and agreed to purchase it for £1,100. Joy was thrilled to bits, but it was in my nature to worry about how on earth we would afford it.

The house, 36 Garsington Road, Cowley, Oxford was just a small, 3-bedroomed, pebble-dashed semi on a road that was fairly busy with traffic and had a rather fanciful name, Krasnova. Today, the house looks rather mean and forlorn, the original homely brown and speckled pebbledash painted over with grimy cream paint. It stands, with its partner, in a small row of faded, 1930s semi-detached houses on a wide and dismal arterial road that has heavy traffic thundering along it all day long. But in 1944, when the house was perhaps only ten years old, there was a hedge along the front and the road was more suburban than urban. It was to be our first home together and for Joy in particular, despite the reality of a war-torn January, there were roses around the door already existing in her mind.

The next day, I made a very anxious telephone call to Tom and Betty Caine to ask if Joy and I could avail ourselves of the short-term loan to secure the house in Oxford. They told me that they would advance it and I felt much relieved. I rang Joy at Buck Lane to tell her the news and she was delighted. It was right then, when so much was going on in my private life that I found that the days at Bulford camp were becoming ever more hectic as well. There was a definite air of something about to happen and we had to carry out a mobilization exercise with kit checks and inspections, which really set the men buzzing.

On a day of platoon training, I found that I was obliged to send for both Tod Sweeney and David Wood and give them a rocket. I even recorded in my diary that I really did not like doing it. This unpleasant duty was to reap rewards a few days later when the platoons tackled the complexities of 'fighting patrols' and both Sweeney and Wood put in sterling performances. We were planning for a whole seven days of night training the following week but I dashed off to London on the Sunday to discuss the house move with Joy. She had obtained an estimate for the removal which, at £12, I considered far too much. Joy was just beginning to learn that I begrudged parting with any more of my hard-earned money than I absolutely had to. The journey back to Bulford was hell, taking an unbelievable seven and a half hours.

The night training commenced on 17 January. I was becoming very stressed and with so much on my mind I hardly knew which way to turn. We had a night exercise the second night with REME (Royal Electrical and Mechanical Engineers) which was chaotic and which I called a circus, and I didn't manage to get to bed until 10.00. Trying to sleep during the day was slowly becoming easier for me, but was not helped on this occasion by being woken up at 16.00 by a telephone call from Joy to tell me that her mother had informed her that they could only advance us the money at 7½ per cent, which was a high rate of interest for those times. I was fraught with worry and felt that they were letting us down and taking advantage of our desperate situation. I was obliged to continue with night exercises with 'D' Company that night but forced myself out of bed for 13.00 the next day, in order to go to the building society in Salisbury, to try to arrange a mortgage, so that we would not need to borrow money from the Caines. But the mortgage would take more time to arrange than was available, since it was vital that we secured the house purchase in a matter of days. There were plenty more house-buyers waiting to snatch the little house from our grasp if we delayed. Therefore, I was obliged to accept that we must go along with paying the 7½ per cent interest to the Caines. But I resolved to organize a mortgage just as soon as possible so that we could pay them back without delay.

I returned to Bulford for a night exercise with twenty-eight Horsa gliders. The weather was kind to us and the flight went well, with no casualties. We did a night attack in the cold, damp air of the January night, and then marched the ten miles back to Bulford. Back at the camp later that day, I telephoned the Caines and, through gritted teeth, confirmed that Joy and I would have to accept their terms on the loan to get us through. Fortunately, there was just one more session of night training to be endured and, to my immense relief on this occasion, the week was over and we could return to what passed for normality in 1944.

After two days of street fighting training down in the bombed-out areas of Southampton, I was counting the hours to my nine-day leave, when I could move my wife and son into our new home. Thus on 25 January 1944, I took the 08.00 train to Waterloo and was indoors at Buck Lane having a cup of tea by 11.00. Despite her increasing size, Joy was happily clearing out and packing up, ready for the move to Oxford. The following day the removal van arrived early and loaded up by midday. It was a good job done and that night, our last in my parents' home, little Terry slept on blankets on the bedroom floor. Joy and I went off to catch the train to Oxford next morning, but before we left I heard Joy say to my mother, 'Thanks Mom – for everything. I don't think we could have managed without you and Pop giving us a home here, and for writing that letter to John like you did.' My parents had mixed feelings about seeing us leave. In a large family there are always bound to be some who stay close to the nest and some who move away. Mom had not always seen eye to eye with Joy, but I knew she regarded her as a wonderful mother and a good wife too and that would have satisfied her.

So we caught the train to Oxford. When we arrived at the house on Garsington Road, we found that the removal van hadn't yet arrived and it finally turned up at about 15.00 with the usual tales of breakdowns, so common in those days. It took several hours to finally get all our possessions piled higgledy-piggledy into the rooms of Krasnova. The couple next door kept popping round with cups of tea and offers of help. They were older people, Mr and Mrs Wormald, and I soon decided that they should be encouraged as they would obviously be company for Joy while I was away. Joy concentrated on putting Terry's cot up and his familiar things around the little room that we had decided would be his – the first time he had ever slept in a room on his own. He was put to bed in his new room, and we waited for the bellows of rage we thought might ensue when he realized that his parents would not be joining him. But Terry was tired after the excitement of the day, and he slept like a log until we crept in the next morning to see if he was still breathing.

The following day, some of our old friends from my police days came round and helped Joy continue the unpacking. Bill helped me with laying linoleum on the kitchen and bathroom floors. The days that followed were of a similar pattern. I dashed into Oxford to sort out the ration books – always a necessity whenever you moved to a new area, and we arranged for coal to be delivered. Only too soon, it was the final day of my leave, but I felt a profound satisfaction looking around our new home already neat and orderly under Joy's magic touch. Now I could go off and concentrate on the bloody war, knowing that my wife and precious child would be safe and settled in our own home. The morning post on this last day brought further good news – the building society had fixed us a mortgage for £800, the maximum they would allow on my salary. Soon I would be able to pay the Caines back and escape that ruddy 7½ per cent interest. A trip to the new doctor confirmed that Joy was well and the pregnancy progressing normally. And so I caught the train back to Bulford camp, but this time Joy waved me off from our own front door.

If only the second front that was being talked about all the time, would actually get going. I was tied to my desk in the company office all day doing administration work and organized a run in the afternoon for 'D' Company just to make sure they knew that I was back. 'D' Company now began a series of exercises that would take us up to D-Day, although at the time we were completely unaware that we were being considered for a special assignment. It was the beginning of February 1944, and although there had been no snow that winter, there was a cold and frosty spell of weather with a very penetrating wind. We were engaged on what was called, somewhat appropriately, 'freeze exercises'. These were essentially anti-tank defensive tactics, where the troops had to freeze in a hedgehog position, taking cover and keeping still. Not ideal training in very cold weather, but my answer to the complaints was to commence regimental cross-country training to warm them all up. Next came a snap exercise where the

Division was given a task without any warning or planning. It involved a quick appreciation of the situation and decisions on all levels. Without a doubt, I felt that it speeded up everything in the field. The platoon commanders and I rose to the challenge and the men of 'D' Company gave us full support. The exercise was commanded by the Battalion 2 I/C, Major Mark Darrell-Brown who, in my rather arbitrary estimation, was not quite up to the job. However, General Gale was observing and full of praise for all our efforts. The eight-mile march back to the barracks – just a stroll for 'D' Company was far too slow in my opinion, the pace being set by Darrell-Brown. Then there was another flying exercise, supposed to be one and a half hours in a glider, but delayed by bad weather and we finally only managed half an hour up there which pleased me for I had not been looking forward to a lengthy flight.

On 26 February 1944, General F. A. M. Browning, Commander Airborne Forces, visited the Regiment and lectured all officers and senior NCOs on the 'Invasion Set-up'. It was a long lecture but delivered in 'Boy' Browning's lucid manner, we all found it extremely interesting. Afterwards, the general feeling was that the plans being made for the invasion were being worked out thoroughly and with enormous care by the highest level of the Allied Command. We also realized that the plans were at an advanced state and that before too long, the command at battalion level would be informed of what was going to take place. It seemed very obvious that the 6th Airborne Division would play an important role.

There was a precious thirty-six-hour leave when I was able to catch the midday train back to Oxford, and I would never forget the pleasure I felt walking into our clean, warm home. Joy cooked a roast dinner on the Sunday and I nearly overdid it, digging in the back garden. Once again, I found it very hard to leave my cosy home and make my way back to Bulford; an appalling journey with one delay after another meaning that I arrived back there in the early hours of Monday morning. I had to grab a few hours' sleep in the afternoon, as 'D' Company were off that night at 21.00 hours on Exercise PAGODA. Once again it was bitterly cold, and this only encouraged the men to 'dig in' hastily to try to get warm. The Regiment was marched back to Bulford but I was able to use motor transport to return with the running team who needed to practise. Next day was spent crossing a river using toggle ropes. There were a few American officers attached to 'D' Company at that time and they particularly enjoyed this training.

Returning to the barracks, I found that the cheque had arrived from the building society – £764. 2s. 6d. I noted it in my diary – and I was able to write a cheque for the princely sum of £800 to send off to Tom and Betty Caine to pay off most of our debt. Feeling satisfied by this, I decided to go over to the officers' mess to celebrate with a drink before dinner and I found the others indulging in one of their 'games'. It was a rule of the 52nd that such games were only to be played in the officers' mess before dinner and, in view of the rough and tumble nature of many of them, it was a sensible rule. The favourite game of the moment, and generally recognized as a game special to the 52nd, was called 'Are you there, Moriarty?' This consisted of one officer, who was blindfolded, lying on the floor with a rolled up newspaper, trying to accurately hit another officer who would be lying somewhere in the vicinity. After a few drinks, this simple game could become extremely funny. After days and nights spent in often very arduous conditions, engaging in dangerous training for active service, this kind of crazy and light-hearted horse-play was a very necessary outlet for the young officers' energy and spirits and we entered into them with enthusiasm and sometimes with a certain amount of aggression. There were other games as well, of a similar nature, but it would be strongly denied that the officers of the 52nd ever practised them. David Wood would recall that once, visiting another regiment, he witnessed their special game which they called 'Submarines' when an unsuspecting visiting officer lay on the floor with an Army mackintosh laid over him with one of the rigid waterproof sleeves poking up above him. There would be much genial chanting of a marine nature and then a pint of beer would be poured down the sleeve of the mackintosh with hilarious results. Woody would never admit to being on the receiving end of this treatment.

Sometimes we officers would run off with each others' letters or some cherished possession in the accommodation hut, and a frantic chase would ensue, over the beds and down the corridors. Once, I put my arm through a glass panel chasing Den Brotheridge, and was left to explain to the medical officer how I had slipped accidentally as I had it stitched and bound up. To get my own back on Brotheridge, the next night I waited until he was in the bathroom and threw a thunder flash in there with him, which was like a large firework. Den emerged coughing madly and with streaming eyes. We were young men away from home and without the restraining influence of the fairer sex to regard us with raised eyebrows, pursed lips and remarks such as, 'Honestly – men! They simply never grow up!' We behaved as men of all ages will always do when in the company of close male friends, with a few drinks to relax us and take away the cares of the day and thoughts of what lay ahead.

The men too had their own way of relaxing. There was a very good pub down in Bulford village called the Rose and Crown, that was much frequented by the soldiers from the camp. Before they went out, the men went through a strict drill of closing all the shutters on the windows of their particular hut, to ensure that the regulations regarding the blackout were adhered to. They would pass a merry time down at the pub, those of them with a little money to spare, and return across the fields to Bulford camp, with much falling into ditches and over tussocks of grass. Upon reaching their hut, it was up to one of their number to open just one shutter, once everyone else was in bed and the lights extinguished to maintain the blackout, in order that there would be just a faint grey light should someone have to pay a call of nature in the night. Tom Packwood, who was in 25 Platoon, commanded by Den Brotheridge, recalled one night when they had a particularly arduous session, one of the lads known to all as 'Swill' Balham because of his heavy drinking, forgot to remove the shutter and in the night he was unable to see to find the toilet. The next morning Tom awoke to find that Balham had relieved himself in his boots. Well, you wouldn't forget a thing like that.

In the officers' mess one night in late February 1944, I was playing a few rubbers of bridge with an American officer named Art Hill who was attached to 'D' Company. I liked Art very much and when I won seven shillings off him, I liked him even more! We had come in third to the Devons in the divisional run that day, up the steepest part of the Beacon, which was the highest hill locally. Already disgruntled at coming third, I received an urgent telephone call in the mess that night from a company sergeant called Les Taylor, saying that his family, who were moving to Oxford, had been informed that they could be billeted in Major John Howard's new home on Garsington Road, as there was a spare bedroom there. You can imagine that I went puce in the face explaining in words of one syllable to the luckless sergeant, that due to my wife expecting another baby within weeks, there would certainly not be room at Krasnova for another family to be billeted. I guess after that poor Art Hill stood no chance facing me at bridge; my senses heightened by this recent confrontation.

At the end of February I managed to borrow a motorcycle to go home to Oxford for the day to see Joy, who was now near her time. It had been thought that Terry would go to his grandparents in London during Joy's confinement in hospital, but the air-raids on London had been particularly severe in recent weeks and I did not want to risk sending our little son there. Our next-door neighbours, the Wormalds, had become very good friends to Joy and Terry was already very content to stay with Mrs Wormald when Joy went to the shops or for a check-up with the doctor. It was therefore decided that Terry would be happiest if he stayed with them.

The following day, 'D' Company had grenade practice and there was nearly a bad accident when one of the men in 24 Platoon dropped a primed grenade and Platoon Commander David Wood was almost caught in the blast. I was very thankful that David escaped injury and returned to the company office to try to put my mind to working out the training sessions for the following week. I found it very difficult to concentrate and come up with any ideas as my mind was on Joy and the prospect of her going into labour. I was profoundly grateful that she had such caring and reliable neighbours, especially since we had no telephone as yet in our new home. In the next few days the training continued with the men doing revolver firing and sniper training, while Brian Priday busied himself dyeing all the toggle ropes dark green. These were the ropes, normally white, that each man wore wound around his waist during operations, in case they were needed in battle to scale a wall or cross a river. Since it was anticipated that 'D' Company's role would involve night fighting, white toggle ropes could have been a target for German snipers, but dyed a dark colour they would not be detected.

During the next week, on 8 March, the 6th Airborne were inspected by General Bernard Montgomery, who was commanding the 21st Army Group, of which we were a part. It was a beautiful day but with a keen and chilly wind and since Montgomery was inspecting us out in the field, I stood with 'D' Company by Dumbell Copse for three and a half hours waiting for him to reach our sector. I described the great man as 'a queer fellow, great exhibitionist' but then I never did take to small men no matter how great they were. But I had to hand it to Monty for having a sure touch when it came to responding to the troops. Instead of the familiar double-badged black beret he usually wore, Montgomery was wearing a red Airborne beret. He explained that it had belonged to our late Brigade Commander who had been killed in action in Italy. We men of the Airborne appreciated this gesture of respect for our fallen leader. I was not to know then that I would next see Montgomery on the battlefields of Normandy, four months hence.

The next day we were all engaged on Exercise PATRIOT when some of the men were cast as spies and infiltrators – fifth columnists we called them then – and these men deliberately tried to cause trouble and mislead the others. The platoons were under the command of their sergeants making guerrilla attacks, which I noted were not very successful. In the field overnight, it was extremely cold and we had to break the ice on the water pitchers at Hyde Farm where we were billeted. Thus, on 11 March, I passed the day listlessly at Bulford completely unaware that Joy was in labour and had been taken into the Radcliffe Hospital in Oxford.

The next morning I went training early and then took off for Oxford with Harry Styles, calling in at our home around midday to see Joy. Instead, I found Mrs Wormald running down the front path of her house next-door, holding Terry by the hand, waving to me frantically, 'John! Joy's in hospital – she was taken in yesterday first thing!' I stopped in my tracks, asking urgently 'Is she OK? What's happened?' Catching her breath, Mrs Wormald gasped, 'It's all fine, John – she had the baby about 11.00 in the morning – a lovely little girl! We didn't know how to contact you 'til this morning and then they said you'd already left!'

I could hardly believe it. Joy had already had the baby. I swung my son above my head and shouted, 'You've got a little sister, Snooks!' I roared off to the Radcliffe in the Army Jeep to visit Joy and see my new daughter. We had already decided to call her Penelope Elizabeth and I called her Penny from the first, usually shortened to Pen. I couldn't believe how small she was. All too soon I had to return to my duties at Bulford, despite feeling a real tug at leaving Terry with Mr and Mrs Wormald, even though I knew the little boy was quite content.

Two days later, I heard from the hospital that Joy had taken a turn for the worse. I couldn't make out what had gone wrong, and was worried to death and longed to go and see her. I rang the Radcliffe again in the evening and, by some misunderstanding, was told that she was improving. I, therefore, decided not to ask for compassionate leave, but to continue with the Army programme, which meant leaving early the next day for Exmoor, where we were engaged on Exercise PRANG. It took five hours to get down there and we were billeted in Dunster Pleasure Camp which was a collection of holiday chalets on the beach. Reassured that my wife and new daughter were quite comfortable in the hospital in Oxford, I relaxed down in Devon and even walked across the cliffs to Minehead, enjoying a fine spell of weather.

The exercise, field firing with the Colonel in charge, took place on Exmoor but it was slow progress as he was unused to the procedure. We were six hours out on the moor and returned to our billets very tired. As we were preparing to leave the next morning, an orderly hurried up to me and said, 'Major Howard, sir. They've been trying to get hold of you – your wife is very ill, sir! You must get back to Oxford immediately!' The bottom suddenly seemed to fall out of my world and I tore back to Bulford and ran to catch the train to Oxford. I found Joy very weak, but slowly on the mend and most anxious to have my reassurance that our little daughter was all right, for she had been unable to breast feed her for several days. It seemed that the hospital had been at best, overly optimistic when they told me that my wife was improving and, at worst, downright negligent. In fact she had been very ill indeed. After a few days, she had had a very high fever, verging on septicaemia, until the afterbirth had eventually come away and the medical staff realized what the problem had been and began to give her the right treatment. During this time, little Penny had been starved until one of the nurses had made the decision to give her a bottle. Unfortunately, the trauma of this setback meant that Joy lost the ability to breast-feed the baby herself, and Penny had to continue to be bottle-fed. I was just thankful to have my wife and child alive and making good progress.

I spent that night at home and the next day weeded the front garden and then took Terry to the hospital to see Joy and the new baby. It was very hard to tear myself away from my cherished family, but I had to go back to Bulford and leave Terry with the Wormalds once more.

Back in camp I was straight into organizing another exercise, this time called 'TIT'.

'Honestly!' I said to an orderly in the company office, 'I don't know where they get these names from.'

'It's a bird, sir' said the orderly smartly.

'Yes, I know,' I replied, raising my eyes to heaven.

Tod Sweeney commanded Exercise TIT with David Wood as 2 I/C and they both put in good work. When it was over, David and Tod went off to Southampton to organize street fighting training in the bombed-out areas of the city. It happened that David Wood particularly disliked this training. It involved all kinds of assault course type of activities, in and out and over the derelict and often dangerous buildings. Sometimes they had to throw a hook over a thirty-foot wall and then clamber up it, gunfire and explosions going off all around them, or jump the gap between two buildings at roof level. Some of the men loved this kind of challenge and others loathed it, finding this kind of training all too realistic and frightening. But on this occasion, David Wood and Tod Sweeney did well and were especially congratulated on their assault course.

Later that same evening, after feeding the men at Durley Manor Farm, they were loaded into trucks and each platoon was dropped off at various locations around the Southampton area, with instructions to find their way to another farm before dawn. This was Grange Farm, near Titchbourne, known to us all from previous exercises. Brotheridge and I travelled on to Grange Farm on this occasion, and arrived there around 01.00 hours to find to our delight that the farmer and his wife had laid on a very comfortable billet for us, thanks to the organizational skills of the Company Quarter-Master Sergeant. We had a cosy room with a fire burning merrily in the grate and bottles of beer set on the side table. That certainly brought a smile to our faces. The platoons slowly crept in out of the night at about half-hourly intervals up to about 04.00 and were accommodated in warm barns with masses of straw piled up for bedding. A cup of steaming cocoa and an Army blanket and they were quickly falling into a sleep of satisfied exhaustion. The platoon leaders reported back to me in the house and were fast asleep themselves in no time, curled up in blankets in corners of the warm room. Mrs Young, the farmer's wife, made fried eggs for our breakfasts in the morning and I found myself reflecting that the kindness of people like that was heartwarming. It gave us all an added sense of what the war was being fought for – to preserve our way of life and freedom.

We all slept deeply at Grange Farm. I particularly enjoyed an opportunity to stay on a farm out in the heart of the English countryside. In the early morning, I opened a window and breathed in the country smell that I loved. It came from the hay in the barns, the unmistakeable, pungent scent of horses, the fresh green of the spring countryside and just a faint whiff of manure. I leaned on the sill and thought with satisfaction of my family. I had heard from Joy a couple of evenings before, to say that she was feeling much better and getting up each day now, and that little Penny was thriving, having taken well to being bottle-fed.

I thought about the day ahead and a meeting arranged for later, with all the 'top brass'. General Windy Gale was going to brief us about an exercise that was planned for the next few days. There had been talk in the officers' mess that it was going to be an important one, and that the senior ranks would be watching closely how each company would perform. Of course, there was talk all the time, rumours and gossip but I felt that all the talk of the invasion being sooner than we thought, might just have some truth to it. If so, then it would soon be decided who did what and I was determined that 'D' Company was going to put on a damn good show. I pulled the window to with a bang, setting the ducks and chickens in the yard outside squawking in alarm and Den Brotheridge to awaken with a shout thinking the invasion had started.

Chapter 8

March to end of May 1944: Preparations for D-Day

On 23 March 1944 I was taken off for a briefing for a full scale divisional exercise that involved 'D' Company landing in gliders near to, and capturing intact, three small bridges near Lechlade in Gloucestershire. This was the very first indication that I had that this was going to be our special assignment for the invasion of Europe. The action was to be called Exercise BIZZ and it took place a couple of days later. The overall military exercise for the rehearsal of D-Day was to become known as Operation DEADSTICK and I would realize in due course that this was the first part.

The following day I briefed 'D' Company and the individual platoons about their role in the exercise where, once they had landed they would have to defend the bridges until relieved by the remainder of the battalion, who were landing two or three miles away. I was very up-beat about it, having been told that such an assignment was a 'VC job', by which I presumed that success in such an operation could mean a distinctive battle honour. I was pleased to note, however, that in this instance we were all to be transported to the landing zone in troop carrying vehicles (TCVs) because there were no suitable areas for the gliders to land. We would then make the attack as if we'd already successfully landed by glider in the right place.

Despite my involvement with Exercise BIZZ, my thoughts were often with my wife still getting over her illness in the aftermath of our daughter's birth. I'd been very relieved to hear that she had recovered sufficiently to be allowed to go home with the new baby, and I wished heartily that I could have been able to help more with the children. But I had little time to dwell on domestic issues for Exercise BIZZ was upon us. On the evening of 25 March 'D' Company was loaded into the TCVs and taken by road up to Gloucestershire. Upon arrival we were led by umpires to the supposed landing zones. For Exercise BIZZ my company consisted of four glider loads, with one rifle platoon and five Airborne Sappers per glider.

1. John Howard in 1942.

2. A sport loving John
Howard, aged eleven.

3. In the garden at Buck Lane, Colindale in 1937.
Left to right: Pop Howard, Joy Bromley aged
seventeen, Mom Howard and Queenie.

4. John and Joy Howard on their wedding day, 28 October 1939.

5. Joy's mother, Betty Caine, Joy holding Terry, and Joy's grandfather, George Sagar, known as the Governor, at Terry's christening in September 1942.

6. Hill Crest, Church Stretton, Shropshire in September 1942. *Left to right:* John, Joy and Aunt Molly with Lorna Caine.

7. On holiday in Ilfracombe, Devon in June 1943. Terry Howard aged eleven months in his 'Pegasus' pram.

8. Pegasus Bridge in March 1944. Aerial reconnaissance photo taken from the
Bénouville side. On the far side of the bridge to the left of the road is the bridge
keeper's house which was demolished in April 1944 to make way for a pillbox.
The café is on the right side of the road.

9. John Howard and his men during the 'Salute the Soldier' week in Oxford in May 1944.

10. Halifax bombers with Horsa gliders in a herringbone formation, ready for take-off, 5 June 1944.

11. John Howard and Corporal Ted Tappenden standing in front of No. 1 glider in July 1944.

12. Aerial reconnaissance photo of Pegasus Bridge showing the water tower of the bridge and the positions of the three gliders.

13. 'D' Company HQ, Château St Côme, July 1944. John Howard is in the front row, second from right.

14. The café at Pegasus Bridge in late 1944 or early 1945.

15. Back in England – July 1945. John Howard with Joy, Terry aged three years and Penny aged eighteen months.

16. John Howard, accompanied by his son Terry, at Buckingham Palace in March 1946 to receive the DSO.

17. John Howard *(left)* and David Wood *(right)* in 1946.

18. On holiday in France, June 1947. The Howard family at a gun emplacement beside Pegasus Bridge.

19. John and Terry at the cemetery in Hérouvillette in June 1947.

20. The tenth anniversary party in Café Gondrée at midnight on 5 June 1954. *Left to right:* Georges and Thérèse Gondrée, Joy and John Howard, Georgette Gondrée, glider pilot Jim Wallwork. In front Arlette and Françoise Gondrée.

21. On location for the
20th Century Fox
film *The Longest Day*
in September 1961.
Left to right: Peter
Lawford, Lord
Lovat, Richard Todd
and John Howard.

22. John Howard and
Hans von Luck,
commander of a
regiment of the 21st
Panzer Division,
exchanging war
memories at
Pegasus Bridge in
the mid–1980s.

23. Thérèse Gondrée, John Howard and glider pilot, Oliver Boland meet HRH Prince Charles at Ranville Cemetery in 1984.

24. John Howard with glider pilots, *left to right:* Geoff Barkway (No. 3 glider), Jim Wallwork (No. 1 glider) and Oliver Boland (No. 2 glider) in Normandy in June 1984.

25. Pegasus Bridge, Bénouville, Normandy 1984.

26. John Howard with Hans von Luck at the Café du Monde in New Orleans for the fiftieth anniversary of D-Day Lecture Tour, arranged by author Stephen Ambrose, May 1994.

27. John Howard with some of 'D' Company in June 1994. *Left to right:* Charlie Gardiner, Wagger Thornton, Ted Tappenden, Wally Parr and Arthur Roberts.

28. Tod Sweeney, John Howard and David Wood in 1994.

29. Penny and Terry Howard in Bénouville in June 1994 for the fiftieth anniversary of D-Day, standing beneath the photo of their father.

30. The unveiling of Howard's bust on the landing zone at Pegasus Bridge in June 1995. *Left to right:* Tod Sweeney, John Howard, Wally Parr, Vivi Malloch the sculptress, Penny Howard Bates, Ted Tappenden and Frank Bourlet.

We 'landed' about 23.00 and took the bridges before they were 'blown up', after what I later described as 'only a brief scrap' with the soldiers who were acting as the enemy at each bridge. It had been stressed to me that it was vital for the Division that the bridges be taken intact, and therefore speed was of the essence.

As was customary on such an important exercise, there were several high-ranking military observers present and I took especial note of them, since my training had instilled in me the need to be suspicious of anyone I saw around the zone of activity. A man who was wearing an RAF uniform made me extremely wary, and my zeal was such that I instructed that the man be seized and interrogated. In a moment, General Gale appeared by my side and quickly put an end to the interrogation by explaining that the Air Force man was an official observer alongside him. I had no time to dwell on this mistake, for the 'enemy' had decided to counter-attack in a spirited manner. Platoon Commander David Wood recalled supplies being dropped by air, for it was a lengthy and intensive counter-attack designed to push my men to the limit. I felt that 'D' Company's hastily assembled defences barely coped, but we still managed to beat the enemy off and keep control in time for the arrival of the 'relieving' forces of the battalion under the leadership of Lieutenant Colonel Mike Roberts. I thankfully handed over responsibility and felt that we had acquitted ourselves fairly well. The whole exercise lasted three days with much patrolling and, since we were unable to sleep properly during this time, we were all very happy when it was time to return to the barracks at 20.00 on 27 March, absolutely dog-tired. After checking that the men were fed and comfortable, all of us 'D' Company officers wearily made our own way to bed. As we reached our accommodation, I said to Brian Priday, 'Did you see that Air Force blighter we pulled in for interrogation just after we took the bridges, Brian?' Priday grinned at me and said, 'Yes John. It wasn't 'til we had our torches on him that we spotted all the scrambled egg!'

'Windy Gale was there pretty damn quick to save his bacon!' I said pulling a face at Priday.

'Yeah – maybe he saved ours too!' added Brian with a laugh. I smiled grimly at him and said, 'I bet the buggers keep their bloody heads down from now on!'

In my opinion, the last thing the infantry needed in the middle of an important exercise was some Wing Commander sticking his ruddy nose in too damn close to the action!

The next day the company was practising firing the projection infantry anti-tank gun, known as a PIAT. This was tricky to use but could be immensely effective, as indeed it was to prove on D-Day. Afterwards I reported to the Colonel who told me I could go off on leave early that afternoon. I ran for the train and was home by 19.00 seeing my family, complete with the new baby, at home together for the very first time.

At a Police dance we attended several people asked me when I thought the invasion would be, but I was able to dodge their questioning easily, for it was generally believed that it would not be for some time to come. History would reveal that Prime Minister Winston Churchill had wanted to defer the invasion, feeling the Allies needed more time to prepare, but General Eisenhower was determined to go in just as soon as possible to ensure the element of surprise. Eisenhower won this particular battle and there was a counter-intelligence operation already hard at work to deceive the Germans into believing that any invasion would be in the region of the Pas de Calais. This ruse appeared to be working when the Germans began to strengthen their defences in that area.

On 1 April 1944, Penny's christening took place. Joy provided tea for everyone back at our new home. It was the very first occasion that we had ever entertained at home. The following day, I had an appointment to see the Chief Constable of the Oxford City Police, who became a good friend to me. However, upon this occasion he could hold out little hope for any certainty of me resuming my police career without having to go back on the beat for a time. I was both irritated and depressed by this and told the Chief Constable that I was considering looking for a job overseas after the war, perhaps with a colonial police force.

I was aware that this could easily be my last leave before going off on active service and although we did not speak of it between ourselves, Joy had reached this conclusion even before I had. This made the end of my leave seem even more difficult and poignant than ever. When we had first moved into the little house I had given Joy a package wrapped in an old cloth. It was a hand-gun that I had 'acquired' along the way, with bullets. I had explained simply how it worked and that it was for her to use in self-defence if ever she and the children were threatened. I was thinking at the time of the possibility of a German invasion of southern England or even of civil unrest and looting. I felt it was the only thing I could do, having to leave my wife and children to fend for themselves while I went to fight for our country and their freedom. Of course Joy was horrified at first. She stowed the gun away at the back of the top-shelf of the airing-cupboard, afraid Terry might find it. But she knew it was there.

On Easter Saturday, 8 April, my leave ended and I said goodbye to my tearful wife. Terry clung to me in a heart-wrenching way as I bent into the cot to kiss the baby. I never went back from leave without cursing the war that took me away. I was on my way to Lincolnshire for Inter-Divisional exercises, and I was billeted at Woodhall Spa. Most of the Regiment were still on leave and I was sent to Lincolnshire ahead to check the arrangements. The men of 'D' Company were to be billeted in the pleasant village of Bardney and they were all made very welcome there, the village people running a canteen in the absence of a NAAFI. Tod Sweeney joined me there over the weekend and my batman, still Evans at that time, produced an excellent rabbit pie. Word came through just at that time that all leave was cancelled which greatly increased the buzz of expectation among us all. The soldiers returned from their leave as well, and I was gratified to note that there was only one absentee among the men, which was a sure sign of their *esprit de corps*. Then it was announced that we were henceforth at what was known as 'a closed address'. This meant that all post had to be censored, which all the officers found time-consuming and extremely boring. Also, everyone had to use an address that would not give away where they were, and our post could only reach us through the Army Post Office (APO).

The 15 April 1944 was an important day for me. First thing in the morning, there was a de-briefing for Exercise BIZZ – our word at the time for this process was 'de-bagging'. 'D' Company's performance was highly praised by General Gale. I so wished that I could tell Joy. The General gave us an excellent lecture, using the word 'verve' to describe the dashing display of 'D' Company's spirited and efficient capture of the bridges. I made note of this word and carried it with me into battle. Another phrase of Gale's, 'what you gain by stealth and guts, you must hold with skill and determination', was also to ring in my ears, as I prepared the company for war. After the de-briefing session was over, I was called over by the Colonel, Mike Roberts and told to report to him that afternoon. I was welcomed cordially by my CO and asked to take a seat. The atmosphere in the room was charged with the anticipation of highly important information about to be disclosed.

Colonel Roberts faced me across the desk and, holding my eye, told me that 'D' Company, plus two platoons of 'B' Company and thirty Sappers under command, were to have a very important task to carry out when the invasion started. The Colonel went on to tell me that our task would be to capture two bridges intact. My force of 180 men was to land by night in six gliders in the areas indicated and he produced a plan of the area around the two bridges which showed a canal running parallel to a river, about a quarter of a mile apart. I sat there rooted to my chair, the thrill of excitement going through me making my very scalp tingle. Mike Roberts knew the effect that his announcement was having on me and he sat back in his chair in order to relax me a little. Then he spoke.

'You realize, John, that your company will be the spearhead of the invasion. It is a great honour for the Regiment to be selected to find troops for this highly important job. But I feel absolutely confident that you will be able to pull it off.'

My mouth felt dry but I coughed and, holding my head high replied, 'Yes sir. You can have every confidence in me and my men.'

Colonel Roberts leaned forward again and said, 'You realize of course that this information is Top Secret and I'm telling you now because at the end of this month you will be involved in a Corps exercise called MUSH, in which your company will be carrying out this job of capturing bridges, and we wanted you to have a little time to think about it.'

'Yes sir. Thank you sir,' was all I felt I could trust myself to say, for I was truthfully overwhelmed by what I had just been told. Colonel Roberts went on to say that I would be given details of the real job soon after we had all returned to Bulford after Exercise MUSH.

Returning to the billet at Woodhall Spa, I was in a state of nervous exhilaration, but could not confide in anyone. It was especially difficult, for that evening, my 2 I/C, Brian Priday was returning after his leave and I would have given anything to be able to discuss it all with him. Brian himself had just come back from honeymoon, and probably did not notice my heightened state of nerves. I was, however, allowed to inform the Platoon Commanders what 'D' Company's task would be on Exercise MUSH, and even to hint that this might be in preparation for our job in the invasion. This news was well received by them all but not without a certain amount of apprehension.

The following day was a Sunday, and all the officers attended Holy Communion at Bardney parish church. I have always had a strongly spiritual side to my nature and that day I knelt and prayed fervently for the Lord's blessing in our task. Later that morning, there was a voluntary Church Parade and I was delighted to see that almost all of my men turned up. I wrote in my diary that those two church services were of great comfort to me.

I had selected two platoon commanders from 'B' Company – Lieutenants Dennis Fox and 'Sandy' Smith. I felt they were experienced and would work well with our existing 'D' Company officers. On 17 April, I attended the Regimental HQ for orders for Exercise MUSH and the following day briefed all the platoon commanders. I recall that day very clearly, when Fox and Smith joined us for the first time. We were obliged to use the small village hall in Bardney for our meeting. There was no blackboard in the village hall and we had to use the back of a blackout board to set out in chalk our plan of attack. There was a very lively discussion between us all, everyone throwing in suggestions and comments and so it was that the foundation was laid of the plan for the capture of the two vital bridges in Normandy on D-Day.

Exercise MUSH began the next day and the Regiment packed up and left Lincolnshire to go by road to a general rendezvous area for everyone taking part in the exercise. This was known as the concentration area and it was to be Oakley Wood close to Cirencester in Gloucestershire. Security was intense surrounding the exercise. It was raining heavily as we arrived and set up camp as best we could, erecting a small log shelter for me which kept me dry and rather pleased me. We were joined there by a troop of Sappers (engineers). For the purposes of the exercise, we would be splitting up into two groups of three 'glider-loads', each group responsible for taking a bridge. Priday took command of one party and since these bridges were smaller than the real ones, I was able to stand in the middle with a wireless set and observe the action on both bridges while commanding the other group. My glider was presumed to have landed first and I could therefore assume control of the attack but it occurred to me that I could not guarantee to land first, or in the right place, and that fact was to cause me many headaches in planning for the real attack. On this occasion, my group consisted of the platoons of Tony Hooper, David Wood and Sandy Smith. Priday's group comprised the platoons of Tod Sweeney, Den Brotheridge and Dennis Fox.

As in Exercise BIZZ, the troops were all taken to the landing area in TCVs, de-bussed half a mile from the bridges and led there by umpires, lying down in the corner of the field to await zero hour when we were told to attack. We were using two bridges at Cerney Wick and I was pleased to note that our group was close by the bridges. The 'enemy' were Polish paratroopers since I had specially asked for troops trained in German methods to act as the enemy. We could hear them talking and moving around with sentries and patrols guarding the bridges. One of these patrols unfortunately stumbled upon us lying in the grass and despite the umpires' frantic entreaties to them saying that the exercise hadn't yet started, they rushed back to their HQ and gave the alert. There was much confusion, not helped by the language problem, and suddenly a Very light was fired up into the night sky and our umpire had no alternative but to tell us that we'd landed and to get going. We all dashed for cover in the hedge and found it full of dannert wire, a roll of coiled barbed wire used in all defences, but thanks to all the training, our obstacle drill came immediately into action. Tony Hooper and his platoon were first across the bridge. They were greeted by much Polish firing and swearing and returned the compliment with English swearing in reply. There was a colossal bang and the umpires all yelled that the bridge had been blown. I fumed and cursed and saw Hooper arguing heatedly on the bridge with an irate umpire who put him out of action along with most of his platoon. They all sat disconsolately on the bridge with their helmets off – the sign that they were dead, wounded or captured. My wireless operator, Corporal Ted Tappenden, managed to reach Brian Priday on the other bridge and found that they had been more successful, managing to capture their bridge intact and get across it, their Sappers already neutralizing the explosives.

Exercise MUSH then degenerated into a free-for-all since the Polish troops, hopelessly outnumbered, refused to take the umpire's decision that the bridges had been captured. When told to lay down their arms, they replied that they 'no speak English' and carried on fighting. There followed several skirmishes, which everyone except the harassed umpires thoroughly enjoyed. We officers stood around grinning as the soldiers let off steam and the consensus of opinion was that 'a good time was had by all'. The relieving forces on that occasion were the Royal Ulster Rifles and the Sappers got on with repairing any damage to the bridges. I had realized by then that it was the intention of the exercise that my bridge be blown and it certainly brought out many questions and lessons for us all to consider in the days ahead. I learned that, above all, my plans must be flexible. It was made clear to me in that exercise that events would take place incredibly fast, but in what order and who would carry out what task, was entirely in the lap of the gods. I realized that the chances of us all getting to our destination in the order we wanted was remote. I had to make plans for this eventuality.

Exercise MUSH drew to a close during the evening and we were all allowed to remain in the Cerney Wick area overnight. Colonel Mike Roberts, who had been observing the exercise, informed me that 'D' Company's performance would have earned me a DSO. I was certainly very pleased to hear that. The next day we all returned to the concentration area in Oakley Wood. The weather had changed to fine spring days and the warmth had brought on the wild flowers in the wood – primroses and bluebells. I always took pleasure in such things and enjoyed the woodland as I sat on a tree-stump and pencilled a note to my beloved Joybells.

We returned to Bulford next day and were again given Spider block in Wing barracks, but it was not in the good order that we had left it. The Borders chaps had been billeted there and the block was dirty and untidy and had to be scrubbed out before we really felt it was ours again. But the luxury of a hot bath after the days out on exercise felt wonderful. The APO had come up trumps and delivered a long letter from Joy to add to my good spirits. The fine, warm weather continued and 'D' Company went back into training, varying it with PE tests to keep the men fit and interested. On 29 April, I stole off in a Jeep to make an unauthorized but glorious trip back to Oxford to see Joy and the children, catching her unawares, her hair tied up in a coloured turban in the fashion of the times and the children in the garden.

I knew that we would be taking canvas assault boats with us in the gliders for the invasion, and so I decided to put in some training for handling them with 'D' Company. We went locally to the River Avon at West Amesbury. Of course, only I knew that the ability to handle such small craft and use them to ferry people and stores over a waterway might be a vital part of our operation. The men just thought it was great fun for a change and inevitably, sooner or later someone would end up 'in the drink' and that person would make sure that he wasn't the only one to get wet.

On 2 May I went with Colonel Roberts to see our brigade commander Brigadier H. M. Kindersley at Broadmoor, which was the codename for the Headquarters of the 6th Airborne Planning Division, situated in the village of Milston, about half a mile north of Bulford village. Divisional HQ where General Gale was based, was only 500 yards or so close by in Syrencot House, and the 6th Airborne Planning HQ was in an old, country mansion called Brigmerston House, set amongst trees on the curve of the river, well away from any roads. I would find myself becoming all too familiar with its rickety staircases and low beams in the coming weeks. On that warm early summer day at the beginning of May, the security surrounding Broadmoor was already very impressive for, as I approached Brigmerston House, Brigadier Kindersley told me that I was now officially on the 'X List'. This meant that I would be given the outline of the whole British plan for the invasion of Europe and would then be told in more detail the 6th Airborne plan, and finally given detailed orders for our own operation. The security classification on the documents I received was Bigot and officers in this category were therefore known as 'bigoted'!

The walls of the room we were in were covered with maps of Europe and, in particular, of Northern France. There were models around of the various landing and dropping zones and huge aerial photographs everywhere. For the first time I was told where we would be landing and shown aerial reconnaissance photographs of the two bridges. I felt my head begin to spin as I looked round trying to take it all in. On that day, I was given the written orders for the operation and the first sentence would stay with me for the rest of my life: 'Your task is to seize intact the bridges over the Canal at Bénouville and the River Orne at Ranville and hold them until relieved by the 7th Parachute Battalion.'

A green pass was given to me which would get me into the planning house. In the following month I would experience great mental strain as I planned endlessly and sometimes far into the night for our part in the invasion of Europe. I saw many Nissen huts springing up around the house, which was really too small for its current purpose, and I would grow used to being challenged by the Military police and armed guards who continuously patrolled the perimeter. Set in woodland by the river in what had always been private land, the house was well away from main roads and the many comings and goings were, therefore, never noticed by anyone outside members of the division. I learned that no orders, or photographs, or even notes, could be taken away from Broadmoor but that didn't prevent it taking over my life in the weeks to come and I found myself thinking endlessly about the many problems there were to solve, and how they could be overcome. However, I was conscious that the mental strain attached to our own small part of the invasion, was as nothing in comparison with those of our senior commanders and I watched them almost buckling under the strain of their weighty responsibilities as the weeks went by.

The 6th Airborne's main task was the protection of the left or eastern flank of the Allied bridgehead. To do this it was necessary for them to gain and hold a small bridgehead of their own, east of the River Orne. The village of Bénouville lay halfway between the large city of Caen in Normandy, and the coast at a small port called Ouistreham. There was a canal running from Caen to the sea, crossed by an unusual steel-girder bridge at Bénouville. Hydraulically operated by a huge water tank at one end, this bridge could be elevated to stand on end perpendicularly to allow quite large ships to pass through it in order to enter or leave the port of Caen. The canal was 150 feet on average wide and 27 feet deep.

A quarter of a mile up the road towards Ranville, there was another regular road bridge crossing the River Orne, which ran parallel to the canal down to the sea. This bridge was long and narrow and the river was wide with steep, muddy banks. Both these bridges were strategically vital to the invasion to allow the movement of troops, military vehicles and supplies inland from the landing beaches on the Normandy coast. They were defended by a small garrison of German troops, about fifty strong, armed with light machine guns (LMGs), four light anti-aircraft guns (LAA) probably 20 mm, one anti-aircraft machine gun (AAMG) and possibly two anti-tank guns (AT) of no more than 5 calibre. Trenches and defences could be seen on the east bank of the canal by the bridge and gun pits on the other corners. Nothing more than two weapon pits could be seen on the Ranville bridge. There was knowledge of one German battalion in the area that would have tanks ready to use and it was also known, and feared, that there was a Panzer division stationed in Caen. From intelligence sources it had been learned that both bridges were prepared for demolition by explosives in the event of an Allied invasion. It had been decided, therefore that the use of paratroops landing to attack these bridges would be inappropriate – the bridges would be destroyed long before such a force could muster and mount an attack. Thus it had been decided that glider-borne troops would have to carry out the job of capturing the two bridges, landing by night in a surprise attack and taking them before the defending German soldiers had time to blow them up. My written instructions contained the phrase 'The capture of the bridges will be a *coup de main* operation depending largely on surprise, speed and dash' and these words were also to remain ingrained on my memory.

A conversation between Army and Air Force authorities had decided that it would be possible to land three gliders in the area by each of the bridges – not ideal, but good enough for first class glider pilots to land on. The designated landing zones lay in-between the two bridges and the more I thought about this, the sounder this idea seemed to me. We were to be under the command of the 5 Parachute Brigade for the operation and I was soon to meet the Brigade's commander, Brigadier Nigel Poett, and to form a good opinion of him. To facilitate my planning, I had been given large and small aerial photographs of the area, maps and intelligence reports and almost exclusive use of the finest model I had ever seen. It was about 12 feet by 12 feet and covered the area of the two bridges. It was a work of model making art; every building, tree, bush, ditch, trench and fence was lovingly recreated on the model, and it was up-dated on an almost daily basis as new aerial reconnaissance photos arrived or intelligence was received. I was most impressed and felt that it was certainly the nearest one could get to personal reconnaissance of the area.

With so many people in and out of Broadmoor, individually working on their own part of the 6th Airborne invasion plan, the place was a hive of activity and lived up to its codename, which came from a well known mental Institution, as they were known in those days. I was to refer to it as 'the mad-house'. I got the Pioneer sergeant to paint a tin mortar ammunition box and took it into Broadmoor and piled all my maps, notes and documents into it, to use when I was there. The place soon had tin boxes piled everywhere containing material for someone's small operation for D-Day. I had a mental image of all these operations, like the pieces of a jigsaw puzzle, fitting together to form the larger picture of the Airborne invasion. After a few days, it all began to make sense and I was aware that with so many senior officers to answer to, I could be in for a harassing time and that any plan I came up with would be sure to be pulled to pieces by many expert minds. I was under the command of Brigadier Nigel Poett for what we came to call 'the bridge party', and then there was our own Brigade commander, Brigadier Hugh Kindersley and my Colonel, Mike Roberts. I also had to answer to the senior Sapper officers, and to Brigadier Napier Crookenden and the commander of 7 Para, Lieutenant Colonel Geoffrey Pine-Coffin, who were to relieve us at the bridges. But in the weeks that followed, I would find that my fears were entirely unfounded, for I was left to get on with it on my own. If I needed help from any source, it was willingly given and I found the shrewd and considered advice from Colonel Roberts, the one closest to hand, most supportive. On 5 May, I was ready to show my outline plan to Colonel Roberts and I presented it to him somewhat nervously. He looked it over and told me that it was 'as sound as a bell'. This filled me with confidence and I only hoped that I could retain that feeling.

I had decided that I would have to rely on my junior officers, and most of all my 2 I/C Brian Priday, to run 'D' Company and keep up the training schedules while I was having to spend most of my days over at Broadmoor. Applying the 'bull-at-a-gate' attitude for which I was famous to my mission, after a few days I thought my brain would burst with all the activity going on inside it.

On Sunday, 6 May I was allowed a day off from Broadmoor and, grabbing a Jeep, drove over to Oxford to see my family. If any senior officers knew about this, they turned a blind eye. In fact, despite the intensity of this vital period of planning for the invasion or maybe because of it, Brigadier Hugh Kindersley took a very enlightened view of his company commanders being allowed some time off to rest and relax.

There was to be an event called 'Salute the Soldier Week' later in May, with the Regiment participating in parades and marches throughout the country. This was to boost morale for, after almost five years, the country was in danger of becoming 'war weary'. It was also used to boost National Savings certificates and encourage people to put their money into them which would, in turn support the war effort. There was to be a big parade through Oxford and I had discussed it with my friends in the Oxford City Police and also with Kingsley Belsten, who was well known in the town. It was an event we were all looking forward to, and I had obtained permission to take a detachment of 120 officers and men who resided in Oxford, to the city for the parade, along with other regimental contingents.

However, I now feared that my commitment to planning the bridge operation might mean that I would have to miss the parade, but Brigadier Kindersley

Defence

1. Road excl. Are. WEST – NE. Patrol canal 500ᵃ. North
   a. Patrols in Port if. not operating.

2. Road inc. Are. WEST – SE. Patrol canal 500ᵃ SOUTH.

3. Astride Road. Ares NW – NE and SW – SE. Patrol
   between Bges. and SOUTH between Canal and River.

4. All round protection. Patrol out to contact 7 Pln.

5. Fighting patrol based on forked roads. Recce
   patrols out to meet enemy from SOUTH v SW.

6. Fighting patrol based SOUTH of le PORT. Recce
   patrol out to meet enemy from NORTH v NW.

7. Sappers if available as a pln. will take
   over 3 area al tasks, leaving that pln.
   in reserve for internal c/a.

Patrol

(a) Harass the enemy and delay the deployment of c/a
    forces of 736 G.R. by offensive patrols covering all od
    approaches from the WEST.

R.E's
Priority of tasks.
(a) Neutralise the demolition mechanism.
(b) Remove charges from dem. chambers.
(c) Establish personnel ferries.

Copy of the original notes written by John Howard in April or May 1944 planning for the defence of the canal bridge after its capture.

instructed me to go ahead as planned. Thus I was able to tie up the details for the 'Salute the Soldier' week procession with Joy and with Kingsley Belsten, and spent a precious night at home. In fact all of 'D' Company had twenty-four hour passes that weekend, it being considered important to let the troops see their families. There was to be a mess dance a week later and I was most anxious that Joy should be able to come to Bulford for it.

Training continued unabated and in one PE test, I set 'D' Company the task of running ten miles in under two hours. I was very satisfied when all the men arrived back in less than one hour and fifty minutes. There was company sports in the afternoon and shooting practice, and then the theatre in the evening with Mollie and Brian Priday. I used to go to Broadmoor in the early morning, when my brain was most active, and it all made for very long days indeed. I even found time to take 'D' Company over to one of their favourite training grounds near Winchester, obtaining permission from Sir John Shelley to use Avington Park for 'snap' exercises, to get the men thinking on their feet, and afterwards for some assault boating in the river there. As on previous occasions, we were accommodated in the barns at Grange Farm where Mr and Mrs Young made us welcome and found a bedroom for me, for which I was grateful.

Next day, we attacked a number of small bridges near Fordingbridge and Brigadier Kindersley turned up to watch. I had noticed how strained the Brigadier looked when we were working at Broadmoor and I realized that coming out to see the troops training provided a break from his mental planning at his desk. I had noticed that the Brigadier always drove his own car down to see us and on this occasion, he took the opportunity of chatting to all the officers of 'D' Company offering them encouragement and stressing to them how very important these last chances of training were. Everyone knew that the invasion wasn't far off.

Just back from Winchester, I went into Andover to meet Joy off the train. She had refurbished a dress to wear that evening at the mess dance and she looked splendid. We all had a wonderful time, forgetting for the time being what lay ahead. The following day was a busy one, not helped by all of us feeling very tired from the night before. Joy was taken back to Oxford with my driver Stock as an escort. Later, after the regimental sports, I followed them to Oxford with the regimental detachment for the parade. I was able to spend the night at home and both Joy and I were up early to be ready for the parade. We were cheered and clapped all through Oxford, a large crowd turning out for the occasion. The Mayor addressed the detachment from the 52nd and I replied on their behalf. It was voted a tremendous success and I found myself very proud to be playing a prominent role in a parade in my home town. We all made the day last as long as possible so that we could prolong our time in Oxford with our friends and family.

Next day we were back at Bulford and I spent all that evening and the next morning at Broadmoor, my break with my family giving me the mental energy and concentration to apply myself once more to the task in hand. Just before lunch I was approached by Brigadier Poett who said:

> I want you to go down to Exeter to report to Colonel Pine-Coffin, John. I've just had a telephone call from him – he's in bivouac with 7 Para and they've been doing some training across the Countess Wear Bridges near Exminster. It occurred to him that they are an excellent replica of the two bridges in Normandy – here's the map reference for where they're camped. I want you to get down there today and get your chaps down there as soon as possible. You can have whatever it takes for this show, transport, ammunition, high priority stuff, you know.

I was genuinely taken by surprise but gathered my senses and saluting my senior officer, I quickly put my paperwork away and hurried off to see the Adjutant to let him know what was happening. 'D' Company and the other officers were out doing a river crossing exercise, so I left the Adjutant to inform them and travelled down to Exeter by Jeep that evening and liaised with Colonel Pine-Coffin. I could see immediately that the area would make a good training ground, although the bridges were a little smaller than those we were to capture in Normandy, and the distance between them was only 150 instead of 500 yards. But like our actual targets, one was over a canal and the other over a river. The local farmer, Mr Pyne at Wracombe Farm agreed to let the 'D' Company officers stay at the farm while they trained and, despite me insisting that I had a sleeping bag with me and could use one of the barns, they made me very welcome in their house, old Mr Pyne even giving me a nip of his meagre supply of Scotch.

The following morning I took the opportunity of talking to Colonel Pine-Coffin, and Major Dick Bartlett, commanding 'C' Company of the 7 Para who, once they had landed and mustered, were detailed to come straight to the bridges to relieve my men. Dick Bartlett had strong ties to the 52nd having once been Adjutant to the Regiment. 7th Para were training that morning at crossing the river and attacking the canal bridge, catering for the worst scenario – that the *coup de main* operation had failed and the bridges were blown. I watched their training, finding it most interesting. I then set off to arrange billets in Exminster for the men. The village policeman, PC Clements, was extremely helpful in this respect and the village hall and church hall were provided for the men to sleep in. I then drove like the wind back to Bulford to organize 'D' Company for the trip to Devon.

The next day, 18 May, all the assault troops were assembled for the first time for training together. This was the two platoons from 'B' Company under Dennis Fox and Sandy Smith and I was glad to see the Sappers were once again the men who had been with us on Exercise BIZZ. They were a troop from the 249 Airlanding Brigade, the officers being Captain Jock Neilson and Lieutenant Jack Bence, and they all got on very well with the infantry soldiers. Since all the men were now fully aware that the intensive training taking bridges must mean that they were being prepared for the invasion, I gave everybody a lecture telling them they had a special job to do but that the usual security practices of not discussing their training with anybody outside those present must be remembered at all times. We were all going to carry out what was known as 'taped rehearsals'. This involved literally taping out both bridges, waterways and obstacles, using rolls of heavy cotton tape and laying it out on nearby fields in order to get the sizes and distances into our minds. It sounds a crude and primitive idea but was, in fact surprisingly revealing. Lengths and distances have imprecise meanings written on a page but look a great deal different when set out on the ground in front of everyone. For one thing, I realized immediately that it would be impossible for me to command the attacks on both bridges once I saw what the distance between them really looked like bearing in mind that the assault would take place at night. I had suspected that this might be the case and had been letting Brian Priday take control of one bridge assault already in training. Now I realized that Priday would be taking command of the attack on the Orne River bridge by himself and it would be vital that he and I could be in contact at all times, either by field telephone or, in the event of the delicate wirelesses being smashed on landing, by runners to carry messages between us. What was hammered out during this training session with the taped out bridges was the various tasks or jobs that had to be done. The first platoon that reached the bridge, relying on surprise, would immediately and as fast as possible go through the inner enemy defences and, crossing the bridge, set about any enemy on the outer banks. The second platoon could expect to mop-up the inner defences while the third, if it got there, under my command at the canal bridge or Priday at the river bridge, would help out whichever of the other two platoons most required assistance. The Sappers, ignoring the battle but protected as much as possible by the infantry, were to neutralize the explosives on the bridges. They were to go straight for the chambers holding the explosive, cut wires, de-prime and remove it. Since the opposition on the river bridge was not expected to be strong, it was hoped that Priday would spare his third platoon to come straight across to the Canal bridge as a reserve. That, in essence, was the plan of attack and, following that, it is easy to see why speed and dash were essential for the success of the operation.

Our taped rehearsals were curtailed by General Gale giving a lecture to all the officers. Without of course, revealing the destination, the General told them that they were in their last days of training for the invasion when they would be carrying out a special assignment that would involve capturing two bridges intact. The officers had realized as much of course, but to have their conclusions con-firmed gave them all the kind of thrill that I had experienced when first told by Colonel Roberts in mid-April. After the lecture, I was given permission to brief my 2 I/C Brian Priday fully on the operation, and I found it an immense relief to be able to share my knowledge and the burden with my fellow officer and friend.

The following day, 19 May, the King and Queen, accompanied by Princess Elizabeth visited the Division and it is an indication of my involvement with the training programme that I, who was a staunch Royalist, tried to get off the parade in order to do some more training. But 'D' Company was expected to be on parade, no matter if D-Day was just a couple of weeks away. I had to attend a 5 Para Brigade conference, which made me late getting away for a twenty-four hour leave. In the pit of my stomach I knew that this would be my last visit home before the invasion, but I firmly turned my mind away from that possibility so that Joy, ever-sensitive to my mood, would detect nothing. I spent the day with my family and then had to return early to work at the mad house of Broadmoor.

It was after I had left, roaring off in the Army Jeep driven by the faithful Stock, who also had a family in Oxford, that something made Joy go to the airing-cupboard and feel amongst the spare blankets and linen for the bulky cloth package. She looked for some time before facing the fact that it was no longer there. The realization that I must have taken the gun away with me came over her. Joy stood on the landing of the little house in Oxford, the sound of Terry's voice prattling to his baby sister in her pram in the back garden outside, and a blackbird in a tree somewhere close by singing in careless rapture in the late spring afternoon and it was one of those heart-stopping moments that she would remember all through her life, as it dawned on her what it meant. The invasion! She had told me that if she got that telegram that everyone so dreaded, to say that I had been killed, she would run upstairs and get the gun and shoot herself. Of course she hadn't meant it and had regretted saying it the very second the words left her lips when she saw the look on my face. I realized that with the two children, she would never really do anything like that. But it had planted the doubt in my mind, and now that I believed that it would be my last visit home before the invasion, I had decided to take the gun away with me. I had hoped that Joy would not have even realized what I'd done, but the bond between us was already very close and Joy had seen something in my eyes as I'd turned to go, my cheery 'Good-bye – see you soon!' not fooling her for an instant. Thus it was that in Oxford, my wife knew the invasion was imminent but, of course, she kept it to herself.

On 21 May, the assault force went down to Exminster. The men were all in high spirits. They had taken with them what I called 'plenty of fireworks' to make the training as realistic as possible. Each platoon took a turn at playing the part of the 'enemy' at the bridges, which gave them the chance to see things from the enemy's point of view, and this raised fresh points. I had been informed that the attack would be carried out in moonlight and, since there was no moon at that time, we carried out a couple of rehearsals at dusk. Brigadier Poett turned up to watch us and loudly commended all of us for our enthusiasm, which did much to encourage the men further. We were all very tired and slept well that night, ready to continue the training next day. Each 'landing' meant another new battle full of bangs, firing, phosphorus grenades and two-inch mortar smoke bombs zooming around. In fact, all this noise fetched quite a crowd of onlookers from the neighbouring houses and we had to frequently request people to 'move on'.

During one especially spirited attack, Brian Priday's mortar men sent a smoke bomb through the roof of a nearby house. Priday saw the owner and gave him as well as the address of the local claims officer, his own particulars, and said he'd submit a report to the claims officer to back up the householder's request for compensation. That closed the matter we thought. However, a month or so later, we were sitting in a slit trench in Normandy up to our eyes in mud and being intermittently bombarded by German mortars, when the mail arrived at Company HQ. Priday opened a letter addressed to him, read it and went completely crazy, swearing horribly. I took the letter from him to read for myself and found that it was from the dissatisfied householder whose roof had been damaged in Exminster – he wanted to know when his house was going to be repaired!

At the Countess Wear bridges, each platoon practised doing each of the jobs, so that no matter who landed where and in what order, they would all automatically know what to do. They practised over and over again until they could do it with their eyes shut. I overheard one of the men, Wally Parr, saying to his mate, Billy Gray, as they washed in cold water, just outside the village hall in Exminster early one morning, 'I flippin' 'ave bin doin' it all in me ruddy sleep, 'aven't I? – dreamin' it all bloody night!' Parr was one of my 'scallywags' and I knew that in battle he would not let us down. I had devised a plan to prevent the risk of the men shooting one another in the dark, and also to identify each platoon to the others. Each platoon had a codeword:

Abel (A)	Hooper's platoon
Baker (B)	Sweeney's
Charlie (C)	Wood's
Dog (D)	Brotheridge's
Easy (E)	Smith's
Fox (F)	Fox's platoon.

It was agreed that each man would shout out his code word, 'Dog – Dog – Dog' or 'Baker – Baker – Baker' so that, over the din of explosions and firing, they could hear men yelling their codewords and know who was around them. This was a lesson learned on Exercise BIZZ when one platoon accidentally 'shot up' a section of another platoon in the dark.

Brigadier Kindersley turned up to see the training at the Countess Wear Bridges as well. By that time we were practising with the assault boats, as if the bridges had been blown up. Captain Jock Neilson commanding the Sappers making up the necessary explosive charge to represent the blowing of the bridge, carrying out the explosions on a spare piece of ground nearby. Neilson was later approached by some canal authority fellow and accused of shaking the foundations of the bridge. This roused his Scots temper and the canal authority retreated with his own foundations shaking severely! Orders to return to Bulford were received the next day, and we finished at 16.00 in order to give the company their pay and the chance of one last evening off in Exeter.

The 'invasion of Exeter' took place that evening, and I had put Tod Sweeney in charge of the party considering him to be the steadiest among them, assisted by a couple of NCOs specially selected by the Sergeant Major, with orders to keep the peace. It was a riotous night with many conflicting accounts of what took place, save to say that the local police were involved, but a decision was made to take no further action.

Back at Bulford we all found ourselves cramming into one day all the accumulated administration and packing that the rest of the Regiment had spent the last three days doing. It was complete chaos and I did not know which way to turn. To make matters infinitely worse, at Broadmoor I received the news, via an RAF reconnaissance flight, that the land defences around the canal bridge were definitely being strengthened. Two huts at the east end of the bridge had been demolished and what appeared to be a pillbox was under construction. Since Priday had also been 'X-listed' by that time, I was able to discuss this worrying news with him. Colonel Roberts put our minds at ease a little by pointing out that it was merely part of the general strengthening of all defences along parts of the French coast.

'God! I hope he's right,' I'd said to Priday as we made our way back to the barracks. 'Supposing Jerry's got wind of what we're planning?'

Back in my room in the officers' accommodation hut, I faced the difficult task of packing up all my personal belongings. This was standard practice for all men going into action, in case they were unable to return to their unit. If they were lucky, they might just have been wounded. I put all my personal kit into my grip and, with a choking lump in my throat, I placed a pair of sunglasses on the top of the pile that Joy had particularly coveted. I had arranged that a friend would deliver it to my home a couple of weeks after we'd gone and, as was customary, I wrote a parting note to Joy and placed it inside the sunglasses case. It was the most emotionally difficult letter I think I ever had to write in my life and I had to look away several times as the tears welled up in my eyes. After my wife had died some forty years later, I found this letter in her writing case and destroyed it. Some things are too personal to pass on to the next generation. The next day, 26 May 1944, I left with 'D' Company for transit camp at Tarrant Rushton.

Chapter 9

May to early June 1944: Transit Camp, Off at Last

Tarrant Rushton is in Dorset, between the towns of Blandford Forum and Wimborne Minster, but it might as well have been on the moon at the end of May 1944 because, once the men were there, the camp was sealed with barbed wire fences and guarded, and they were unable to leave until D-Day. The transit camp was under canvas, on farmland near to the airfield. Tom Packwood, who ended up as a corporal and was in Den Brotheridge's platoon, recalled the big ash tree by the gate at the entrance to the camp, and it was still there when he returned to look for the site in the 1980s. Tom spoke to the farmer, who was the son of the man there in 1944, and he told him that his father had been checking up on his cattle one evening in early June 1944, when he found himself arrested by the military police, suspected of being a spy!

The extended group of 'D' Company, numbering 180, was not on its own for there were some 140 Anti-Tank Gunners and eighty men of the Airborne Reconnaissance Corps there as well. The remainder of the battalion had gone to another transit camp at Harwell, Oxfordshire. Since the troops were to be there for an unknown period of time, some effort had been made to minimize boredom. There was a fair-sized NAAFI, a small marquee set up as a mobile cinema, which the men had to take turns in using, and some ground for recreation. When one considers the large number of soldiers that were sealed into transit camps at that time, awaiting orders to depart for the invasion, it is not surprising that not all the arrangements were perfect. Due to inexperienced cooking staff, the food was a constant source of complaint amongst the men. I had always adhered to the belief that 'an army marches on its stomach' and was one of the first and most demonstrative of the officers to demand an improvement. I gave them hell and as a result, became rather unpopular with the camp staff and higher Quartermaster personnel. A disgruntled Lieutenant Colonel came to inspect the 'messing arrangements' and annoyed me intensely by calling the complaints complete nonsense but the standard did improve over the time we were there, although the rations were singularly uninteresting.

By contrast, the information and briefing arrangements were splendid. There was a Nissen hut specially set-up for briefing in the middle of the camp, and I found that all the maps, documents and aerial photographs had been brought down. The magnificent model that had been made for the operation was with the 7th Para Battalion, but arrived at Tarrant Rushton a couple of days later. On the first day in transit camp, Brian Priday and I began by unpacking and sorting out the maps and photographs in the briefing hut. As we were engaged in this task, I received an urgent message to report to Broadmoor and duly sped up there in a Jeep, a distance of some thirty miles. Once there, I reported to Brigadier Poett and was introduced to Staff Sergeant John Ainsworth of the Glider Pilot Regiment who was going to lead our Wing of the Glider Pilots on D-Day. Although not 'X-listed', Ainsworth was there to inspect the model of the area of the two bridges, so that he could see the details of the two small landing zones and he was told that he and the other glider pilots would be landing on them by night. Ainsworth was most encouraging, telling us that he and his Wing of the fourteen specially selected pilots had been practising landing their gliders on similar landing zones for the past months, often at night. I would learn that the glider pilots had been training intensively for the D-Day landings and were immensely skilled at their job. Their training had been part of Operation DEADSTICK and they had been doing it for many months. Many problems had been ironed out during this training. The tug aircraft had been changed from the Albemarle to the more powerful Halifax. One night, practising landing three gliders on a small landing zone in two areas, they had smashed into one another. Fortunately there were no fatalities but five of the six gliders were written off. There was no other way to learn than to keep on training. Eventually their performances had improved dramatically and the glider pilots found they could consistently land three gliders one after the other by night on the areas indicated. Ainsworth told me that they were all confident that they could carry out the job. The glider pilots were regarded as a valuable commodity, being required for all the landings of the invasion and it was hoped that there would be the minimum of injuries to them. They would not, therefore, be expected to take part in the battle at all but would help with unloading the gliders and running messages. They would then be repatriated as soon as possible to fly on further missions. Sergeant Ainsworth travelled back to Tarrant Rushton with me and impressed me further with his confident manner. The pilots were stationed at an airfield near the transit camp and would be joining the *coup de main* group for briefing.

During one of the conference sessions that had been held throughout the last few months to discuss tactics generally, and at which every man in the force had been present, one of the troops asked if we could have a medical officer with us, as well as the usual two nursing orderlies at Company HQ and one trained stretcher bearer for each platoon. I thought the idea a good one and forwarded the suggestion to my senior officers. So when, after a couple of days in transit camp, a tough-looking captain reported to me saying he was the medical officer assigned to the *coup de main* group, I was very pleased to see him. He announced himself as Doctor John Vaughan of the Royal Artillery Force Medical Corps and I noticed his large droopy moustache at once, commenting to Priday later that 'the Doc's moustache looks as if it needs de-lousing'. The Doc had been trained as a paratrooper and had never before flown in a glider, but he became very popular with all the men and they were certainly glad to have him along.

On 27 May Brigadier Kindersley came down to see us all in camp and informed me that I could brief my platoon commanders. I therefore called them all over to the briefing hut and gave them the details of their assignment. Recalling how bewildered I had been a month before when the information had been given to me all in one go, I decided to tell the platoon commanders slowly and clearly, giving them the whole picture first of the invasion, and continuing the following day with the full details of the assault on the two bridges. There was much competition to guess exactly where the invasion would begin. Before starting the briefing, Priday and I held onto all the maps and ran a one-shilling sweepstake for the platoon commanders to make a bet on where they thought the invasion would take place. The guesses stretched from Denmark to Bordeaux; only two of them said Normandy or the Cherbourg Peninsular, and shared the pot. We were still briefing at 23.00 that evening, and were all hoarse from constantly talking in a room full of smoke.

A parade for prayers was held by the Padre on Sunday, 28 May, after which all the 'D' Company officers plus the officers reinforcing them, repaired to the briefing hut again and were there well into the night. I was the only one allowed to leave and I went over to the transit camp at Tilshead to collect the model of the bridges area from 7 Para and while I was there, was glad to have the opportunity to detail my plan to the officers and NCOs of 7 Para which I regarded as time very well spent. I then returned with the model to Tarrant Rushton and had it installed in the briefing hut to general amazement and acclaim from my platoon commanders, who were seeing it for the first time. It naturally led to many other discussions and objective comments. I was to find that in the week that followed, I never left the briefing hut without leaving somebody in there, pondering over the model or aerial photographs, or comparing ideas on some detail or other. The Brigade Major, Napier Crookenden sent over a message written in his own hand which said, 'You may brief ALL your men on model and air photos, WITH-OUT' giving place names or relation of area to coastline'. Napier Crookenden had a pragmatic approach to Army bureaucracy that particularly appealed to me. On the same note, which was security classified 'Overlord. Secret', the Brigade Major referred to some copies of 'Glider Forms' he had sent over for me which were 'in addition to the normal ones, now meandering through the usual channels!' It was apparent that even the imminence of the invasion could not speed up the official Army procedures.

I got all the men together and addressed them, telling them that they were going to be shown a model of their objectives but that the location would still remain unknown to them. The men were then summoned to the briefing hut, one platoon at a time. They stood round the model, at first struck dumb by its complexity, fascinated and impressed by its detail, and before long they all seemed to know every inch of the area on which they would be working. Their interest was easy to maintain for they were all totally absorbed by knowing so much information in advance.

Just at this moment, when I needed to be completely focussed on the operation ahead, I had a most unwelcome situation to deal with. Mike Roberts informed me that a sergeant in the Glider Pilot Regiment over at the Tarrant Rushton Air Force camp, had been overheard in the bar there talking about matters he should have not been discussing or even have known. Hauled in front of his senior officers he told them that he had learned it from Major John Howard while on their way to Tarrant Rushton from Broadmoor in a convoy of Army trucks on the day of their arrival, 26 May. Asked by his senior officers to explain further, this man, Sergeant Garner, had stated that during the journey I had discussed the coming operation and given him information regarding the distance between two 'objectives' and had mentioned types of glider that were to be used in a second wave of the invasion. One must imagine just how appalled I was when informed of this accusation, which came totally out of the blue. The shock that I felt at first, very quickly turned to outrage and then to anger, at this attack on my integrity. Given that I had actually been in charge of the convoy to Tarrant Rushton on 26 May, the chances of me striking up any kind of conversation with a strange NCO from the Glider Pilot Regiment, let alone discussing details of a Top Secret operation, would seem very unlikely. I had kept all the details of the operation to myself for over a month, before even discussing it with my trusted 2 I/C Brian Priday, and only then when given permission to do so. Naturally, I refuted the allegation immediately and demanded to confront the man concerned but, knowing my temperament only too well, Mike Roberts decided that such a meeting would definitely not be a good idea at that time. He must also have known instinctively that I was completely innocent of such a lapse and realized that Sergeant Garner, cornered by his own senior officers, had just blamed me because he knew my name and had travelled in the same truck with me. It was obvious that he was covering up for his mates in the sergeants' mess who had been gossiping and speculating after a few drinks.

The Glider Pilot Regiment was bound to report the matter to the Airborne and it had to be investigated. Colonel Roberts would doubtless have let the matter drop there and then, knowing only too well that I had much more important matters to consider but he did not reckon on my energetic zeal to get to the bottom of the accusation, leaving no stone unturned.

Therefore, while giving my fellow officers the impression that I had nothing other than the invasion on my mind, I began an investigation into what had led this sergeant to accuse me of a breach of security. I talked to my own sergeants, carefully concealing my real interest in what had taken place in the sergeants' mess. Unusually for someone of my rank, I was known for going into the sergeants' mess and relaxing with them and these men were prepared to be much more forthcoming with me than they might have been otherwise; they knew me and trusted me. I learned that Sergeant Garner had been in the Airborne sergeants' mess, actually on our camp, on the night of 26 May. It seems that they had all been discussing the recent exercises at the Countess Wear bridges and my men admitted that they'd probably mentioned the distance between those two bridges and that it had been intimated that the 'real bridges' were further apart. That would have been all it took for Garner to learn that piece of information. In respect of the details of the glider types to be used on future missions, I certainly had no knowledge at all about this matter and therefore, it followed that I could not possibly have been the one to pass on such information to him. However, since the sergeant had been living with the pilots of those gliders for some time, it would have been easy for him to jump to conclusions. Viewed from this distance, it was a storm in a teacup, but right then it had serious implications for my integrity and disturbed my state of mind deeply just when I least needed a problem like that.

The Glider Pilot Regiment gave no further information after they had passed on this allegation to the Airborne. It was up to me to defend myself and I was unbelievably angry and frustrated. I told no one else about it and carried on with my job as if nothing had happened. When Brigadier Kindersley came down to talk to all of us on 3 June, I discussed the matter privately with him and despite him telling me that 'from our point of view the matter is closed', having accepted totally my innocence, I nevertheless wrote in my diary that I felt that I was being given the benefit of the doubt only because I was commanding the *coup de main* attack.

It was as late as 4 June that I was finally shown a statement made by Garner and I felt compelled to leave a statement of my own with my brigade major, which I wrote the same day. In the light of the invasion and all that happened just after this time, no mention of this matter was ever made again but it added to my burdens immeasurably and I found it impossible to understand what had made this NCO accuse me. In my letter I gave my own explanation for the sergeant's indictment and added that I could not leave the country without making some kind of a reply as it must have been apparent that the seriousness of security regarding this part of the operation was very clear to me. I further said that I trusted that my point of view would be considered and that the NCO would be dealt with.

By 29 May the glider pilots that were to fly us into battle had come over from their camp to meet the extended 'D' Company group. From the first we all got on very well. I introduced each one in turn to the whole company and they were soon familiar faces in the bar of the sergeants' mess. I wrote in my diary that 'the Glider Pilots are magnificent – damn good crowd,' careful not to let my problems with Sergeant Garner affect my judgement. But on 30 May, a scare began concerning the weight of all the men and equipment that the gliders were to carry.

It began with the leader of the Sappers' group, Jock Neilson, weighing one of his men loaded for action. He found to his horror that the man weighed nearly 300 lb instead of the allowed 240 lb. Neilson reported this concern immediately to me, and I quickly got one of my troops to dress and load himself ready for action. We found that he weighed 250 lbs instead of the average allowance of 210 lb for an infantryman. When we considered what this overload would amount to for twenty-eight chaps in each glider, it came to about 1,400 lb overweight. This caused a real crisis for us. It didn't take much imagination to realize that this overloading of each glider would be extremely dangerous, especially when it was considered that we had to land in such a small area. I decided that the problem was so great that the advice of my senior officer was called for and I jumped into a Jeep and drove at my usual breakneck speed over to Keevil, near Trowbridge in Wiltshire to where Brigadier Kindersley was stationed. The result was that the Brigadier came down to Tarrant Rushton the following day with Laurie Nicholson, the Battalion Loading Officer, and the whole problem was discussed in depth along with myself and Jock Neilson. It was decided that certain items would have to be left behind such as some ammunition and stores, and the biggest items to go were two of the assault boats. The decision was also made to cut down the load on each glider by one man from each platoon, as well as one Sapper from each glider. An 'arrester parachute' was fitted to each glider as well, that could be deployed to help bring the aircraft to a halt.

I found Brigadier Kindersley's advice invaluable and the problem was solved once we had whittled down the load in each glider, item by item and weighed each of the men in full battle order, although it was noted by the men that none of the officers was weighed. There was much joking between the men about the weigh-in and suggestions for quick weight loss in some cases. The handwritten lists of each man's weight would remain in my archives in the Overlord file, gathering dust over the years, but at the time it was a very real problem and if Jock Neilson hadn't thought about weighing one of his Sappers, the overloaded gliders could well have smashed into the ground by the canal bridge or even into the water. As it was, on take-off the pilots felt that the gliders were still overloaded, but not dangerously so. I was tremendously relieved at the weight problem having been detected and solved and that evening I went over to Harwell transit camp where the rest of the Regiment was based, for up-to-date intelligence on the area round the bridges. To my dismay I learned from both the air-reconnaissance flights and from intelligence sources that operated in that area, that what were known as anti-air landing poles were being erected on the landing zone by the canal bridge, although none as yet were seen beside the river bridge. This had been one of my worst fears, and to have it confirmed so close to the invasion really was a dreadful shock.

There was a French resistance cell operating in Bénouville, led by a gallant lady, Madame Vion, who lived at the chateau in Bénouville, which was used in those days as a maternity hospital. I'd been told that there was a café by the bridge on the Bénouville side of the canal, owned and run by a Frenchman named Georges Gondrée. This man had once worked for Lloyds Bank in Normandy and spoke perfect English, a fact not known to the Germans. His wife Thérèse, had come from Alsace and had been forced to learn German as a child during the First World War. Due to the unhappy history of Alsace Lorraine, on the border of France and Germany, she had grown up with a profound hatred for the Germans, which she hid with difficulty during the occupation of France, not letting anyone know she understood German. They continued to run the café throughout the occupation, serving the German soldiers who manned the garrison by the two bridges, and keeping their ears and eyes open. They had two daughters, one a girl of nine and the other just an infant. Like so many people in occupied France they just carried on doing their jobs and keeping a roof over their heads and food on the table. The Germans sat in the Café Gondrée and became loud and careless when they drank too much 'calva'; the local apple brandy, Calvados, which substituted very well for schnapps. Thérèse Gondrée understood their conversation and would tell her husband anything of interest when the café was closed and the despised Germans had gone back to their billets. Georges translated it into English and passed it on to Madame Vion who sent it on to British Intelligence. This was how it was known and confirmed that the Germans had organized a work-party who were busily erecting these anti-air landing poles by the canal bridge. They were known as 'Rommel's Asparagus' in the slang of the time. It had been the German General Rommel who had suggested these poles be erected at various points along the Normandy coast, where it was felt that the Allies might try to land. Regular white dots could be clearly seen on the latest aerial photographs around the bridge. I had frowned as I looked at the photos and said to the team who expertly interpreted them, 'Do you think that this means that the Boche know this part of our plan and are deliberately strengthening the bridge's defences to meet our party?' One of the officers tried to reassure me: 'They can't possibly know about your operation, John. Our feeling is, that this is just another part of them building up their defences generally in the coastal area.'

'But you've said that there are more trenches now, by the bridge and that the pillbox you suspected was being built a week ago, is now definitely there,' I'd replied.

'Honestly John. It's happening all along the coast – not just in the bridge area. We've just got to get in there as quickly as possible before they have a chance to do much more. Would you like another cover flown, to get more pictures of the area?'

I said at once, 'Yes, absolutely! And can you get them to take some oblique shots to definitely confirm the erection of poles? It's difficult to tell from these dots whether it's just the prepared holes or actually the poles already in place.'

I remember driving back to Tarrant Rushton more slowly, for I had much to ponder. When I arrived I unloaded my anxieties onto Brian Priday who took the news in his calm, practical way. The first thing next morning, I sent for the glider pilots, keen to see their reaction to the news about the anti-air landing poles. One of them was especially full of himself – Staff Sergeant Jim Wallwork, a young chap of only twenty-two, from Manchester. A veteran of the Sicily landings, he was a witty fellow, with a smiling, open face and slicked back dark hair. He was always popular in the bar. I found myself liking him instinctively and was glad to know that he was to pilot No. 1 Glider with John Ainsworth, in which I was flying. I showed them the aerial photographs, pointing out the poles and informed them of the intelligence reports. I ended, 'So that's what we face on the LZ, I'm afraid chaps.' My words hung in the air, already full of smoke from many of them puffing away on cigarettes and pipes. There was a pregnant silence for about five or six seconds, and then Wallwork stepped forward and said unexpectedly, 'That's just what we want, sir!' I was frankly stunned, but before I could speak, Wallwork continued, 'You see, one of our main worries has been running into this embankment on landing if we over-ran the LZ,' and he jabbed his finger at the steeply sloping embankment shown on the model, which abutted the road-way. 'We knew if we had a bad landing and even just a grenade went off, sympathetic detonation could cause the whole bloody lot to go up – just like what happened in Sicily! What will happen now when we come into the LZ' and Wallwork seized one of the small models of the Horsa gliders, ' is that, those poles will take that much off one wing, and that much off the other.' He made a slicing movement on the glider's wings as he spoke and concluded, 'That'll pull us up nicely!' He beamed at us all, turning the doubtful and worried frowns into relieved smiles with his infectious enthusiasm. I truly couldn't have wished for a more positive reaction from the pilots and I was immensely grateful to them. All the men were assembled and I went through informing them of this new hazard and got Wallwork to tell them all how it would be dealt with.

There was an amusing postscript to this story – on 6 June, after the force had landed and captured both bridges, we found that the poles had not been erected, but only the holes had been dug ready for them, which was what had showed up on the aerial photos. During the morning of the 6th, I noticed a group of rather weedy-looking Italian workmen engaged around the canal bridge, busy placing the poles into the prepared holes. I went up to one of them and got one of my French-speaking officers to ask what the hell they thought they were doing. The fellow said that the Germans had told them they must put the poles up and had paid him in advance for the work. I pointed out that the invasion had arrived and the gliders had landed. The Italian said that in his opinion, the Germans could very well return and he didn't want them to find that he and his men had not completed their task. I gave up and, shaking my head in disbelief, left them to it!

In transit camp, the men of 'D' Company spent the first day covering every inch of the ground, for it was in their nature to try to find some means of escape. It emerged later that in fact two men did manage to get out for a night, and those two men were the platoon commanders from 'B' Company, Sandy Smith and Dennis Fox. They had chatted up a couple of WRNS visiting the nearby airfield at Tarrant Rushton, who had gone into the Airborne transit camp on official business. Smith and Fox must have been very fast workers for they met the girls for a drink in nearby Blandford Forum and then sneaked back into the camp in the early hours of the morning, never revealing quite how they did it. The men of 'D' Company settled for the more mundane pleasures of taking their turn to go to the camp cinema. Men who were off to 'the flicks' could be easily identified by the pillows and blankets they were carrying to make themselves comfortable, since the cinema had no seating provided. The weather was good for the first few days at Tarrant Rushton and the men became suntanned as they usually did living under canvas. They played soccer and other games, and cards in the evenings. In fact the interest in cards increased substantially once the men were fully briefed on Thursday, 1 June and were each given a small 'survival kit' which included some French francs. Most of the men quickly lost this money in card games. Also in the kit were maps of France beautifully printed onto silk squares, which the men were instructed to sew into the linings of their battledresses. These were intended to help the men to find their way home if they became lost but France is a big place, and Tom Packwood said since his map was of the south of France, he would have got lost finding that first! More sewing was involved with special trouser buttons that could be removed, set onto a pin and used as compasses. Jokes were made about the theoretical efficacy of magnetic fly-buttons! There was also a pack of toffee that contained eight vitamins and could keep a man going for forty-eight hours but not much of that reached France either. And there were files, and a hacksaw blade and even fishing hooks to also sew into their battledress, and the men were kept occupied for some time competing with each other to see who could hide these items best. The men were immensely pleased with all these acquisitions, which were eagerly received and studied. The only drawback from my point of view was that all the francs had to be signed for by the company commander and I, therefore, hoped sincerely that I would not be held to account for them.

I was diverted by being taken over to the airfield and shown a film that the pilots had all mentioned to me, which had been especially made for their training. I was told that it was 'a film of the landing' and was not sure what to expect but was, in fact, overwhelmed by it. The film had been made by carefully linking together the sand-table models made from aerial reconnaissance photos, and filming them in sequence with a camera ingeniously hoisted over the models by a system of pulleys and levers so that you got the effect of flying over the exact route they would have to follow from cast-off over the French coast, down to the landing zones by the bridges. One of the pilots, Peter Boyle, said he'd been told that smoked glass was used over the projector lens to give the impression of a night flight, and everyone who saw it said that it was certainly most realistic. The pilots sat through this film several times a day all through their training in the final weeks. Although they did not know where they were going on D-Day, they all got to know the pattern of the countryside. Watching that film, I realized how the pilots would bring us onto the landing zones. The drill was – cast off from the Halifax bombers that were to tow us over the Channel, then so many minutes and seconds on a bearing of 180 degrees, a right-hand turn and so many seconds on a bearing of 270 degrees, then another right-hand turn and a run in. They called this timing dead reckoning. The co-pilot would have a stopwatch and be responsible for the timing. The first pilot would hopefully see the ground and get his bearings – the film showed exactly what he should be able to see – at first the Bois de Bavent, a large wooded area, then the river and canal, Caen to the right at the front. Then a turn over the Orne River and then another turn over the Caen Canal, getting a clear view of the fields, for by that time the glider would be low, then the ponds beneath them in the final approach. I found that I could actually recognize the fields, hedges and ditches from the long hours spent poring over the aerial photographs and the model and gasped as the film ended just before touch-down. I could certainly see how invaluable it was to the pilots.

On 1 June when the men were all briefed on the operation, they drank in all the information I was able to give them and the discussions afterwards were intense and lively. Colonel Roberts came down and addressed us all. He told us that spirits were high everywhere and the feeling in the Regiment was of envy of us being the vanguard of the whole division – of the invasion in fact. As the first few days of June went by, the weather, which up until then had been so good, began to deteriorate; a wind got up and it became overcast. We had all realized by that time, that the invasion would take place when the moon was full and each night we would all stare up at the sky, watching the moon rise earlier and fuller, and a tingle would go through each of us thinking 'Not long now!' I found myself looking at the moon and thinking of Joy in Oxford and wondered if she was also looking up at it with me on her mind. She had faithfully written to me every day and I wished with all my heart that I could see her and tell her what I was doing. It was the same for all the other men, but more so for those who were married and had children. Naturally, Brian Priday thought longingly of Mollie and Den Brotheridge, who had been married for almost four years to Maggie, was especially thinking of her as she was in the final stages of pregnancy and would give birth to a baby girl, Margaret, only two weeks after D-Day.

On Saturday, 3 June, Brigadier Kindersley came down to speak to us all. Our spirits were so high and everybody so keyed-up and eager to go, that his rousing address hit just the right spot and he was spontaneously cheered at the end. The endless briefing continued, using every hour left to discuss and plan for action, and on Sunday 4 June, I received the codeword I was waiting for – Cromwell. This meant that the invasion would take place that night! Orders were issued that every man could write a last letter to his loved ones that would be posted straight after they left. These letters were very difficult to write, not knowing if it would be the final contact with their wives, parents or sweethearts. We were told that although the letters would have to be censored, we could tell our families that by the time they received the letters, we would all be in France. But as the day wore on, heavy rain and gales set in and I received word that the invasion was cancelled for that day due to the conditions. I was devastated but had to pass on the news to my junior officers and to all the men. The Padre arrived and a short church service was held. The weather was so dreary and we were all very downcast.

I was profoundly worried that the longer the delay, the more chance there would be that the enemy would receive information of the plan and that the defences on our landing zones would be strengthened. As I tried to sleep, I found myself repeating the prayer over and over again that the weather would clear on the following day so that the invasion could go ahead. One can imagine just how many tens of thousands of men were all sending that same prayer heavenwards on the night of 4 June 1944.

On Monday, 5 June the weather was still bad and word came through the 'jungle telegraph' that the English Channel was rough, and our thoughts went out to the hundreds of men waiting on ships being thrown around on the seas. Everybody was extremely tense but in the afternoon the codeword Cromwell was received again and I was told that the meteorological boys had confidently predicted a spell of clearer weather overnight. Excitement and apprehension rose to fever pitch as the day wore on. Due to the high winds on the previous night, nobody had slept very well and many of the men tried to get their heads down for an hour's nap in the afternoon, but with so many thoughts and fears running through their heads it was impossible to sleep. The men listened to their shared wireless sets for more news and tried to pass the time. Brigadier James Hill, Commander of 3 Para Brigade addressed his men, saying: 'Gentlemen, in spite of your excellent training and orders, do not be daunted if chaos reigns. It undoubtedly will.' His words were to prove only too prophetic for some of them.

In the evening, we were all given a fatless meal to minimize the chances of airsickness. Aware that on the battlefield we would all be existing on 'compo rations' the men tried to relish this last meal. Then it was time to check our kit and to dress. The platoon commanders were all busy checking that the men had all their equipment, weapons, ammunition and provisions. Some of the smaller chaps were visibly sagging at the knees under their heavy loads. I was glad to see them busy for it left no time for reflection. We all had to blacken our faces because of attacking at night and the men fooled around amongst themselves as they were doing this. I ordered the company on parade for the last time at 21.30 as darkness fell on that cloudy evening, but it was not the Company Sergeant Major who did this, for he was among those men to be left behind. The task fell to the Senior Platoon Sergeant, Sergeant Barwick, who was Acting CSM. He was a tall, good-looking young Londoner with a happy-go-lucky attitude. It was an amazing sight! Everyone was grossly overloaded but they would not be attacking the bridges in all that equipment, it would be left in the gliders and retrieved later.

So I addressed my men for the last time. I wished them luck and thanked them for all their hard work and untiring cooperation during training. As I ran my eyes over the faces of the men before me, I was immensely pleased to see that all of them looked confident and excited and I knew that every man under my command would give of his best. I am an emotional man beneath the surface, a fact that would have surprised many who knew me then, and I found addressing the men as they went into battle very moving. I found my voice breaking several times as I wished them all the best.

The men were shepherded into Army trucks by the platoon leaders. There was much hilarity over the way they scrambled on board the trucks, some of the men losing their balance with all the extra gear they were carrying and falling into the arms of their comrades; others having to be given a good shove from behind to get on board. The journey to Tarrant Rushton airfield was about a mile up a hill. As we passed the RAF administrative buildings many WAAFs and airmen waved to the men. They had all been confined to the camp for several days and knew that something big was in the air. The gliders were tucked unobtrusively away in a corner of the airfield; six Horsa gliders being chalk-marked with numbers 91 to 96. My party for the canal bridge was in 91, 92 and 93 and Priday's group for the river bridge was in 94, 95 and 96. A little way off were the tugs; six battle-worn Halifaxes. At the last moment three white stripes had been painted on the wings of the gliders and of the Halifaxes. This was so that all Allied aircraft could be identified for the invasion. The glider pilots came to meet us all as we scrambled out of the lorries and I was pleased to note that the men greeted them by their first names, their sense of comradeship strong on this memorable occasion. They had been supervising the loading of the gliders in the last couple of days and were now just waiting for what they called 'the bods' – their passengers. The pilots helped us to load a few more odds and ends onto the gliders and then hot tea was issued to everyone to help fortify us for the trip. There was no official send-off for this, the vanguard of the invasion, because of the high level of security, but Colonel Mike Roberts had made the sixty-mile journey down from Harwell to see us all off and wish us 'God Speed', and we warmly appreciated this gesture. He was to follow us to Normandy, along with the rest of the Regiment some twenty hours later. As we stood around the gliders, talking nervously to one another, I went round checking the blacking on their faces and told several of the men that they hadn't put enough on. They had to use anything to hand, sticking their fingers up the exhaust pipes of the lorries or motor-bikes, to smear more greasy blacking over themselves. They still had blackened faces days later in Normandy, having not had the opportunity to remove it and Thérèse Gondrée would remember ending up with a black face herself after vigorously kissing her liberators!

The pilots of the tugs, the 'Hallys' as the glider pilots called them, also joined us for a smoke and a chat and one of them said to me, 'I've got to hand it to you boys. We've flown on some sticky jobs in our time but what you lot are going to do – well, that takes some guts!' Somehow I found that I really did not want to think of our mission in those terms, not at that moment, so I looked down at my watch and called on everyone to synchronize their watches. It was precisely 2240 hours when I called out, 'Now!' and everyone set their watches at the same time. Suddenly it was time to get on board and I gave the order. Just before we boarded the gliders, I went up to each one, calling encouragingly to the men and shaking the hands of all the officers. I recall hearing shouts of 'Ham and Jam!' from them all; those were the success signals for the capture of both bridges intact and the men had already adopted the phrase. I felt a terrible lump in my throat as I shook my junior officers by the hand and wished them good luck. Cigarettes were stubbed out and all the men piled onto their gliders, men from each platoon calling to the others and wishing each other 'Good luck' and 'See you over the other side'. We sat in the appointed place down each side of the glider and fiddled about fastening the belts that held us on the side of the aircraft. None of us had parachutes, for glider borne troops never carried them. As I climbed into the glider, Colonel Roberts had called out, 'See you on the bridge tomorrow, John' in so calm and matter-of-fact a tone that I felt confidence and certainty flood my senses.

The glider pilots were in the cockpits of each glider waiting for the moment of take-off. Geoff Barkway in what was to be known as No. 3 Glider with Peter Boyle beside him, remembers marvelling at the incredible organization of the mass take-offs, the Halifax tugs in a herringbone formation alongside the runway and the gliders waiting for each Halifax to set off down the runway with its appointed glider in tow behind. That night they left at intervals of one minute. As each glider took off behind its tug, the next Halifax would take to the runway, tugging the next glider. The coordination was incredible. The Halifax towed its glider up to 6,000 feet. It occurred to Barkway, watching the exhausts of the 'Hally' ahead of him, that this really was it, they were off to France and not just back to Netheravon. It was a moonlit night with ragged patches of cloud and as we left the English coast over Worthing, Boyle recalled looking down to see if they could spot the invasion fleet but he saw nothing, for it was dark when the moon was concealed behind the clouds and the Navy's blackout was very effective.

As it happened, much as I cursed the constant clouds shrouding the moon that night, and the wind that sent them moving so swiftly across the skies, unknown to me, the uncertain weather played into our hands, for in Berlin on the previous day, the chief German meteorological officer had said that in his opinion, there would be no invasion on 4 or 5 June due to the unsettled conditions. The enemy were therefore lulled into a false sense of security for those two days and were all the more surprised when it did take place.

In No. 1 Glider John Ainsworth and Jim Wallwork were in the cockpit concentrating hard on the job in hand. They were aware of the soldiers in the back of the glider singing and joking amongst themselves to keep their spirits up and also, surprisingly, most of them smoking cigarettes. When you consider how much ammunition we were carrying, this seems very hazardous, but it was as natural to us then as eating or drinking. Most of the men were Londoners and the song I would always remember them singing was an old one called 'Abey, Abey, Abey My Boy'. There was just enough moonlight coming through the round windows that ran along the sides of the glider above the heads of the seated men, for me to make out the rows of dark figures. The glider gave a lurch and my stomach turned slightly and I remembered with regret, not taking the anti-sickness tablets that Doc Vaughan had given me. I had been sick on almost every glider flight I'd taken in training and indeed, one of the wags at the back of the glider called out, 'Has the Major laid his kit yet?' But this was to be the only flight that I never even felt airsick; the adrenalin surging through my veins kept it at bay.

There were two doors on a Horsa glider that slid up in to the roof, one door at the front and the other at the rear. I was sitting opposite the front door with Den Brotheridge to my right and Platoon Sergeant Ollis on the left. The three of us made a bet as to who would step on to French soil first. When the glider straightened out, I released the clip on my belt and went forward unsteadily to talk to the pilots. I stared out through the cockpit windows and to my surprise found we were all alone in the sky and I could see no other planes. Knowing that we were being taken over under the cover of yet another 'Thousand Bomber Raid' and that the Halifaxes would be going on to bomb Caen, I had really expected to see more aircraft. I learned afterwards that none of the gliders saw any of the others on the way over.

About forty minutes after take-off, Jim Wallwork saw the white line of surf breaking on the beaches of Normandy, and he said to Ainsworth, 'Two minutes from cast-off!' From the Halifax tug, he then received the windspeed, height and heading and they ended their communication wishing each other good luck. Wallwork called back to us, 'Prepare for cast-off' and I gave the order for all the singing and chatter to cease. Complete silence had to prevail as we approached the target. We were crossing the French coast at a known gap in the German air defences. We all re-adjusted our safety-belts and waited for the jerk that always indicated that cast-off had taken place. It came almost immediately as Wallwork released the Horsa from the tug, and the glider went into a steep dive. I realized that Wallwork and Ainsworth were losing height to get below the clouds so that they could see the ground and get their bearings. It took me back to watching the training film at Tarrant Rushton, but I could not afford to let my thoughts wander for we had to open the doors of the glider. This could be a fairly perilous manoeuvre, but we'd practised it several times and Den Brotheridge, whose task this was, released his safety-belt and, as I gripped his left hand in a double wrist-grip, and his platoon stretcher bearer held firmly onto his straps and equipment, he leaned forward and heaved the door upwards. The other man and I then yanked him backwards and he sank back into his seat with a sigh of relief and re-fastened his safety-belt. Suddenly we were all aware of the sweet, damp night air over the Normandy countryside as it filled the glider and we all breathed in, for the first time, the smell of France. The glider was now down to 1,000 feet and, looking down through the open door, I could see the dark and unbelievably peaceful fields of Normandy with cattle grazing in them. The patchwork of fields was so similar to the countryside of England, it was hard not to believe that we weren't just on another exercise. The silence was uncanny and all we could hear was the air swishing past the sides of the glider; it was a sound that none of us would ever forget.

Up in the cockpit Wallwork and Ainsworth saw the silver threads of the river and canal in the moonlight. Their training film made it seem so familiar and Ainsworth went through their routine of counting the seconds off on the stopwatch, lit by a small hand-held lamp, giving the instruction to 'Turn'. Ahead of them and to the right they could see Caen, as on their training film, but now it was already ablaze from the bombing raid, lighting up the skyline. More counting, another instruction to 'Turn' and they were on the run-in to the landing zone. Ahead of us we could see the large structure of the canal bridge exactly like the model we had studied.

Behind us in the glider, everyone was quiet, preoccupied with their own thoughts. I thought of Joy and the two children, sleeping peacefully in their beds in Oxford, and felt the small lump in my breast pocket that was a little red leather shoe belonging to a pair that had been my son Terry's first shoes. Suddenly, I was shaken from my thoughts by the instantly recognizable sight of the River Orne beneath us through the door, and my heart leapt as I realized that the glider was right on course. I wanted to stand up and get immediately behind the pilots, as I had done so often on exercises, but we were losing height rapidly and swinging about, so I sat back in my seat. Ainsworth yelled back 'Hold tight' and all of us automatically adopted our landing positions, linking arms in a butcher's-grip, and lifting our feet off the floor to minimize the chance of breaking our legs on impact. I gritted my teeth and tried to pray but all I could think was 'Please God, please God' as we came in to land with a terrific crash, a splintering noise and sparks flying past outside the doorway.

Chapter 10

6 June 1944:
The Capture of the Bridges

S taff Sergeant Jim Wallwork of the Glider Pilot Regiment, who was at the wheel of the Horsa glider that would become known as No. 1 Glider to land at Pegasus Bridge, fought with the controls that night to perform the most accurate and skilful landing of his life; a feat later described by the Allied Air Force Commander-in-Chief as 'the finest piece of pure flying of World War II'. But it didn't feel like it at the time. The glider was too high as we came in, and Jim Wallwork deployed the arrester parachute and adjusted the flaps as he tried to control the unwieldy aircraft and to steer it precisely where he wanted it to come into land. He had cheekily asked me where I wanted the glider to finish up and, never imagining that he would take me seriously, I had told him, 'Ideally Jim, right through the wire defences of the bridge!'

'Right-ho, sir' Jim had replied and now here he was, intent on doing just that. The Horsa seemed to skim the tall trees at the end of the field and came in to land with an ear-splitting crash that shook us all to our bones.

Both the glider pilots realized that we had lost the wheels and had landed on the skids. Briefly, the glider seemed to bounce and we were airborne again for a second or two. Then we hit the ground once more with another enormous crash, rose briefly and came down for a third and final time. That is when I saw the flashes flying past the door and for a second feared they were tracer bullets fired at us by an enemy ready and waiting for our arrival. In fact, the flashes were caused by the skids striking pieces of flint as the glider hurtled along the uneven ground at 80 mph. We were going too fast for a completely perfect landing and came to a sudden and stupefying halt with the glider's nose right through the barbed wire defences, just as I had requested. The cockpit disintegrated, injuring the pilots who both left for the UK on stretchers later that day, although before he left Wallwork managed to unload the glider during the night.

The door opposite me seemed to collapse in on itself as we came to a halt and the tremendous impact caused me to pass out. As I came round I found to my horror that I couldn't see anything. For a frightful second I really believed that I might have been blinded, and then just as quickly realized that my helmet, the battle-bowler, had rammed itself down over my eyes as I hit the roof or the side of the glider. Pushing it up I took in my surroundings – the smashed doorway, the air full of dust, the holes torn in the sides of the glider and the sound of the pilots groaning in the smashed cockpit. And then the glorious realization came to me that otherwise there was silence, complete silence, no gunfire at all – we had achieved our first objective of complete surprise.

I wrenched off my safety-harness and ran my hands over myself to check that I was not wounded and then, getting a grip on my Sten gun, I rolled forward head-first out of the wreckage of the glider. The first thing I saw was the large water tower of the bridge that I had studied so many times. Now here it was less than 50 feet away from where I stood. I realized in that instant what a fantastic job the glider pilots had done.

Not all the gliders had benefited from such a straightforward flight. Pilots Boland and Hobbs were on their final approach to the landing zone when Boland saw behind him and to his right, another glider bearing down on him that he knew must be Barkway and Boyle. Boland flashed his landing light and banked to avoid a collision, then rounded out and came in to land, losing his undercarriage just as we had done. The glider careered across the field and landed almost intact. The third glider landed in between the first and second, Barkway probably encountering some sideslip and being forced to land very hard and at an angle. The troops in Boland and Hobbs' glider, David Wood's platoon, were out and in action almost immediately, but Barkway and Boyle's glider and passengers did not fare so well. The glider broke up on landing and finished up on the edge of, and partly submerged in, the pond. Both pilots were thrown through the smashed up cockpit and into the pond. Barkway, soaked to the skin, came to and struggled back through the water to his glider on the bank. He saw the body of one of the men in the wreckage but in his confused state his only thought was for the first job he was supposed to do on landing, which was to find the PIAT gun and get it to the command post. Boyle wasn't aware of seeing Barkway but both of them saw the body of the dead lance corporal and, still confused from the crash, they each set off to find a stretcher bearer for the casualties. Barkway was hit by a burst of machine-gun fire, which almost severed his arm just above the wrist, and his recollections thereafter were understandably hazy as he was put on a stretcher and taken to the casualty command post or CCP as we called it. He later lost his arm. Boyle continued to help with the unloading of ammunition from the glider. The platoon was shaken about badly on landing and suffered casualties; one man died and two were injured. It therefore took them longer to muster and they were last onto the bridge.

There was unbelievably still no firing from the Germans on the bridge. In fact, the sentries on watch had heard the crash landings and thought that they were

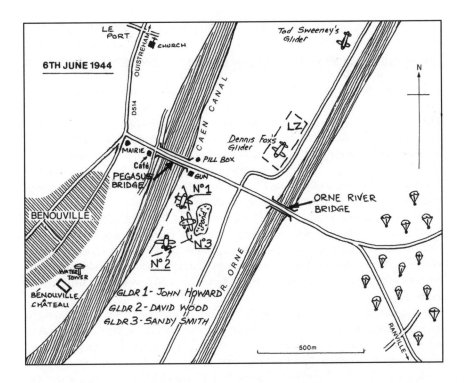

something that had dropped from one of the bombers. They were just looking around in bewilderment. Brotheridge had broken his way out of the other side of my glider and as he came round to join me, I realized that he was limping. 'You alright, Den?' I asked and he replied that he was OK. So I said, 'Get cracking with your first section' and he ran off in the direction of the bridge with his platoon in close pursuit, to tackle the first task; securing the area on the other side. Almost immediately, one man lobbed a phosphorus bomb at the pillbox across the road, to give cover for Corporal Bill Bailey's leading section to run in and drop thirty-six grenades through the slits. While this was happening, the rest of the platoon charged across the bridge. Den Brotheridge limped as he ran but was oblivious to the pain in his leg and was firing from the hip as he went.

My wireless operator, Lance Corporal Ted Tappenden, and I began making our way towards the bridge to the place where I'd arranged to have my command post. Firing had begun the second the soldiers had appeared over the embankment and, as I went, I was watching Den Brotheridge and his platoon doing their splendid dash across the canal bridge with the courageous Brotheridge valiantly at the front. Alerted to my position, an automatic machine gun had opened up at Tappenden and me from the trenches across the road and we both dived for cover. Just at that moment, I heard what I learned later was a Spandau machine gun firing at Den and his platoon from the direction of the café on the other side of the canal. Almost simultaneously I heard the familiar babble of 'Charlie, Charlie, Charlie' from David Wood's platoon and Wood himself came panting up to me out of the darkness. He and his platoon were ready for action and I quickly gave the order for them to carry out task No. 2, and they immediately went in, firing from the hip to clear the inner trenches on their side of the canal. The air was rent with gunfire and explosions and, much later, a German soldier was discovered dead. He had been in the act of laying ready-primed mines in the trenches and I was profoundly grateful that he had been prevented from accomplishing his task. The calls of each platoon identifying themselves could be heard above the sound of gunfire. Stray bullets whipped past them and red, green and yellow tracer, making patterns in all directions.

Just then Platoon Leader Sandy Smith, from No. 3 Glider, informed me that they had made a bad landing and there were some casualties. He had suffered a broken wrist and his arm was tucked into his battledress. I quickly brought him up to date and gave him his platoon's task, which was to cross the bridge and reinforce Brotheridge's platoon, taking the right of the road and leaving Brotheridge to the left.

It was just after I'd sent Smith off that I was informed that Den had been hit in the neck by the machine-gun fire and was badly wounded. My first instinct was to go over there and check on my friend's condition for myself, but the CO should never leave the command post without leaving another officer in charge, and this made me realize that I had heard nothing at all from the river bridge, where my 2 I/C Brian Priday was supposed to have landed. Tappenden confirmed that he had heard nothing over his wireless and we both wondered if the set had been damaged in the landing. I considered sending a runner to see what had happened on the river bridge, but just then I was informed that David Wood and his platoon sergeant were both out of action, having run into machine-gun fire from the trenches. It occurred to me then that within a few minutes of landing, I had only one infantry officer left and that was Sandy Smith who only had the use of one arm.

Of the three gliders that were to land alongside the bridge over the River Orne, only the one piloted by Roy Howard and Staff Sergeant Baacke landed in the right place. And that was only after Roy Howard had realized, immediately after release from the Halifax tug, that his glider was seriously overloaded and unstable. He shouted back to Lieutenant Dennis Fox, whose platoon he was carrying, 'Two men move to the back – on the double,' and Fox had immediately seen that this order was carried out. Howard was then able to control the Horsa again, but it seemed to Baacke that they were still coming in too fast for the landing. At that moment, their sudden arrival out of the night sky startled a herd of cattle that had been grazing peacefully on the landing zone and they proceeded to stampede across the glider's path. With the deployment of the arrester parachute, the glider came to a halt right on target, Baacke never being quite sure whether the nose-wheel hit an obstacle to aid their deceleration or whether that obstacle was an unfortunate cow! Baacke also recalled being very disconcerted to find they were the only glider there. The other glider, piloted by Pearson and Guthrie made it to their destination, but landed 500 yards short, a couple of fields away and Tod Sweeney's platoon were therefore obliged to make all haste across the dark countryside to the river bridge. This took them about ten minutes and Sweeney approached the river bridge cautiously, for it all seemed suspiciously quiet there. He found Dennis Fox standing on the bridge with his platoon already in control, and said urgently, 'Everything all right, Dennis?' to which Fox had casually replied, 'I think so, Tod – but I can't understand why there aren't any ruddy Umpires about!' He was referring to the army umpires who had directed all their exercises.

Thus within a few minutes, a message was received on Tappenden's wireless from Dennis Fox and Tod Sweeney at the river bridge to say that they had captured it without any opposition but that there was no sign of the third glider containing Brian Priday and Hooper's platoon. They reported that the enemy had run off, leaving their guns in weapon-pits, still warm from the sentries' occupancy. That the river bridge was secure was good news for me and I instructed Tappenden to send out the success signal for both bridges being captured intact. Jock Neilson and his Sappers had searched the bridges, cut all wires and found the chambers ready to receive their charges of explosive, but in fact, no charges had been laid. They were later found in a magazine near the canal bridge.

It was just ten minutes after we had landed. Tappenden began sending out the success signal, 'Ham' for the canal bridge and 'Jam' for the river bridge. We were hoping that this message would be picked up by Brigadier Poett who had a wireless set on our net, having dropped with a special stick of Pathfinder Paratroopers ahead of the main force at about the same time as we landed. Tappenden continued to send out this message with monotonous regularity positioned alongside me, and I well remember his voice repeating over and over again, 'Hello Four-Dog, Hello Four-Dog, Ham and Jam, Ham and Jam' and I am certain I heard Tappenden eventually say 'Ham and Bloody Jam!'

Naturally I had been concerned to know that there was no sign of the sixth glider over at the river bridge, containing Brian Priday and Tony Hooper and his platoon. I hoped they had landed nearby and would turn up, but for the present I had other matters on my mind. Sandy Smith had reported back with the situation on the other side of the canal bridge, saying that things seemed to be going fairly well there, although he felt sure there were Germans holed up in some of the houses. I ordered Smith to coordinate the defence of both his and Brotheridge's platoons and added that I would send someone over to deal with the Germans. Smith charged off back over the bridge, after I had enquired if he had seen anything of Doc Vaughan. He said that he thought he might have been injured on landing. I wanted to make sure that the casualty command post had been established at the agreed place, a small tree-lined lane between the two bridges.

Things seemed quiet in the trenches that Wood's platoon had cleared and I yelled across the road to Corporal Godbold, who had taken over Wood's platoon, asking him to go over the bridge and clear the houses there in front of Smith's platoon and making sure he liaised with Sandy Smith. Godbold did a very good job of commanding the platoon and carrying out his orders. Then I gave orders for Sweeney to remain on the river bridge and Fox and his platoon to report to the canal bridge to lend a hand, as I now feared that counter-attacks from the enemy could not be long in coming. Next I sent the 7 Para Liaison Officer, Macdonald, off to make contact with his CO. He had all the information to pass on and I was already scanning the skies for the welcome sight of the paratroopers dropping. I watched Macdonald steal away into the night and as I did so, two stretcher bearers came past carrying Den Brotheridge to the CCP. They told me that he was still unconscious. I bent over and felt for his pulse and tried speaking to him, but Den was mercifully completely insensible, although still alive. I watched them carry him away with a lump in my throat. Brotheridge had been incredibly brave and had been the first man to be wounded in action in the invasion, and his platoon had then made short work of the gun crew that had fired the Spandau.

While all this was happening, the glider pilots who had not been injured had been carrying out essential work ferrying arms and ammunition from the gliders to my command post by the bridge. I heard one of them struggling up the bank and went to assist him and found myself looking into his face, the moonlight revealing it to be covered in what I realized was blood. He had a bad cut on his head. It was Jim Wallwork and he dumped the box of ammunition at my feet and said, 'What next, sir?' Another pilot was running messages for me to the forward platoons. They refused to keep clear of the battle and did stalwart work to aid the troops.

Dennis Fox's platoon arrived from the river bridge and I sent them over the canal bridge to form a fighting patrol out beyond the perimeter defences facing west, in order to detect any enemy reconnaissance parties, or to stop any enemy forming up to counter-attack. Jock Neilson and his Sappers, their most vital job to deal with the explosives on the bridge having been completed, were patrolling between the two bridges and I decided it was safe to leave my command post so that I could visit the forward platoons and assess the situation for myself. I found Sandy Smith had done his job well and was in control on the other side of the bridge. But at Brotheridge's Platoon HQ all was not well, for his platoon sergeant, Ollis was in great pain, having been injured in the back and ribs on landing. So I sent him off to the CCP for treatment and put his senior corporal, Corporal Caine in control. This meant that out of three original platoons, I had one

124

commanded by a platoon commander with his arm in a sling, and the other two commanded by corporals.

I returned to the command post and found Tappenden still 'Ham and Jamming' close by. Just then, I noticed Doc Vaughan wandering about in a dazed condition. He was covered, head to toe in slime and mud and stank to high heaven. It appeared that on landing, he'd been thrown into the pond and had received a blow to the head and was obviously concussed. I took him by the shoulder and said 'Hey Doc! Have you seen Brotheridge or Wood or any other casualties?'

He frowned and said, 'No John. Where are they?'

I replied, 'At the casualty command post!'

'OK' said the Doc and wandered off over the canal bridge in completely the opposite direction to the CCP. I yanked him back and he overheard the patient Tappenden still sending out his success signal.

'What's all this Ham and Jam about, John?' he asked, still confused. He had sat in on all the briefing sessions and had taken a tremendous interest in everything. He certainly would have known the significance of those two words if he hadn't been so dazed. So I gave him a shot of Scotch from a hip-flask I was carrying which seemed to help him collect his senses, and then sent him off with a runner to make sure he found the CCP down towards the river bridge. I then allowed myself to lean back against the steel panels of the canal bridge, my gun at the ready and ever alert to pick up any signs of the enemy. I heaved a sigh of relief – so far, so good.

In Oxford in the middle of the night of 5/6 June 1944, Joy was awoken by a loud droning of aeroplane engines overhead. She lay there in bed, the realization slowly coming to her through her drowsiness of what this meant. She slipped out of bed quietly, so as not to disturb our three-month old daughter Penny, asleep in the cot by her bed, and went to the window and drew back the curtain just a little. Looking up into a night sky of partial cloud, the moonlight streaming through them intermittently, she saw what appeared to be hundreds of aeroplanes flying south and whispered, 'It's the invasion!' I had told her that when she knew that the invasion had started, my job would already be over. That was all she knew, and she went back to her bed and prayed that I had been successful and would be safe.

As I was taking a moment's rest I heard the increasing drone of many engines and, looking up, saw the skies full of countless aeroplanes coming from the direction of the sea. I can recall checking my watch and it was just 00.50 hours. Ground flares suddenly appeared at various points about a mile to the east and north-east of the canal bridge. These were to mark the dropping zone or DZ for 3 and 5 Parachute Brigades. Then we all saw the parachutists begin dropping and the skies to the east of the bridges became full of parachutes. It was a sight none of us ever forgot, as they drifted to earth illuminated by the ground flares. But we could also see the German tracer going up to meet them. Even though this sight was terrible to watch, knowing that many of those young men would inevitably be killed or wounded, for me it remained one of the most awe-inspiring sights of my life. I began to send out the 'Victory-V' signal on my pea-whistle at this point, the three dots and a dash carrying as clear as a bell on the night air. Many para-troopers who were blown off-course in the drop would say afterwards that they were able to take their direction only by hearing the unmistakeable sound of the 'Victory-V' being blown by Major John Howard's whistle down on the canal bridge.

Soon after this spectacle, we received our first visitor down at the bridge in the shape of Brigadier Nigel Poett, Brigade Commander of 5 Para. He quietly materialized out of the night at my side and asked how things were going. I was pleased to give him a full report. The bold Brigadier told me that he had lost a couple of sticks of his men – a drop of paratroopers is known as a stick – and his wireless had presumably been smashed and would not work, which accounted for why Tappenden was receiving no acknowledgment to his constant signals. We were to find out much later that the wireless operator had been killed in Ranville and thus Tappenden's tireless signals had been sent to a dead man. Brigadier Poett did not linger at the canal bridge, but sped off to join his men. Having confirmed the position on the bridges, his tall figure vanished into the darkness as quickly as it had appeared.

It was then that we heard the first sounds of the enemy preparing to counter-attack. Noises came from the other end of the village of Bénouville, in an area known as Le Port to the north up by the church, towards the coast road to Ouistreham. We realized that it was the sound of tanks clanking about up there. Then we heard firing coming from the direction of Ranville and the river bridge. I learned that Sweeney's platoon had spotted a patrol of four men approaching them along the towpath from the direction of Caen. Sweeney's scout section waited until the patrol could clearly be seen and then stepped out of the darkness and halted it. There was a scuffle and a guttural exclamation of 'Englanders!' and the patrol opened fire and wounded one of Sweeney's men. The scout section replied with its Bren gun and annihilated the lot. Upon examining the bodies, they realized that unfortunately, only three of the bodies were Germans, the other belonging to an English paratrooper who had obviously been taken prisoner. Almost a year later, that same scout section leader was visiting me in hospital in Oxford and still bitterly regretting that they had killed one of their own boys that night by the River Orne. But such tragedies were bound to happen in battle.

Five minutes later Sweeney's platoon was again confronting the enemy. This time they heard the sound of a car and motorbike approaching the river bridge at speed, coming up the road from the direction of Ranville. It was a German staff car and escort and was moving so fast that they flashed through Sweeney's outer defences and were immediately engaged with light machine-gun fire, which brought the motorcycle crashing to the road. It slewed right into the river, killing the rider instantly. The staff car careered on over the Orne River bridge, but a further burst of fire punctured the tyres and it skidded to a standstill. Three men jumped out and tried to escape but were soon stopped by Sweeney's platoon. Two of the Germans were killed. The other one turned out to be the commander of the garrison at the bridges and he was badly wounded in the legs. He declared, in excellent English, that he had lost his honour and demanded to be shot. Sweeney's men took him along to the CCP where he lay propped up against a tree, haranguing Doc Vaughan about the futility of the Allies believing for one moment that they could win the war against the master race. He asked the Doc to shoot him and, tempted as he might have been to do so, Vaughan later recalled sticking the largest needle full of morphine he could find into the fellow, which Doc said 'induced him to take a more reasonable view of things and within ten minutes he was thanking me profusely for my medical attention!' An investigation of the staff car proved most interesting because it was found to contain wine glasses, plates that had evidently been used for a recent meal, and also ladies' lingerie and cosmetics! Evidently, the British troops unexpected arrival on his patch, had resulted in 'Herr Commandant' being interrupted during a most intimate soirée with an obliging local lady in Ranville. One can only imagine his panic hearing the fighting going on at the canal bridge, and the lady being unceremoniously dumped as his staff car sped down to the bridges to find out what was happening.

Back on the canal bridge we had our own excitement. Tanks were heard approaching from the direction of the chateau, clanking and rumbling along the road to the T-junction at the end of the road leading to the bridge in Bénouville. One of them began slowly and menacingly to grind and clank its way down the road towards us. By this time Fox's forward platoon had got a PIAT gun assembled and ready by the roadside. PIAT guns could be most effective when well-aimed at a tank by daylight but it was very dark then, and since a PIAT could only be usefully fired at a range of about fifty yards, the platoon sergeant, Sergeant Thornton, who was in charge of the gun, was obliged to wait a nervously long time as the tank came into range before he could fire. What the rest of us also knew was that the bomb fired from a PIAT had a high trajectory and would then only explode if it hit the tank directly, a miss-hit would see it bouncing harmlessly away. I was almost at the point of giving the order to go in with grenades to attack the tank when, with remarkable control, 'Wagger' Thornton took careful aim and fired his PIAT gun at the tank, scoring a direct hit. The tank exploded with a mighty bang. It must have been carrying a full load of ammunition, for it continued to explode for a long time, creating an amazing firework display accompanied by deafening cracks and thuds, that could be seen and heard over a large area. Tom Packwood, who had been with Brotheridge's platoon and was ordered with his mates to 'dig in' in the garden behind the café, recalls that they nearly jumped out of their skins when the tank was blown up, having no idea what could have caused such an explosion. They all feared it could be the Germans counter-attacking. He said he remembered the explosions went on for over an hour. It is understandable, therefore, that the two German tanks that had been following quickly retreated thinking that there must have been several heavily armed companies of Allied troops down at the bridge. The paras who were beginning to muster in the surrounding countryside thought we were having a hell of a fight at the bridges. I reflected later that the successful destruction of just this one tank certainly bought the *coup de main* force precious time holding up the German counter-attack at the bridges.

I stood watching the tank exploding, feeling very proud of how my well-trained men were dealing with the enemy. But my satisfaction turned to immense sorrow when Doc Vaughan sent word to inform me quietly that my platoon leader and dear friend, Den Brotheridge had died without regaining consciousness down at the CCP. With Brian Priday lost God knows where, and Brotheridge gone, I was without my two closest friends. Doc Vaughan had very quickly regained his senses when he had left me at the command post. He had first of all been taken to where David Wood lay, close to the trenches from where he had been fired at, with his thigh shattered by a machine-gun bullet. The Doc said, 'He had no thoughts for himself, but kept asking how Denny Brotheridge was getting on.' Arrangements were made to take Wood down to the CCP on a stretcher where the Doc could patch him up and give him a shot of morphine to help with the pain. Wood was later repatriated to an English hospital and was unable to play any further role in the battle for Normandy. Doc Vaughan carried out his duties magnificently and no doubt saved lives and eased the suffering of many others that night.

The continuing firework display of the exploding tank helped to guide many of the members of 7 Para who were lost in the Normandy countryside down towards the bridges. The plan had been that our assault party would be joined by a contingent of 7 Para within an hour of the gliders landing, but in fact due to being blown off course and having a very scattered drop, they took much longer to muster than anticipated. The liaison officer for 7 Para, Lieutenant McDonald, who had arrived in one of the gliders, had been obliged to return to the canal bridge having failed to meet up with any of his chaps. I began to wonder just when the main force of 7 Para and its officers would arrive, for at about this time odd paratroopers started to turn up at the bridges unable to find their rendezvous point. At 02.50 I received a message saying that 7 Para were finally on their way and shortly afterwards a Major Fraser appeared with some of his company. He was followed by his CO, Lieutenant Colonel Geoffrey Pine-Coffin, along with more men at 03.00 hours. It should be remembered that the Army was operating by British time that night. It had been hoped that Major Dick Bartlett and his paratroopers would have arrived at the canal bridge shortly after 01.00 hours. However Bartlett and his men were dropped in the wrong area completely and thus we were eventually relieved at 03.00 by 7 Para, two hours late as recorded in the official record of the Airborne Division.

I wrote, in early July 1944, an account of the event which said that, as the paratroopers crossed the bridge in the early hours of 6 June, there was a lot of banter among them and the glider lads of 'D' Company. Our lads asked if the paras 'had enjoyed their crafty forty-eight-hour passes', implying that the 'paraboys' as they called them, were definitely late on parade. One can imagine that there were some very smart replies from the chaps of 7 Para having been blown off course and shot-up, and then having to find their way cross-country to the bridges. However once they had crossed the canal bridge, they were straight into action alongside the glider-borne troops. Lieutenant Colonel Pine-Coffin took over command from me at this point and gave the order for me to form my company as his battalion reserve, while 7 Para moved out to their allotted positions. I commented in my first military report, shortly after the assault on the bridges, that the paratroops 'soon made up for lost time and despite their depleted numbers, nobly pushed out the bridgehead towards the west'.

One might pause to wonder what the effect of these events was on the inhabitants of Bénouville. On a visit there in 1946, I persuaded Georges Gondrée, the proprietor of the café by the bridge, to recount his memories of the night of 5/6 June 1944. I had already realized that it would be useful for posterity to have these things set down. Georges was becoming a close friend to me by then and I typed his account out on my faithful typewriter. Naturally, Georges dictated it to me in his near-perfect English. He told how he and his wife Thérèse were woken up at about 01.15 as the first glider landed. They heard the crash landing and assumed that it was the noise of an English bomber crashing and that the crew would have baled out and been captured by the Germans. Gondrée had immediately taken cover in the cellar with his wife and two small daughters. They heard gunfire. Then there was pounding on the front door and a German shouted for them to come outside. The Gondrée family remained hidden in the cellar. They were wise to do so, for the retreating Germans seemed to have taken retribution against some of the inhabitants of Bénouville, shooting one old man against the door of the café. Gondrée commented in his account, 'You can see the splashes made by his brains on the door if you look'.

After some time, Thérèse, shivering in her nightdress, persuaded her husband to go upstairs to take a look, which he did cautiously. Opening the shutters of one of the first-floor windows a little, Gondrée called out in French to two men he saw below, 'What's going on?' The men replied in a mix of languages but Georges could not really work out what they meant and was alarmed by their black faces which he took to be masks. So he went to one of the kitchen windows and opened it, finding two more men crouched there, who asked him in bad French, if he was a civilian. Gondrée affirmed this but decided not to speak any English just in case the soldiers were German. When they signalled that he should close the shutters and withdraw, he did just that and retreated to the cellar. They all waited some time, and then heard sounds of digging in their back garden and Georges looked out of a gap in the cellar wall. His words give us a very clear impression of what the dawn of D-Day was really like: 'There was a wonderful peaceful air of dawn coming up over the land . . . I saw vague figures moving among the vegetables in my garden.' It was Tom Packwood and the remains of Brotheridge's platoon 'digging in' in the garden of the café. Thérèse and Georges listened intently to the soldiers' conversation and Thérèse felt that they were not speaking German. Georges thought one of them said 'All right!' in English but they still decided to err on the side of caution and to remain in their cellar. However, when there was knocking on the front door of the café, Georges felt emboldened to go up and open it, and saw soldiers with 'coal black faces'. He took one of the soldiers by the hand after assuring him there were no Germans there, and led him down into the cellar to show him his wife and children. The first soldier took one look at the little French family and said to his mate 'It's all right, chum!' and, sure at last that this was indeed the liberation of France, Gondrée burst into tears of joy and the soldiers and the family all embraced! This is when Thérèse got black camouflage paint all over her face. The soldiers gave the little girls some chocolate.

Georges Gondrée allowed his café to be used as a casualty post in the days that followed. Doc Vaughan was forced to partially evacuate his CCP in between the bridges, because at first light German snipers, situated around the chateau of Bénouville about half a mile away, began firing with deadly accuracy and hit several of the wounded. Somehow they managed to carry some of the casualties up to and over the canal bridge and into the Café Gondrée where the Doc could treat them in safety. Georges Gondrée also showed the English soldiers where the telephone lines ran so they could cut them to further confuse the enemy. He finished his account by saying that throughout the occupation, the only drink he had sold to the Germans was beer, his store of wine never having been found. Just beer, he declared, and once some homemade liqueur they had 'brewed out of rotting melons and the remains of a rather dusty packet of sugar we discovered, half mouldy, one day in the garret. This disgusting concoction was drunk with avidity by the Germans who paid me 25 francs a glass for it.' This final sentence being the typical Norman sentiment of delight at making a fast buck, especially out of a despised army of occupation!

Georges Gondrée had, in fact, hidden his wine by burying it in the garden and later in the day on 6 June, he quickly disinterred bottles of champagne and opened them, much to the delight of the Doc and his patients and causing me to declare that 'half the company want to report sick!' David Wood was not one of those taken to the Café Gondrée and Doc Vaughan mentioned that Field

Ambulance personnel arrived at the bridge after being parachuted in and surgical teams turned up to assist them. David Wood was moved to a First Aid post in Ranville with Sandy Smith, who was having his broken wrist, and a knee injury, treated. Thus they both missed out on the champagne.

The *coup de main* party was busy setting up a company command post in the pillbox, which had by that time been cleaned up after the carnage caused by the grenades. I went into the pillbox and found a Nazi flag that had been on the wall, having been torn down by my men and thrown to the floor to be used as a door-mat. Realizing its worth as a memento, I picked it up and took it back to England with me where it was displayed in the regimental museum at Oxford after the war. By then dawn had broken and the canal bridge area was under constant attack from sniper fire coming from the direction of the chateau. We tried to work out where it was coming from and thought it might be from a hedgerow, from the roof of the chateau itself or even from a water-tower to the right of it. This deadly accurate sniping made all movement perilous over and around the canal. The snipers were about 550 yards to the south-west of the bridge.

When dawn had broken, an air bombardment began from the Allied ships off shore, shelling both the enemy coastal defences and Caen, as a 'softening up' measure, prior to the seaborne landings. The noise was unbelievable, and occa-sionally the bridge areas received shells that had gone astray, falling dangerously close to us. I felt that we were getting the 'overs' from the coastal shelling and the 'unders' from the Caen bombardment. Even in the relative safety of the pillbox where we now had our command post, the noise deafened us and the ground shook repeatedly, sending showers of dust down onto us all. After one particularly close explosion, which had shaken us all and left our ears ringing, one of my Cockney chaps said to me, 'Blimey sir! They're firing Jeeps!'

I might not have felt like joking if I had known then how close our small force was to total annihilation. A decision had been taken at a high level of command, not to inform me of the belief held by British Intelligence that the German 125 Panzer Regiment of the 21st Panzer Division, under the command of Colonel Hans von Luck, was stationed in Caen in June 1944. It was a crack force, specially trained to counter-attack and by 01.30 hours on 6 June, von Luck was already receiving reports of enemy paratroopers landing in the area towards the coast. However at that stage of the war, much dissension and mistrust had built up in the German High Command and Hitler, himself, had taken control of the armoured divisions. He was in bed asleep and no one dared to disturb him. The initial reports into the German HQ were unclear and it was decided to wait until they could be sure that it really was the invasion of France and not just a diversion. Therefore, von Luck received no orders from Berlin and he was obliged to sit back impatiently and wait until Hitler could be awoken and orders issued to counter-attack. Thus it was, that as Hitler slept, the assault group, under my command, consolidated our positions and were joined by 7 Para under the command of Lieutenant Colonel Geoffrey Pine-Coffin. From then on the Allied invasion unfolded.

Close by the pillbox lay the gun pit containing a 5-cm anti-tank gun. It was not long before Wally Parr, Billy Gray, Bill Bailey and Charlie Gardner were examining it and finding the ammunition stored in small cellars, which had been excavated off the gun pit. They were keeping their heads down, for the sniping had become highly dangerous as full daylight was replacing the dim light of dawn. It did not take long before the lads had figured out how to load the gun and fire it and Wally Parr was desperate to 'have a go' at getting the snipers. Bill Bailey had told him, 'Better not fire it without the CO's permission, Wal' with a nod towards the pillbox where I was working out my next moves. Down in the gun pit they were all safe from the constant sniping and Wally had to be quick about it as he scrambled out and ran across to the pillbox, bent double. Once inside he saluted me smartly and said breathlessly, 'Please sir, permission to fire the anti-tank gun, please sir – we know 'ow to fire it an' there's loads of ammunition down there!' I was engrossed in deciding how to follow orders from Pine-Coffin when all three of the platoons at the canal bridge were now being commanded by corporals, and I was a platoon down with my 2 I/C Priday still missing, his glider having never arrived. I had glanced at the excited Parr and said, 'OK Parr – but just be careful where you aim it'. Parr rushed back to his mates.

Back in the gun pit, Corporal Bill Bailey had decided that it would be an excellent place to brew a cup of tea. He was known for his addiction to 'a nice cuppa' on all occasions, and he was trying to brew the tea on the little Primus stoves we used to heat water. This process could take almost twenty minutes of fiddling and he was relishing the thought of his hot drink, with a large spoon of tinned condensed milk stirred in, when Parr decided to fire the anti-tank gun. The mighty explosion it made caused dirt and earth to shower everything in the gun pit, and Bill's precious mug of tea was full of good Normandy soil before he'd had so much as a mouthful! I was told that his comments were best left to the imagination, while the other men there who had been watching his performance, fell about laughing. I remember that a minute or so after I had given Parr permission to fire the gun, I heard, above the bombardment which was still going on, Parr shout, 'Number One gun . . .' as if he had a whole barrage of cannons at his disposal, and then, 'Fire!' I recalled afterwards, 'The most God-awful blast followed as the gun fired', and, glancing quickly through the slit in the pillbox, I saw the large water-tower to the right of the chateau explode as the shell went right through it and out the other side, showering water and debris all around. Parr then aimed at the chateau itself, being convinced that the snipers were using it and the water-tower from which to fire. He sent one shell to its upper floor before I could stop him and I hurled myself out of the pillbox, over the road and into the gun-pit. In my best sergeant major bellow I roared, 'Stop that, Parr!' He was most put out for he was just beginning to really enjoy himself. I quickly explained that the chateau was being used as a maternity home during the occupation, and even if the roof was being used as a sniper's nest, we could not fire on it. Parr hung his head, but only for a few moments.

'But I can go on firin' around the chateau?' he asked me, brightening. I relented. Parr was one of my 'scallywags' and I didn't want to dampen the lad's initiative.

'All right Parr,' I said, 'You can fire in the direction of the snipers and put the wind up them a bit – but only when they fire at us.' With that I returned to the command post, leaving a very happy Wally Parr in control of the biggest gun he'd ever fired.

Bill Bailey and the others raised their eyes heavenwards as Wally began firing at the trees and anything else in that direction, but the sniping did not cease and continued to be accurate and very hazardous for us holding the canal bridge. Eventually, even I got fed-up with the extra din caused by the anti-tank gun and ordered Parr to cease firing.

It must have been shortly after this, at around 06.00, the unmistakeable sound of Spitfires took everyone's attention skywards and we observed three Spitfires circling high above us, unsure whether to come down lower. We could see the three white stripes on each wing that had appeared overnight on all Allied aircraft for easy identification during the invasion and immediately I deployed some men to put out the 'recognition signals' – parachutes and scarves in a pre-agreed pattern. Spotting these, and realizing that the bridges were indeed in the hands of the Airborne, the three 'Spits' flew low over the bridges and to the men's delight did the now famous 'Victory roll' above us to great cheers of delight from the party at the bridges. As they left, a package was dropped, landing in the fields beyond and I sent out a party to retrieve it. They discovered that it was the morning newspapers from England! The men scanned them for news of their success at the bridges but there was no word yet of what we had achieved.

At about 07.00 a small German gunboat came slowly up the canal from the direction of Ouistreham on the coast and started to fire its 20 mm gun at the HQ of the 7th Para Battalion up near the church, in the area known as Le Port. Wally Parr could not use the anti-tank gun because the superstructure of the bridge was between him and the gunboat. However, Corporal Godbold's platoon took cover on the Bénouville bank of the canal and waited until it came in range of their PIAT gun. This time it was fired by Private Cheesely and he had a direct hit on the gunboat and it slewed round and became grounded on that side of the canal, allowing Godbold's men to capture the Germans on board. They were then taken up to the POW 'cage' up in Ranville where General Gale had set up his HQ.

Shortly after 09.00 Tappenden received a message on his radio and said to me, 'It's Lieutenant Sweeney sir, from the river bridge. He says to go and look down the road in their direction.' 'Tapp' was grinning, so I knew that it wasn't a warning, and I left the pillbox, bending low so as to avoid the bullets from the snipers, and ducked into the relative shelter of the bridge's girders. I saw an amazing sight for, marching precisely in step in the centre of the road in between the two bridges, were three tall figures. In the centre was General 'Windy' Gale, Commander of 6th Airborne Division, on one side of him was Brigadier Hugh Kindersley, commander of the Air Landing Brigade and on the other, Brigadier Nigel Poett, Commander of 5 Para Brigade. I could hardly believe my eyes. Each commander was immaculately turned out in battledress and, to see them marching down the road heedless of the snipers, was just the lift the men needed. It was the start of a day that we would remember as being one of the longest days of our lives.

Chapter 11

6–19 June 1944:
Escoville and Fighting for
Normandy

S eeing the three commanders striding down the road from the direction of Ranville and approaching the canal bridge I set out to meet them half way despite the bullets from enemy snipers whipping past me. If the General and the two Brigadiers could take a chance, then so could I. Coming up to the three tall figures about 250 yards short of the bridge, I saluted them smartly. Gale frowned at me, gesturing to where a PIAT gun lay on the grass verge where it had been left in the chaos of the previous night. 'That shouldn't be left lying around, Major – could fall into the wrong hands,' he said, staring down into my eyes, for he was a very tall man. If I was hoping for a word of praise from him for a successful operation, I was to be disappointed. The three commanders continued over the canal bridge to the 7th Para HQ where they went to confer with Colonel Pine-Coffin.

At about 10.00 the sound of an aeroplane was heard above the noise of the continuing bombardment, and a German bomber was spotted approaching, diving out of the sky towards the canal bridge. Everyone jumped for cover into the pillbox or the trenches and watched helplessly as the aircraft dropped a bomb with fatal accuracy onto the bridge. It hit the side of the bridge's tower with a dull clang and then, unbelievably, dropped into the canal with a splash. We had all braced ourselves for the inevitable mighty explosion which would blow the bridge sky-high and were open-mouthed with amazement as it failed to explode. 'My God,' I said to Tappenden in the pillbox, 'it was a dud!' The mark made by the bomb on the side of the bridge was to be there for evermore, pointed out to the families of those of us who survived in the years afterwards. At the time thanks were offered to the prisoners of war who, working in the German bomb-making factories, tried to deliberately disable some bombs they manufactured, in order to undermine the Nazi war machine. 'That one's for Poland' they might have thought, and thus the bridge that was to become known as 'Pegasus' survived intact, and many British lives were saved.

But we had little time for reflection as two enemy frogmen had been sent up the canal from Caen to arrive at the same time as the bomber and, whilst their undoubted bravery was acknowledged, nevertheless, they were quickly dispatched by the members of the group on the canal banks.

All through the morning of 6 June and on into the early afternoon, the enemy were piling on the pressure, counter-attacking the soldiers at the bridges. 7th Para was fighting bravely in Le Port and in Bénouville under the command of Major Nigel Taylor. One platoon of my men was ordered in to assist them, and all the street fighting training they had done in the bombed out houses of Southampton certainly paid off. By noon, Colonel Hans von Luck finally got orders for his 125 Panzer Regiment of 21st Panzer Division to counter-attack from Caen. But von Luck knew it was too late for, as he had feared, their positions were quickly spotted by the Allies and came under heavy attack both from the sky and from the war-ships off shore, doing heavy damage and considerably lessening the thrust and impact of their armoured divisions.

For those of us who had arrived by glider just after midnight the previous night, and for the 'paraboys' too, the day wore on interminably as we struggled to hold off the German tanks and artillery attacks. Many of us wondered just how long we could hold out on our own at the bridges, and began to feel that it was just a matter of time before the enemy overpowered us. I kept checking my watch constantly, it was past midday and the time was ticking by. I said to myself under my breath, 'Come on lads – where are the bloody Commandos?' for I knew that we were supposed to be relieved by midday by more forces from the sea-borne landings.

I was finding it one of the most difficult times in the whole operation. 'Hold until relieved' kept repeating in my mind. 'But how long for?' I asked myself. It was then that several of us thought we heard a strange sound above the noise of the gunfire and bombardment – a wailing sound, then a tune; it was bagpipes! Several of the men thought they were definitely dreaming but I was straining my ears in the pillbox and knew at once that it was the signal I'd been waiting for – young Bill Millin, piper to Lord Lovat, leading the Commandos, marching up the tow-path along the canal from the coast. They were the first sea-borne troops to reach us at about 13.00 hours on D-Day. A bugle sounded in reply from 7th Para and the skirl of the bagpipes became louder. We could see Lovat striding ahead of his men, clad in his trademark Aran wool jumper with Millin beside him blowing away for all he was worth. The column of men in green berets had brought on a fusillade of snipers' bullets from the fields south-west of the canal bridge.

But Lovat didn't know the meaning of fear and insisted upon striding straight over the canal bridge alone, despite my shouted warning. There was a reenactment of this moment in a famous film, *The Longest Day*, made twenty years after the war, in which the American director, Daryl Zanuck, demanded that Bill Millin play the bagpipes as he crossed the bridge alongside Peter Lawford, the actor who played Lovat. I was unable to prevent this piece of dramatic licence despite protesting at the time in my capacity as a Technical Advisor for the film, that it had been far too dangerous for such a thing to have actually happened on D-Day. Lovat may have refused to alter his pace and upright bearing, but the other commandos had run across the bridge single-file and even so, several of them had been unfortunately hit by the snipers.

However this did not diminish their welcome by the soldiers holding the bridges. Lovat and I memorably shook hands and Lovat later claimed to have said 'Today history is being made' but I can only remember greeting him with 'About bloody time!' Lovat and I remained on very good terms for the rest of our lives and I always felt an immense respect for the courage and panache that he displayed on D-Day.

Several Churchill tanks had arrived by sea with the commandos and they split up, some to go up to reinforce the defences in Ranville, and others into Bénouville to backup the troops there. Shortly after this, a gunboat was seen approaching up the canal from Caen, loaded with enemy troops. The moment it was seen, Wally Parr, Billy Gray and Charlie Gardner manned the anti-tank gun and made ready to fire. Unsure of the range of the gun, they fired a little early the first time and the shell landed thirty yards short of its target but stopped the gunboat mid-stream and it attempted to turn back. Wally took aim and fired again and this time hit the stern of the boat and it headed back towards Caen as fast as its engines allowed, billowing black smoke behind it in a manner most satisfactory to the lads in the gun pit, who whooped and yelled in glee.

By mid-afternoon the enemy attacks on the bridges were waning. An uneasy peace seemed to settle over them and naps could be taken and meals heated up over the small Primus rings. At around 21.00 hours as dusk fell on a glorious evening, we saw many gliders coming in to land around Bénouville and Ranville. This was the Airlanding Brigade plus other members of my own battalion, carrying the heavy equipment, Jeeps, lorries and anti-tank guns, as well as stores. After some time they began coming across the bridges in the Army vehicles and the soldiers who had already been there for almost a day, shouted good-naturedly to their comrades, 'You're a bit late on parade, mate!' Tom Packwood saw one young soldier leaning out of the cab of an armoured truck and yelled 'Hey! Where've you been? – the war's over!' But the next day when we were under fire in Escoville, running for our lives while company men were being wounded and killed around us, Tom told me he recalled this lighthearted sally and wished fervently that it could have been true.

My orders were to hand over to a seaborne battalion when it arrived and then to rejoin our battalion in Ranville. I would no longer be under orders from

Colonel Pine-Coffin of 7 Para, but would await instructions from Colonel Mike Roberts. Thus when the Warwicks of 3rd Division finally arrived at the canal bridge in the late evening of 6 June, I briefed their commander and made ready to leave. Regretfully, Wally Parr instructed one of the Warwicks' chaps how to use the anti-tank gun and handed it over. The men found a wooden farm cart in the village of Bénouville and they dragged it down to the canal bank and filled it up with the items they wanted to take with us, including a fair number of German guns and other 'liberated' articles, not all of them vital to the war effort. The cart was very heavy by the time this was all on board and after struggling to push and pull the unwieldy object for a few miles, it was too difficult and arduous to drag it across the countryside, especially as we got lost for some time. Eventually the cart was abandoned, the men carrying what they could themselves.

'D' Company was now depleted. We had lost five officers, two being wounded, one killed and two more missing, in the assault on the bridges and one soldier had been killed and fourteen wounded. In addition Tony Hooper's platoon was still missing. I was without my 2 I/C, Brian Priday and had only Sweeney left of my original four platoon commanders. The injured had included two of the platoon sergeants and therefore two platoons were still under the command of corporals. The glider pilots were under orders to get themselves down to the beaches to be taken back to England as quickly as possible, for they were needed for further missions. On the beach Pilot Oliver Boland gave a short interview to a reporter from *The Times* who got his article into the paper the next day, this being the first publicity for the 'Pegasus Bridge' operation. Pilot Peter Boyle found himself back in Blighty so fast that when he was on leave a couple of days later in his native Nottingham, a woman, seeing his uniform, said to him, 'Why aren't you over in France with the invasion forces?' and when Boyle replied, 'I've been and come back!' she just shook her head in disbelief.

Jock Neilson and his Sappers had returned to their units, and I knew that once I'd reported to the battalion in Ranville, I would lose Sandy Smith and Dennis Fox and their platoons as well, back to 'B' Company. Thus it was almost exactly twenty-four hours after the party had been the first to land in occupied France to spearhead the invasion, that I, and what remained of my men, left the bridges' area and headed off towards Ranville. As we marched over the canal bridge in the middle of the night, the snipers having been put out of action by the dark, I found myself glancing back at the distinctive bulk of the bridge that had come to mean so much to me. We all felt a kind of sadness at leaving this place where we had achieved so much only to hand it over to the men of the Warwicks. Bill Bailey described it rather well in the years that followed when he said, 'You see, we rather felt that it was ours'.

We made our way in the pitch black of night over the Orne River bridge and came to a division in the road. There is a roundabout there today with numerous helpful signs, but in 1944 there was no indication which of the roads went to

Ranville and, after a discussion, a decision was taken to carry straight on. But in fact it was the right hand fork that we should have taken. In this way we missed Ranville and skirted around the outside of the village, ending up at another junction, at which my instincts told me we should turn right. We found we were approaching a hamlet but there was no way of knowing which one it was and I decided to send Sweeney ahead with a corporal to see if there was any sign of the battalion. As the two men went into the hamlet, which was in fact, Hérouvillette, they saw a large bulk in the road ahead and realized to their horror that it was a German armoured vehicle. Tod Sweeney realized in a second that this couldn't be Ranville and began to retreat hurriedly. A sentry challenged them and firing started. Covered by the corporal's fire, Sweeney managed to return to me and the 'D' Company group. I realized our mistake and we went around the other way and eventually found Ranville. It seemed that the Regiment had been obliged to be in a different place to the one that had been agreed back in England, because the chateau they had selected as a suitable HQ was being fired on by the enemy. We reported to Battalion HQ in Ranville in the early hours of 7 June and, shortly afterwards, my spirits were given the most tremendous boost because shortly after we arrived in walked Brian Priday and Tony Hooper. I cannot express my delight at seeing them. Priday told us their story over a welcome cup of tea and something to eat.

Their glider had taken off from Tarrant Rushton, just like all the others and crossed the channel and the coast of France. Unfortunately, it turned out that a navigation error was made by the tug aircraft, which resulted in their glider being released in the wrong place. The pilots had been confused by cloud and darkness as they went through their landing sequence, but had spotted a river and a bridge and brought the glider down right by the river and up against the bridge. At that point, they had no way of knowing that they were in the wrong area completely, and it wasn't until Priday got out of the glider and looked around, that it dawned on him that they had landed by the wrong river. They were unable to retrieve any of their stores or equipment from the glider as the Germans manning the small bridge came to their senses, and began to fire rounds of machine-gun fire into the glider. Priday's men took cover in the nearby hedgerow and decided what to do. The pilots were distraught at landing in the wrong place, but Priday assured them that it wasn't their fault and that they had, in fact made an excellent landing. At that point, they saw paratroopers dropping close by. Contact was made with them and six men joined the group. With the maps that Priday had managed to bring with him and in conference with the glider pilots, telling him exactly what they had seen as they came into land, they were able to work out where they were. They had come down on the River Dives in the area of Varraville Bridge.

Priday then worked out a plan of action. He realized that they would, of course, have missed the assault at the canal and Orne bridges by that time, and so he decided that they would first take the nearby bridge from the small force

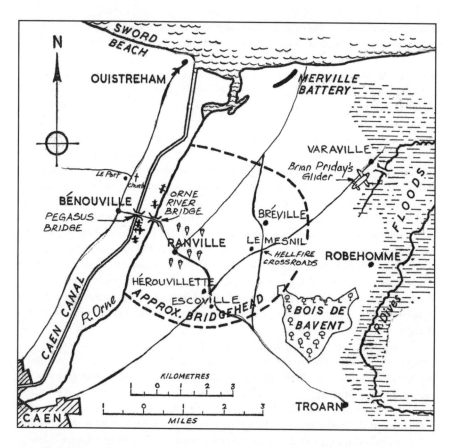

guarding it and then they would attempt to make the cross-country journey to rejoin the battalion at Ranville. The men succeeded in taking the bridge after a short battle during which the enemy guarding it were killed. After that was accomplished, Priday decided on their route and sent Hooper and two men ahead to recce a small wood they needed to pass through. After a short while the two soldiers came back, gave the 'all clear' and said that Lieutenant Hooper was waiting for them in the wood. Just then they all heard the sound of boots coming down the roadway and jumped for cover in the hedge. Priday heard Hooper's voice talking unnaturally loudly and realized why when he saw that Hooper had his hands in the air and was being prodded along by a German soldier with a gun. Hooper contrived to have the German clearly silhouetted against the skyline and Priday took aim with his Sten gun, shouted 'Jump Tony!' and then fired. Hooper leapt aside and the German fell dead, but he must have pressed the trigger of his gun as he fell and Sergeant Titch Rayner got a bullet in the shoulder, the next round hitting and ricocheting off Priday's map-case. Titch would live to a ripe old age to tell the story of being the only British soldier to be shot on D-Day by a dead German.

Alerted by the gunfire, enemy troops approached, firing at them, and Priday and his men all made a run for it, just one of their number being killed. The area around them in the Dives valley was then an area of swampland, since the Germans had flooded it. Therefore, they were obliged to wade and occasionally even swim as they made their way with difficulty in the right direction. They found it very tiring, trying to hold their weapons and ammunition up out of the water and it was a chilly night. After about two hours they saw a farmhouse that had been left marooned on a higher piece of ground in the marsh. As they watched, an Allied aircraft crash-landed close by them and Priday sent out a party to rescue the pilot, who subsequently joined the group. Approaching the farm cautiously, they found a French family living there and were able to tell them who they were and to obtain information on the enemy presence in the area. The family were very poor and had nothing to offer the soldiers except a hayloft where they all covered themselves in hay to soak up some of the damp in their clothing, and became warm enough to sleep a little until it was light.

In the morning, the French farmer gave them some milk, which they drank gratefully, having eaten and drunk nothing since landing. The farmer's niece offered to guide them to Robbehome, which was in the direction of Ranville and they set out. In Robbehome the group were joined by some lost Canadian paratroopers and other stranded soldiers. By now around forty-five men strong, Priday's group headed off for the Bois de Bavent, which meant more swimming and wading through the flooded areas. Suddenly, the wet and exhausted men saw at some distance the unmistakeable sight of the Ulsters and the Regiment flying in, which was very encouraging for them at that moment. Many of the men cheered. Finally, the group made it to Ranville via the hamlet of Le Mesnil. It was dark by the time they arrived. There Priday reported to his battalion HQ and declared that he and Hooper's platoon were missing no more! They found the rest of us there, having just arrived ourselves, and a joyful reunion took place. But the men had to be allowed a few hours' rest and so they were directed to a house used by the Germans as a bunkhouse. We then found some mattresses for ourselves to have a rest in the nearby chateau for the remaining two hours of the night.

When we'd reported to battalion HQ in Ranville, I learned to my dismay that Colonel Roberts had smashed his leg in a bad landing in the glider and was unable to walk. He had handed over command to his 2 I/C Mark Darrell-Brown and had been invalided back to England. I was not too sure how I felt about this, for I did not have the confidence in Darrell-Brown that I had in Colonel Roberts. This was a personality problem peculiar to myself, for no one else ever voiced any misgivings about him and he was well liked in the Regiment. However, like it or lump it that was the situation and I just had to put up with it.

141

On the morning of 7 June 'D' Company awoke in Ranville and made ready to move out. From my original force of 181, I was now down to 110 men, whom I reorganized into four platoons – the remnants of 23 Platoon under Lieutenant Tod Sweeney, 22 Platoon under Lieutenant Tony Hooper, 24 Platoon under Corporal Godbold and 25 Platoon under Corporal Caine. I decided that I would keep an eye on 25 Platoon and Brian Priday would do the same for 24 Platoon. The battalion left at around 05.00 with 'C' Company leading and orders to occupy and hold the village of Escoville along with 'A' Company.

The battalion moved through Hérouvillette very slowly. It had been decided that 'D' Company should be kept in reserve, being already 'blooded' by our battle experience at the bridges, and because we'd only had a couple of hours' rest. 'C' Company reported Hérouvillette clear of the enemy, and were then left as a firm base there as 'A' and 'B' Companies advanced cautiously towards Escoville, which was a typical Norman hamlet with a main street of cottages and farms and many small lanes crossing it. But the Germans were already there, concealed and waiting until the leading platoons arrived, when they opened fire with Spandau machine guns sited on a slope south-east of the village. Under heavy fire, the battalion continued to advance into Escoville, with 'A' Company to the west of the village, and 'B' Company in the centre. 'D' Company was obliged to spread out and advance by what was known as 'fire and movement' tactics through 'C' Company in Hérouvillette and to take up positions to the east of Escoville. It was around 11.00 when 'D' Company reached the centre of the village. It was deserted, the villagers having taken to their cellars, aware that a battle was about to take place around their homes. It must have been terrifying for them as they heard the British soldiers occupying the houses above their heads on either side of the village street.

I quickly set up a makeshift company HQ in a farmyard on the main street. There was no communication with regimental HQ because they had lost all their wireless sets in the glider landings and communications therefore depended on runners alone. If a runner couldn't make it through to them then the company was stranded with no information from the commanders. This is effectively what happened to us that terrible day in Escoville. I set out to check up on 25 Platoon as I had planned, and found it in a farm building. From the top-floor of an outbuilding, I spotted some movement and saw that the soldiers there were dressed in camouflage flying smocks like we wore. Assuming that it was men from 'A' Company, I sent a man out to make contact, but he was immediately fired on. It was then realized that the men we'd seen were 21st Panzer troops and I briefly wondered why Army Intelligence had neglected to warn us that the Panzer Divisions were similarly dressed to British troops. I sent a runner off to RHQ to confirm the identity of the enemy troops.

I then visited my forward platoon, some of whom were pinned down by enemy snipers in the centre of Escoville. We were sheltering in the lee of a stone wall and could hear the sound of vehicles. I wanted to see what was going on and tried to look round the end of the wall with binoculars. Sweeney said hurriedly to me, 'Watch out, John – those snipers are deadly' but I was already moving out of the cover of the wall as a shot rang out and they saw me fall backwards, unconscious and bleeding from the head. At first, they all thought that I was dead but after a minute or so, I began to groan and Tod shouted 'He's alive! For God's sake get him back to the RAP!' I was assisted, dazed and stumbling to the farmyard where we'd set up the company HQ. Priday had the medical orderly look at my wound and it was discovered that I'd had the most amazing escape. The sniper's fatal accuracy had pierced my helmet from front to back, the bullet actually grazing the top of my head. Photographs 'in the field' would show that my hair was particularly abundant on the top of my head at that time. A man with less hair would have been killed. As it was, I could legitimately claim to have had my hair parted for me by a German bullet. The scar on the top of my head could clearly be seen into old age and my helmet, or 'battle bowler' as they were known, with its bullet holes back and front, was to be displayed in future years in the Airborne Museum, for visitors to marvel at the survival of the man that had worn it that day in Escoville.

But I found myself no longer able to fully command 'D' Company for I'd lost much blood from the head wound and was probably concussed. By that time it was evident that 'B' Company was nowhere to be seen and 'D' Company seemed to be surrounded by the enemy. We had heard nothing from RHQ. Word was received from an NCO from 25 Platoon that he and another man had managed to crawl forward towards the enemy gun that was causing so much damage, and to the south-west of the village had sighted German armoured vehicles that they thought must be from 21st Panzer. A runner was sent off to RHQ for artillery backup, or even to get the naval bombardment from the coast that was still being used to shell the enemy lines, to target the German advance into Escoville. I recall that later on the area was indeed bombarded – 'stonked' was the word we used, but at that time in the early afternoon we had no feedback from the Regiment at all. Lacking wireless communication and surrounded by the enemy my men were as helpless as any forward infantry company would have been almost thirty years before in the First World War. In the Ox & Bucks' *Quarterly Journal* for February 1945, when a detailed account of the fighting during those days was reported, 'D' Company was described as ' heavily engaged at the time, became cut off and had a spirited battle with the enemy'. The reality to those of us finding ourselves in that situation was not quite so cut and dried.

At about 15.00 hours the enemy attacked from the east as well as the south and all platoons suffered many casualties. At 16.00 a runner from RHQ at last managed to get to my beleaguered company and told us that we should have withdrawn to Hérouvillette through 'C' Company who had been brought forward to cover the withdrawal from Escoville. There were many casualties from all companies, and Priday and I organized the withdrawal of 'D' Company as quickly as possible, taking with us as many of the wounded as we could under fire. Once back in Hérouvillette some of the men were sent back to salvage some of their precious stores that had been left there in our hurried withdrawal. We desperately needed the food rations, ammunition and medical supplies and it was considered a priority to retrieve them as well as any wounded men. The troops moved with extreme caution, but found the enemy had withdrawn to the south of the village. Thus they were able to pile all the stores into a cart and drag it back to Hérouvillette. Despite being spotted by an enemy fighter aircraft at one point in their journey and fired on, they managed to get the stores back to the company.

Brian Priday and I established an HQ in Hérouvillette in a wooden caravan parked in a farmyard and counted up our casualties. It was to be the saddest reckoning of my life, for we had lost fifty-eight men, killed, wounded or missing. That represented nearly half of my company, and I nursed my head wound feeling a profound grief and depression. We were holed-up in Hérouvillette for about four days, which was time enough for me to sink into a deep trough of near-despair over what had befallen 'D' Company since our glorious success of capturing the two bridges. It had happened so damn quickly and I was engulfed in an agony of remorse and bewilderment.

I had been led to believe back in England, that the superbly trained crack-force that we had become, was to be repatriated as soon as possible to be used again to attack bridges. Instead we found ourselves fighting an old-style infantry battle, ditch to hedge, house to barn, under intense fire from an enemy that was highly trained, motivated and armed to the teeth. We'd been cut off from the Regiment and found ourselves surrounded by the enemy, totally unprepared to fight under those conditions, just a few hours after taking the bridges. I felt bitterness and confusion in those days worse than I had ever known in my life and I found myself unable to sleep, so tortured was I by my thoughts. Somewhere deep inside me I suppose I realized how lucky I had been to survive the sniper's bullet through my helmet and I must also have worked out that strategically things were not going quite the way that Eisenhower and Montgomery had planned. The Germans' counter-attack had been much more ferocious and effective than the Allied High Command had anticipated. They had been confident of having the enemy on the run and retreating towards their homeland within days; a week at most. Instead it would take us almost three months of gruelling fighting to secure Normandy, and 'D' Company, or what was left of it, would be part of that campaign.

I sent a party of men back into Escoville to retrieve the bodies of our dead troops. They were buried in the cemetery in Hérouvillette and their graves would be visited and their memories honoured for over sixty years afterwards. I never got over the devastating shock of what happened to 'D' Company in Escoville on 7 June 1944. I never again entered that village without experiencing a feeling of loss and grief and it even overshadowed the triumph of 'Pegasus Bridge' for me, although I rarely shared this emotion with others. To this day, the shell damage and bullet holes can be seen in the stonework of the old barns and houses of Escoville, and the inhabitants of the village have long grown used to seeing visitors standing among them, pointing out the scars left from that distant battle. I took my daughter Penny through there when she was in her late teens in 1962, showing her the bullet holes and where we had sheltered from the enemy. I had been grim as I pointed out to her the wall where I had so nearly met my death. Penny sensed my distress and must have wondered at the contrast in my demeanour from the relaxed confidence I displayed when I was in Bénouville, sitting outside the Café Gondrée with my good friends Georges and Thérèse Gondrée, sipping champagne with them. I never cared to talk very much about Escoville and indeed, only ever wrote about it after some fifty years had passed, realizing that for archive purposes an account should be set down. I asked Tod Sweeney to help me with what was a very short account. I left it for other officers to make their reports and preferred to dwell on the success of Pegasus Bridge.

On 9 June, or D+3 as we called it, a fighting party from 'C' Company was sent back into Escoville to assess the situation. A battle ensued, pushing 'C' Company back towards Hérouvillette into the defensive positions of 'D' Company. My men had constructed some pretty impressive trenches there. The attacking enemy were reinforced with tanks, armoured vehicles and infantry backed up with Me109 fighter aircraft which strafed the area. Fortunately, the battalion had the support of heavy artillery that had arrived from the beaches and was able to repel the enemy, destroying several Panzer Mark 4 tanks with the bombardment. This was encouraging for the Airborne troops and slowly I felt my leadership qualities rising to the task in hand and my enthusiasm begin to return as I talked over my concerns with Brian Priday. Supporting 'C' Company in this battle, some of the men of 'D' Company came across a German armoured car that had been abandoned in a ditch. This was a prize indeed! There was a lot of interest in the vehicle, but it was Priday who managed to get it out of the ditch and drive it back to 'D' Company's HQ in Hérouvillette. It was complete with 20 mm guns and machine guns. I contacted my Adjutant, John Tillett, and asked for permission to try the guns out. Permission was granted. The other companies were not warned about this and there was a fair amount of shouting and consternation until the groan went up 'Stand down! It's only ruddy 'D' Company again!'

Thereafter, this vehicle was used in battle by 'D' Company who also used it to store some of the treasured items that had been 'liberated' by the men. On one of the changes of our position in the coming weeks – 'tuppenny ha'penny moves' I called them – as 'D' Company was moved from forward fighting positions at Château St Côme and Bréville, and then back to a rest area for a few days, the vehicle was 'raided' by another company for souvenirs. Unfortunately the set of tools that the Germans had, in their efficient way, left with the armoured car, disappeared at this time and when somebody had a minor crash in it, we were unable to get it going again. It was left with a REME sergeant who allegedly 'swapped it for a packet of fags' and 'D' Company never saw the vehicle again. I was very disappointed about this and remarked regretfully in a letter to the *Quarterly Journal* that it would have been 'grand to have got it home with our many other odds and ends, although getting it up that scramble net at Arromanches would have been a bit of a job!'

On 10 June the Germans moved forward from Bréville towards Ranville but were driven back by the tanks and artillery of 7th Para Battalion who were joined during the night by the 51st Highland Division. They had been fighting in North Africa and were perhaps battle-weary from their experiences there, and were to suffer for it. The task of the Airborne Forces was to protect the bridgehead east of the River Orne, but the enemy held the village of Bréville which stood on a ridge overlooking the British positions in Ranville, the Orne Valley and towards the beaches at the mouth of the River Orne. The Divisional Commander of the Airborne, General Gale was determined that Bréville must be taken and set out to do so with the Black Watch attacking from the south-west. But they failed in their attempt. General Gale then decided to use a company of the already depleted 12th Battalion Para. Regiment, the Devons, to assist, along with a squadron of Sherman tanks and they attacked when the enemy might least have expected them to on the evening of 12 June.

For 'D' Company, waiting for orders in Hérouvillette and constantly enduring heavy bombardment from the nearby enemy, this was a difficult time. On 13 June the Regiment was ordered to move to Château St Côme, about one mile south of Bréville to relieve 9 Para Brigade. As we moved into our new positions we encountered problems from enemy snipers and night patrols were organized to try to find them. The patrols found devastation and carnage everywhere from the battles that had taken place attempting to capture Bréville. There were bodies of both British and German soldiers lying all around in various stages of damage and decay, and the patrols saw sickening sights that would stay imprinted on their memories for the rest of their lives. Many of the dead belonged to the 51st Highlanders. They appeared to have been practically massacred. Tom Packwood said that the lads thought they were easy targets for the snipers because their uniform had a white webbing band diagonally across their backs, often with their white enamel mugs slung there as well, and these made ideal targets, even in the dark. But many of the dead had not a mark on them, just sitting eerily still and silent, caught by the mighty blast of a shell exploding close by and killed by concussion, forever at rest half-way through whatever they had been doing when the shell landed. I particularly remember coming across one group of dead soldiers in a trench who had been passing the time having a game of cards. The playing cards were still held in their hands and their lifeless eyes stared at them. The patrols retrieved the bodies and buried them as best they could in graves, taking the men's identity tags back for records. But there were also many bodies of farm animals killed in the fields and farms overtaken by the battle, and burying them was much more difficult. The stable block of the chateau had been set alight by the shelling and many pedigree racehorses had perished in the fire, trapped inside their loose boxes. They had been there some days, there was an appalling stench and we had clouds of flies to tolerate, as the men dragged the bodies across to a deep shell hole and covered them with enough soil and lime to prevent the flies becoming even more of a problem. These were the dreadful tasks that all the soldiers found themselves dealing with, in between the continual bombardment, and the harrowing memories lived on within each of us.

We called the heavy enemy shelling 'stonking', and I found that over the weeks that followed, some of the men broke down and could not take the constant noise and threat of imminent death during a raid. They became 'bomb happy' – a strange phrase to describe a man who broke down and lost his senses with the incessant barrage of heavy artillery and explosions that showered dirt and shrapnel and left our heads ringing with the deafening noise. Most soldiers got used to it day after day, but some did not and went mad, and became useless for duty and a burden to the rest of the company. They were dealt with by the medical officer and evacuated. But it affected me badly to see good lads turn into quaking, hysterical wrecks and this period of 'stand-off' with the enemy put immense pressure on all who took part in it.

On 16 June a German shell hit a tree close to one of our trenches and some shrapnel landed on Gammon bombs lying in the nearby trench. Although the men had orders to keep the Gammon bombs close by them for use in the event of a tank attack, most of those in charge had placed them in a cache close by their trench, just in case they were hit by shrapnel. But our Company Sergeant Major Flexon, in charge of the trench near where the German shell had landed, was known to carry out procedures to the letter, and he had placed his Gammon bombs in the trench with him. They exploded and Flexon was killed outright. He had been an excellent CSM and a stickler for duty, coming down hard on any of the men who tried to cut corners or did a job sloppily. A group of the troops watched as Flexon's body was carried past them on a stretcher. His arm was hanging down and as the stretcher bearers made their way across the uneven ground, the dead man's arm swung back and forth rhythmically. 'There he goes,' I heard one of them say. 'Good old Sergeant Major Flexon – regimental to the last.' I realized that they meant no disrespect for that brave man, rather the reverse in fact, but used to so much destruction and carnage all around them, the men used black humour to conceal their feelings.

There was another casualty on the same occasion, for shrapnel from the Gammon bombs had flown in all directions when they had exploded and a piece of it had hit me in the back. I was dispatched to a First Aid post where a surgeon cleaned me up and dressed the wound. I had been left unconscious on the table after this treatment and listed for evacuation to England. Just at that moment, there was another heavy 'stonk' and I came round with the noise of the raid to find everyone had run for cover and left me lying there quite alone. I decided very fast indeed that I would be better off back in the trenches with 'D' Company and I heaved myself off the table and went out of the tent to find my driver who was taking cover beneath the Jeep. I ordered him to drive me back to Château St Côme immediately, and this is what he did.

However the paperwork at the First Aid unit had recorded me as having been sent back to a hospital in England and, in consequence, all my mail was redirected to the UK. The Army considered it vital for the morale of the troops that they receive their mail regularly and I had been receiving almost daily letters from Joy. However, after this incident, when I was wounded and in pain, the letters from Joy ceased. With news of bombing raids and the 'doodlebug' or V1 rocket attacks on southern England, I was terrified that my precious family would be killed if the *Luftwaffe* attacked the Morris Motor Works so close to our home. My daily letters stopping so suddenly could have meant that something terrible had happened to Joy, and I was very anxious about my family. My diary for the days just after I was wounded state bluntly 'acute depression'. My junior officers confirmed that I was laid very low for several days as I tried desperately to rest-up, and give my wound a chance to heal and accept the adversities of war and the loss of my men. Brian Priday assumed command of 'D' Company again for a couple of days to give me an opportunity for my energy to return and spirits to lift once more.

It took a fortnight before it was realized that I had left the First Aid post and instead of being evacuated to a hospital in England, had returned to my unit amidst the battle for Normandy. Eventually the mistake was put right and I received a parcel of Joy's letters about two weeks later, that had been held at the Army Post Office while my whereabouts was established.

Low as I was at that time, it was fortunate indeed that I did not know that while I was recovering from my wound in France, in Oxford my wife had received a telegram from the Army. The telegram should have read that I had suffered a 'mortar wound' but the telegraphist had made a typing error and Joy read that her husband had received 'a mortal wound'. After her initial shock, her instincts told her that there was something odd about this piece of blunt information, and she ran next-door to her kindly elderly neighbours, the Wormalds, for their advice. It took them about an hour to get through to the right person at the War Office who apologized profusely for the error and confirmed that Major John Howard had been wounded in a mortar attack, receiving a shrapnel wound in the back, and had been sent back to a hospital in the south of England. Joy asked which hospital so that she could visit and, after much rustling of paperwork, the War Office clerk said that, for some reason she really didn't know, but said she would 'look into it and telephone back'. It took several days for Joy to find out that I had never left France and was, in fact, once more commanding my company in Normandy.

The heavy 'stonking' continued around Château St Côme, keeping us all in the trenches for hours at a time. Patrols were sent out at quieter times and they returned to report that German troops had been sighted in the area of the chateau. At 20.00 hours on 19 June, a frightful whining and howling sound was heard coming from the skies and we realized that the enemy was using the terrifying new weapon that had been euphemistically nicknamed 'Moaning Minnies'. These rocket-propelled shells were deliberately designed to strike fear and dread into the recipients. They were launched several at a time on a high trajectory into the sky, packed with shrapnel to do maximum damage when they landed, and emitting a screeching, wailing sound as they fell back to earth. It was a fiendish invention and intended to terrify and demoralize as well as cause death and damage. The attack lasted for around half an hour on this occasion leaving those troops not killed or injured, with shattered nerves. Afterwards we brewed tea in mess tins, stirring in the condensed milk, some of the men with very shaky hands indeed, and cigarettes were lit and inhaled gratefully. Billy Gray said that even those chaps that didn't smoke, started at that time.

There was a three-day period of very stormy weather and all of us were soaked to the skin by heavy rain, having no way of drying our clothes, which added to the discomfort. Sometime on 19 June, the leader of 'B' Company decided to move towards enemy positions in the nearby wood to carry out a 'feint attack', theoretically in order to discover the enemy positions by drawing their fire. 'B' Company's OC, 'Flaps' Edmunds, was wounded in the attack and repatriated. The OC of 'S' Company, Teddy Favell was told to take charge of 'B' Company and as he made his rounds, introducing himself to his new company, he too was hit by enemy mortar fire and killed. Thus, it was decided that Brian Priday would be promoted to take command of 'B' Company and I was thrust back into command of 'D' Company, barely three days after my shrapnel wound. I did not have time to dwell on losing Priday, both a companion and trusted junior officer. This was, in fact, to be the end of my military association with Brian Priday, because he was wounded later during a platoon raid with 'B' Company and ended the war in hospital back in England.

One by one my junior officers, all good friends to me, would be wounded or transferred and 'D' Company was left in the Normandy trenches not knowing how long it would take to break through the enemy lines.

Chapter 12

20 June to November 1944: Normandy, Returning Home and the End of the Road

On 20 June 'D' Company was ordered back from the battle front to the 'rest area' half a mile or so behind the lines at Le Mesnil. The weather changed for the better and in warm sunshine the men were able to wash lighter items of clothing and dry them in the sun as well as drying out their battledress. I remember it being a great relief to be able to sort oneself out in this way. On occasions, a tin bath in a barn partly filled with shallow water, might serve as a wash house for us all but there were actually some showers rigged up in a large orchard at Le Mesnil. However, being so close to the front meant that we were still subjected to 'stonking' from the enemy, who did not intend that we should be allowed to rest properly. The one event to cheer me up at this time was the return to duty of Colonel Roberts, who took command of the battalion again. I had sent a letter to the Ox & Bucks *Quarterly Journal* which appeared in November 1944's issue, written in the rather breezy, stiff-upper-lip tone we all adopted and was typical of the time. It read, 'The Regiment's still in very good form, rather disillusioned about not being relieved but nevertheless wearing the disappointment well. At least the Division has the record of having been in the line for thirty-six days without a break!' This quote shows clearly how we had all anticipated that fairly soon after the successful attack on the bridges, we would have been returned to the UK for our expertise and training to be utilized again attacking other bridges, rather than being left in the field, used as just another infantry company in the 6 Airborne Brigade. After the all too brief excitement of our success capturing the two bridges, I was inclined to be 'disillusioned' indeed. Although I had dated this letter 10 July 1944, I stated that it had been begun on 'D+14' while in rest camp, and that would have been Tuesday, 20 June at Le Mesnil, 'my very first opportunity to sit down for a minute'. I went on to say that

I 'threw together some notes on the capture of the bridges', which I had wanted to send to be published in the journal but that permission was not granted. However I wrote about the assault on the bridges in my letter to the *Quarterly Journal* saying:

> It was a grand party. Gosh, I was lucky to be selected for the job. My chaps were magnificent, from the moment we pranged, everything really went according to plan ... Intelligence reports were first-class, no stone was left unturned for our show ... we have agitated for one of the bridges to be called Light Infantry Bridge, [now called Horsa Bridge] the other has already been elaborately sign-boarded 'Pegasus Bridge' ... Our Glider pilots were absolutely magnificent ... put the gliders down in the exact spot indicated by me during briefing. I am told that Russian General Staff who have seen the gliders would not believe they were put down at night on such uneven ground and suggested they'd been put there as a show piece. My chaps are furious.

I had also mentioned the difficulties faced by 7 Para Brigade with bad weather, saying:

> ... they came down all over the place, so they never actually reached us first; for the same reason our relief was nigh on two hours late, 3.30 am instead of 1.30 am.

These words to the *Quarterly Journal* were written at the end of June 1944, and should be especially noted by those later members of 7th Para Battalion and indeed, the lady who was then a two year old infant, whose home was liberated by 'D' Company and who, some fifty years after the events, was to claim that my *coup de main* force at the two bridges was relieved at 01.30 by 7th Para. Even allowing for these later claimants deliberately using the discrepancy between French time and Greenwich Mean Time to confuse the timing, this testament stands true as the earliest account of the Airborne assault on the two bridges. About my own wounds I referred only briefly as having had 'a couple of near-misses but I'm too thick skinned'.

'D' Company were to remain at the rest-camp at Le Mesnil from 20 – 26 June. Tom Packwood, who had been in Den Brotheridge's platoon and had been promoted to corporal on D+4 in Hérouvillette, recalled the average soldier's life in the field in Normandy with great clarity. Tom said that the 'compo rations' consisted of tinned bacon, stewed steak, and the 'bully beef' which was what we now call 'corned beef'. He recalled with particular fondness a tinned vegetable mix that was, for some reason called 'Maconnachies'. There were also sweet items in tins, like rice pudding and fruits such as apricots. The platoon sergeant was in charge of the food, having '28 Man Compo Rations' issued to him for distribution to his men. But there were no potatoes and in particular, no way of obtaining fresh bread.

On 26 June the Regiment was ordered back to the front line, to occupy the village of Bréville, over which a fierce battle had been fought with the enemy in the days following D-Day. Once more, the men were set to work digging trenches and tidying up the area. We were to stay there until 8 July when we were ordered back to positions at Château St Côme. On 4 July, I was informed that I was to be awarded a Distinguished Service Order for the bridge operation and that the ribbon would be presented to me in the field in two days by no other person but Field Marshal Montgomery himself. Monty duly arrived and inspected the men, his words of praise and encouragement on such occasions always proving very popular with the soldiers he met. I commented in my letter to the *Quarterly Journal* dated 10 July 1944 that, 'I felt rather self-conscious about my own ribbon, I felt it ought to have gone to Den Brotheridge, who was killed dashing across the bridge. He has an MC.' It is interesting to note that the other DSO awarded in the battalion went to Mark Darrell-Brown as CO, even though he did not arrive in Normandy until the evening of 6 June.

The Army moved in a mysterious way when it came to handing out its battle honours and it was the custom to award medals according to rank other than in very exceptional circumstances. An OC was supposed to submit a recommendation list for medals for his company within a day or so of the event, often while still in the thick of battle. The importance of doing this and making sure all the names on his list were included was often not appreciated by such an officer until it was too late. Sometimes a group of men assigned to another company for a particular operation, such as the Sappers and glider pilots were for the assault on the bridges, might 'slip through the net' where battle honours were concerned, since their own commanders were not present to put forward special recommendations, and they would just end up with a relatively minor award. I confess that in later years I felt at that time that I was still possibly regarded as a bit of an upstart and a rough diamond in certain quarters and my recommendations for battle honours were not given as much attention as they might otherwise have been. I felt particularly bitter about this in respect of the glider pilots who landed five of the gliders so accurately, especially the pilots of No. 1 Glider and in particular Sergeant Jim Wallwork, whose flying earned him such high praise from the Air Chief Marshal. I also felt very strongly that my platoon leaders should have received higher awards for their leadership and bravery, and that Den Brotheridge should certainly have been singled out for a high honour. There was some later technicality that ruled that Brotheridge had died as a result of 'wounds received in battle' and not been killed outright. I have to say that I have no time for that kind of nonsense. In my time left in the Army after we returned to the UK, I did my best to put right what I considered to be a notable wrong, and to get the medals awarded to Brotheridge, Priday and Wallwork in particular, upgraded. I wrote many letters to the War Office on this matter but to no avail. It grieved me very much that Brian Priday wrote to me in 1945 asking why I had not recommended him for a higher award, and I always felt that it soured our relationship thereafter. But the fact remains, that the actual decisions about which medals would be awarded and to whom, were beyond the control of an officer at my level of command.

Back at Château St Côme, once again the men were obliged to dig new trenches. They took care with this task knowing that the continual bombardment would require them to spend much time in them. They would roof the trenches where possible using anything lying around the site, from branches to wooden planks and corrugated iron sheeting. I strongly believed in keeping the men in the picture as much as possible on the current positions of the enemy and Allied forces. A photograph exists of me at Château St Côme, bending down to a make-shift board leaning up against a low wall, with a hand-drawn diagram pinned onto the board, and a pointer in my hand; behind me lie the blackened and charred remains of a burned-out building which was the stable block.

The camera that took this photograph was a German one 'liberated' at some point from a dead soldier. Removing valuables from the bodies of the enemy was considered the natural spoils of war on both sides. The camera was used to record those exceptional times, giving brief, often blurred glimpses of the men of 'D' Company at Château St Côme. In one shot four soldiers are standing around a motley arrangement of barbed wire and a small wooden hen coop housing three flop-eared rabbits which were being kept to supplement the 'compo rations'. Fresh meat was a very welcome addition to our diet as any livestock discovered if they strayed too close to the soldiers' camps.

On 11 July, Wally Parr was hit by shrapnel and taken back to hospital in England, and all of us found ourselves missing his ready cockney wit. The following day was my son Terry's second birthday and I recall feeling very blue about not being at home for it. Also, my good friend and platoon leader, Tod Sweeney was injured by mortar fire at this time and disappeared to the First Aid post and thence to hospital in England. But the day did bring some relief in the shape of fresh bread that was sent out to us. The day before had seen the arrival of real tea instead of the cubes we'd all been using until then, and the men were considerably cheered by the improved rations.

Two days later the news came through that Caen had finally fallen to the Allies. This was a considerable morale-booster for all the soldiers on the front. So much so that on 16 July, I decided that some of the men could accompany me on a quick visit on foot down to the newly named Pegasus Bridge. I had a strong urge to return there to see again the scene of our triumph and revisit the wrecked gliders; I wanted a last look before time erased the traces of our landing. So I took a small group of the men and we walked cautiously down the three or four miles to the bridges, taking the German camera with us to record the occasion.

One particular photograph was taken on that occasion that was to become very famous, of No. 1 glider with two figures standing by it – my wireless-operator, Corporal Ted Tappenden of 'Ham and Jam' fame and me. We also took shots over Pegasus Bridge from the Ranville side and a long shot, taken from the other side of the marshy pond back towards the bridge with the three smashed-up gliders in the field next to it and the café just visible over the canal. At some point in the following month, fighting our way up the Normandy coast towards the Seine, the camera got wet and the film was damaged. I took it to an expert film processor in Oxford and he managed, remarkably for the time, to enhance the negatives. The photographs were saved for posterity as a unique and historic record of 'D' Company's time in Normandy.

On 23 July the Regiment was once again sent back to Le Mesnil to the rest-camp, which at least gave us all time to clean up and sort out our kit again. After periods of very wet weather followed by hot sunshine and, being so close to the marshes created by the Germans to hamper an invasion force, we were plagued by mosquitoes. After all the flies that had flourished with so many dead farm animals, horses and men around, it was a real burden to have to deal with the buzzing, biting insects that arrived in clouds. One of the wags said it was like the seven plagues in the bible – 'It'll be locusts next – you see!'

We were back in the trenches in Bréville by 30 July where we spent the following week being bombarded at intervals with shells, mortars and 'Moaning Minnies'. Then, on 7 August, the men were ordered to pack up ready to move again and were glad to be leaving Bréville. Had they known as I did, that they were being moved down to the notoriously dangerous area known as 'Hellfire Corner' they might not have been so ready to move out. Hellfire Corner was a crossroads about a mile to the south of Château St Côme, situated on the roads that led west towards Caen, north to Bréville and south to Troarne. The trenches there were constantly occupied by one force after the other, steadfastly defending this strategic position from an enemy equally determined to overrun it. It was well named. At this time, the battalion took over from the Devons, known to all as 'the Swedes' because of their rural associations. There no one could leave their trenches and move freely around because the 'stonking' was almost continuous and it was far too dangerous and pointless for even the usual sniper patrols to be carried out. Thus it was a relief when the orders came for us to return to the rest area at Le Mesnil on 13 August for two days. The men obeyed orders but amongst themselves had begun to wonder what was going on. But it was, in fact, good news – the best news, for it seemed apparent that at long last the Germans were failing in their determination to hold onto their positions and were giving way.

I finally received the orders to 'paddle' on 19 August 1944, after several frust-rating days waiting to be told to move. The expression, 'paddle', was used to describe the eastward advance up the coast of Normandy towards the Seine, crossing the flooded areas of the Dives valley. Our orders were to go towards Varaville where we would find lorries waiting to transport us to the town of Troarne, so that we could cross the River Dives. All the bridges in that area had been blown by the Paras in order to make the German retreat as difficult as possible. The area was still occupied by pockets of German resistance and many snipers and the men of 'D' Company had to move with great caution. A day later we were in Varaville and boarded the trucks that took us the six miles or so south to Troarne. There the bridge had also been blown up, but a pontoon bridge had been erected over the river and the men crossed it on foot. We proceeded to make for a village called Grangues and then to Gonneville-sur-Mer. In my diary I recorded the route we took, moving through a small place called Le Croix d' Heuland towards Vauville, Bionville and Tourgeville.

By 23 August we were approaching the village of St Arnoult, aiming for the River Toques just beyond it. The men called this part of the Normandy countryside 'Hellfire Hill' and several of them remained there for evermore, buried in a small and serene cemetery overlooking the sea. We had to advance up a hillside that left us completely without cover of any kind and being continuously fired on by self-propelled guns, probably 88 mm, by the enemy in a nearby hilltop position. There were many casualties before we reached the outskirts of St Arnoult. I recorded that we were the leading company to cross the river at the small town of Touques and 'were fêted all the way', spending the night at a hamlet called Le Parquet where we were fed chicken legs. However, there was little time for enjoying the fruits of our victory for the next objective was the village of Manneville-la-Raoult.

The battle for Manneville as it turned out, was to be our last encounter with the enemy in Normandy, but it was ferocious and in some cases fatal. I remember with regret that we lost Lieutenant Pat Bulford in the fighting there and that we were all exhausted afterwards as we spent the night in the village. We reached our objective of Foulbec, and the town was taken by the Airborne Forces on 27 August. Standing on the ridge, we could see the estuary of the Seine ahead of us. Reports reached us that the retreating Germans were scrambling to get over the Seine but by then they were being captured or were surrendering in their hundreds.

The men were exhausted and we rested in Foulbec awaiting final orders. In our elevated position overlooking the Seine estuary we could see the battle being played out beneath us, as the retreating Germans received a pounding both from the air and from the artillery. Naturally the enemy was still firing back on the Airborne troops and we had to remain alert and keep our heads down. On 29 August I received the orders I had been waiting for and could now hardly believe and wrote in my diary 'News of going home – can't be true!' We had fought our way up to the Seine, a distance of some forty-five miles, in ten days.

The following few days, waiting to be returned to the UK, seemed endless. On 31 August we handed in some of our kit and then on 2 September, we received orders to proceed to transit camp at Arromanches back down the coast beyond the bridges where we had landed so dramatically. The weary men of 'D' Company boarded the lorries to take us to Arromanches, but the transport annoyed me by being badly arranged and the lorries had hard seats that were hell to sit on for so long. But the men didn't seem to mind; they were just grateful to be going home.

It seemed strange to bump our way back through the countryside that we had so recently been fighting for and the men seemed to sit almost in a dream, feeling that this could not really be happening. The villages and farmland seemed eerily still. If it hadn't been for the occasional bombed-out houses and barns, and the abandoned military vehicles along the roadsides one might have just been able to imagine that the past three months had been a nightmare and we would wake up tomorrow with all our old friends around us again. Eventually we came over the hill and down into the little port of Arromanches. That is when I first saw the Mulberry harbour that had been towed across the channel in sections and erected just offshore at Arromanches to provide the Allies with a floating harbour that could manage the large ships necessary to service so vast an invading army. It was an amazing sight and the men were suitably impressed. But the weather was bad by the time we reached Arromanches, overcast and raining with an increasing wind. We were taken to the beaches and left in a camp there overnight.

The next day the weather was even worse, but we went out to the Mulberry harbour and boarded a landing craft to be ferried out to the troopship which was anchored a mile or so offshore. The sea was very choppy and some of the men started to be sick. They were heavily laden with full kit and it was a miserable business. Then it went from being miserable to being highly dangerous. The only way to board the troopship in such a swell was to wait until the landing craft was taken up on the crest of one wave, and then jump across to grab the rope scramble nets hanging down the side of the much larger vessel. The men then had to climb frantically up the netting, as the landing craft fell away beneath them into the trough of the next wave. They had to get well above the level of the landing craft's next lunge upwards very quickly, in case the two boats struck each other. Reaching the top of the rope netting they were hauled into the troopship. Some soldiers sadly perished during this perilous operation, but fortunately none from my company. Eventually the embarkation was called off for the day in the deteriorating weather conditions, but I reported that I had boarded the troopship at 15.00 hours and that I was 'quite comfortable on board'. We spent that night offshore of Arromanches and the boarding was concluded the following morning. The ship sailed for Southampton at 11.30 on 4 September. Among those soldiers returning home were the forty remaining men of 'D' Company, all that was left from a force of 180 men that had taken off from Tarrant Rushton in gliders, three months before.

We spent the night on the troopship lying offshore and docked at Southampton the following morning, disembarking at 14.30. The Regimental Band was on the quayside playing in the pouring rain to welcome us all home. I recognized at once the figure of Harry Styles waiting with the TCVs and the men scrambled gratefully aboard, out of the rain, to be driven back to Bulford. A couple of the trucks had a detour on the way back and didn't arrive until 21.00 but my Jeep made it back to Bulford much earlier. There was a hot meal waiting for every man after we'd gone back to Spider block to leave our kit. The food tasted wonderful to the tired and disorientated men. I wrote in my diary that I 'had a wonderful call to my Joy, still can't believe it'. Going back into the familiar accommodation huts after their meal and a shower, the men were suddenly made painfully aware of the vacant beds, where the lads who had not returned from France should have been. Some were still in hospital with wounds, but even more had been left behind in Normandy, their names only living on to be carved on to endless rows of white gravestones.

I went to the officers' accommodation and sat heavily in the chair in my old room. I was the only original officer left with 'D' Company, for none of my friends or junior officers returned from Normandy with me. I had lost all of my sergeants and most of the corporals. I had seen my closest friend killed in the first minutes of action in battle. I found myself home, unscathed but for a couple of scars, and I couldn't wait to see my family again. I can remember trying to pray – to thank God for bringing me back alive – but, instead, I put my head in my hands and wept.

The next day, we were all off on disembarkation leave and were to find, on our return to Bulford, that all traces of the men who had not returned were gone and new recruits and officers had filled their places in the accommodation huts. I spent that first day back sorting out the company office but like all the rest, I was longing to get away. I managed to do so by the middle of the evening and gave Johnny Busher and Nick Nicholson a lift back to Oxford. I was home by 23.00. Joy was already pulling the door open and threw herself upon me. We were to enjoy several weeks of bliss at being together again, our pleasure only tempered by the knowledge that I was certain to be posted abroad again fairly soon, for the war was not yet over.

The following days tumbled by in a rush of excited visits and homecoming welcomes. I took Terry out in the Jeep every morning, proud of my little son who stood on the front passenger seat holding onto the frame of the shallow windshield over the dashboard. We visited all my old friends and at the Police station received an especially ecstatic welcome, with many congratulations, for the news of the successful assault on the bridges was becoming well known already. I did not forget to thank my neighbours for all their support for my family while I had been away fighting; Pop and Mrs Wormald and Harold and Mary Collier, who owned a fishmonger's shop locally, had been very kind to Joy. Harold generously offered me the use of their Austin car if I could get hold of the petrol. I looked round at my family and friends and tried to put the bitter losses and arduous struggle in the trenches, the constant bombardment and stink of war, to the back of my mind.

Thus on Sunday, 10 September, we took the Colliers up on their kind offer, having managed to get an allowance of petrol for 300 miles. Our little family set off early for London to visit my parents who were thrilled to see us all. The following day, I used the Jeep to call in on the offices of the Ox & Bucks *Quarterly Journal* to see my friend Graham Greenwell who worked there and was known to all as 'Smoothy' on account of his urbane manner. I gave him the notes on the bridges' operation to be published in the regimental journal and Greenwell was fascinated by this first-hand account.

Back at home Joy was giving the children their tea as well as packing for a quick visit to Church Stretton the next day. I had to pitch in and help her and I think that this was quite possibly my very first taste of hands-on family life. However, we managed to be on the road early, once more borrowing the Colliers' little Austin to drive to Church Stretton where we arrived in time for lunch. Tommy, Betty and Lorna gave us a most tremendous welcome, Lorna quite beside herself to have a new niece as well as a nephew to play with. The weather was kind to us and I recall nostalgically those particular golden days of that fine September, when Joy and I were on top of the world. We were only able to stay one night at Church Stretton before driving carefully back to Oxford the following evening.

On the Thursday, we heard that I could have four extra days' leave and I wondered if this meant that the Regiment was being posted sooner than we'd thought. There had been talk amongst the officers of a posting to Burma to assist in the war in the Far East but this never materialized.

I had no time to dwell on the future for I'd been booked to give a talk on the bridge assault to the Police the following day. It was the first of many such lectures that I would give in the following years. In fact, I would become very used to lecturing on the operation, and was much in demand in later years. But in those early days, I recall being diffident and nervous about my performance and had to force myself to stand in front of an audience and address them. The talk to the Police went down extremely well and I was immensely buoyed up by a standing ovation and shouts of 'Jolly well-done, John!' as if I'd pulled it off single-handed!

As I heard church bells ringing from a nearby steeple the following Sunday, I can remember standing out in our little garden, watching a host of aircraft flying overhead. I recognized immediately that some of them were tugging gliders. 'They're off again,' I thought to myself and went in to tell Joy. It was 17 September and I found out later that it was the 1st Airborne Division off to Arnhem, once again to take bridges and to chase the 'Jerries' out of Holland. My leave was drawing swiftly to a close and I felt the familiar blues descending on me at the prospect of returning to camp. But I made a visit the next day to the family of Lieutenant Pat Bulford, who had been killed just days before we'd left Normandy, and to share their grief.

I made the best of my last day's leave, arriving back at Bulford late at night. I found the rumours of an overseas posting rife. Dick Osborne had been appointed as my new company 2 I/C and there were also new platoon commanders to meet, among them an American called Phil Bordinat. Also I had fifty new recruits to swell the ranks and be trained, most of them having no battle experience. Once again I felt the old enthusiasm welling up in me as I surveyed my new men and was keen to see what they were made of. Because the next day was a Saturday and I had been summoned to see Brigadier Poett to discuss first-hand their experiences at the bridges, I was able to use the Army Jeep once more to slip off home to Oxford for the afternoon. I got home at 14.00, catching Joy by surprise, and we had a lovely evening together before I left at 23.00 to drive back to Bulford.

At a Thanksgiving Church Parade the following morning, I was suddenly and painfully made aware of the gaping holes in our ranks. After the exhilaration of homecoming, it hit me anew just how many friends had gone. My prayers were thus sadder, wiser and my thanks profound.

In the week that followed I found myself once more in the routine of training and administration that had filled my time in the years before the invasion, and it gave me an unsettling feeling of déjà vu. On the Wednesday news came through of the disastrous glider landings at Arnhem, and I wondered how our pilots, who were sure to have been in action again for that raid, had fared. The Airborne had been pulled out I recorded in my diary, and later Montgomery said that the operation had failed due to lack of backing from the American generals; their forces arriving too late. I wrote '1,800 left out of 8,000!' A lot of mistakes were made at Arnhem, and the American historian Stephen Ambrose, writing forty years later, would comment that it was a pity that 'D' Company of the 6th Airborne had been 'wasted' fighting in the trenches of Normandy, and had not been utilized to take the bridge at Nijmegen instead. 'If the *coup de main* party had landed to take that bridge, then the American paratroopers would not have had to fight a desperate battle for it' wrote Ambrose in his book *Pegasus Bridge*.

But it certainly did not occur to me at the time to think that way, and back at Bulford I went into the old routine of company training, platoon training and NCO training with my new troops, and was pleased with what I saw. One afternoon was spent with the Colonel looking at a model of Escoville and learning what had gone wrong there, but I found myself unwilling to dwell on that experience, which was still very raw for me. I drew a veil over those painful memories in my mind for many years afterwards. At the end of this session Mike Roberts informed me that he was leaving the battalion, having been promoted to be a general staff officer, Grade 1, at HQ 6th Airborne. I was naturally pleased to see my Colonel's leadership qualities appreciated, but nonetheless felt a real sense of personal loss to see him go. It was like the last straw to me – the whole chain of command unravelled. And, of course, I realized what it meant – that Mark Darrell-Brown would be promoted to head-up the battalion. I honestly tried to be natural in my congratulations to the amiable Darrell-Brown, but it felt forced even to me. I had invited Jock Neilson, the leader of the Sappers who had accompanied my company on the bridge assault, to dinner in the mess that night and it took my mind off things.

I had a thirty-six hour leave and dashed back to Oxford and took Joy shopping. I revelled in the days at home with my family. On the Sunday evening I took Harry Styles back to Bulford in the Jeep I'd once more borrowed for the weekend, but Monday found me frustrated and disillusioned. The euphoria of the return from Normandy had evaporated all too quickly. It wasn't the new recruits and the necessity to train them that got me down – I'd applied myself to that with my usual enthusiasm for the task in hand. It was, in fact, the regimental hierarchy of the Ox & Bucks; the 'old boy network' that appointed favoured sons to the higher positions regardless of their aptitude and suitability. It seemed to me that it was always the same type of chap in the county regiments that was promoted and whose path would be smoothed regardless of performance on, or off, the field. I realized that Mark Darrell-Brown would eventually become the Colonel of the battalion, but was very irritated to find out that the position of 2 I/C was to go to 'Flaps' Edmunds. I commented in my diary, 'What a hopeless combination!' I have to admit that I could be extremely judgmental then and I'm afraid that once I'd made my mind up about someone I seldom changed it. I never did take to Mark Darrell-Brown who was a long-serving officer with the Ox & Bucks and was held in very high esteem by his contemporaries. That he was an 'old school-tie' sort of chap was undeniable of course, and that did not endear him to me. But there was more to it than that. I simply did not admire the man nor did I rate his leadership qualities. It was not a clash of personality because, if he was aware at all of my dislike of him, he was evidently too much of a gentleman ever to show it and, indeed, he was to offer me a job alongside him in due course. In the field, Darrell-Brown was known for courage and an almost careless disregard for personal danger, and the other officers regarded him with affection and loyalty.

'Flaps' Edmunds had impressed me with his debonair attitude, being very much a young man of his times, well-heeled and privileged, with a passion for horses and those kind of 'county' pursuits, the enjoyment of which were totally beyond the experience of someone with my background. Edmunds was the kind of young officer who might be regarded as devil-may-care or downright irresponsible, according to your viewpoint. In Normandy he had carried out some fairly wild schemes, planning attacks on the enemy that were considered by some of his contemporaries to be ill-conceived and, in some cases, thoroughly dangerous. He had ended up being wounded on one of these occasions when leading 'B' Company, and had been invalided back to hospital in the UK. His fellow officer, Teddy Favell, had taken over command of 'B' Company from Edmunds, and was unfortunately killed almost immediately. It had been then that 'B' Company had been placed in the sure and steady hands of Brian Priday, my own 2 I/C. However, 'Flaps' Edmunds had bounced back from hospital and rejoined the Regiment before we left Normandy, and had returned to Bulford with the rest of us. I truthfully could not understand why this officer was selected for 2 I/C of the battalion. Looking back, it was this decision that was the final straw for me with the Ox & Bucks. I decided to look elsewhere to further my career in the Army and my sights were set on the newer regiments of the paratroopers.

Despite my airsickness, I was determined to learn to become a paratrooper and leave the infantry behind, for I considered that this section of the modern Army would go from strength to strength and I wanted to be a part of that progression. I believed that the Paras were not steeped in the tradition of the county regiments, and their officers would, more realistically, represent the new social order in Britain that would emerge after the war. I felt that I would definitely have a future in the Paras. I wrote in my diary on 3 October, 'I want to go to the Paratroopers – must talk Joy round,' for I had been turning it over in my mind for some time. I had discussed it with Joy but she was against me training to become a Para. Because, with the war still going on, she felt it was too risky. Having recently so nearly lost her husband, it was understandable that she just wanted me to take it steady and reach the end of the war in one piece!

Thus my entries in my diary show a restless irritation with the situation I now found myself in with 'D' Company. I missed my old team of junior officers and almost resented the fact that I was still there without them around me. I had tried to contact Brian Priday in hospital but had heard nothing back and I took the company on a fifteen mile route march to try to work my frustration out in rigorous exercise. Although I had begun to form a bond with my new platoon leader, the American officer Phil Bordinat, I reflected in my diary that I 'had my first row with Flaps! I wish Tod would come back.' Tod Sweeney, too, was still in hospital getting over his wounds but, by 7 October, he was back with the Regiment but not looking very fit according to my reckoning. It was, however, good to see him back. My new company 2 I/C, Dick Osborne, took command of an advance exercise held at Newton Tony and I was furious that Mark Darrell-Brown turned up late to oversee it.

On 9 and 10 October I had two days at home in Oxford in order to promote the Airborne Fund, and attended a special exhibition in Oxford. I also addressed a Rotary Club lunch which the Duchess of Marlborough attended. I was once more riding on the crest of a wave, for the story about the bridge assault appeared in the *Oxford Mail* and I began to be well known in the city. When I addressed the Morris factory workers, I was enthusiastically cheered and met the managing director for the first time, a man called S. V. Smith, who impressed me very much and was to become a strong influence on me in the months to come. That night there was a Police dance. Joy wore a new gown and looked wonderful. I had to return to Bulford afterwards and didn't get back until 02.00 hours. My late night did not prevent me taking the company for a sixteen mile march in driving rain next day. When I got back I was pleased to hear from glider pilot John Ainsworth and was delighted to know both he and Jim Wallwork had returned safely from Arnhem although others had not been so lucky. Another old friend, Digby Tatham-Warter, was missing. The fact that Digby had joined the Paras did not deter me for I had, at last, talked Joy round to my point of view and had applied for a jumping course in preparation for joining the Paras myself.

The Regimental Ball was held on the evening of 13 October and was an opportunity for the officers from the Pegasus Bridge operation to have a reunion. Unfortunately Joy's train from Oxford was late arriving at Bulford and she didn't get there until 20.30, with me chafing at the bit to meet her. I still had time to notice that she looked lovely in her new black dress, before hurrying her through the rainy October night to the Ball. David Wood was also there, his leg still strapped up and on a crutch, but looking his cheerful self again. However, I commented in my diary that Tony Hooper 'looked awful'. It was the first time we had all been together since 6 June and I found the evening went all too fast. I had arranged for Joy to stay overnight with friends locally and next day, was able to borrow a Jeep and take her home to Oxford, with Harry Styles coming along for the ride since his family lived in Oxford.

Back at Bulford, company training continued in a spell of appalling autumn weather. All this time, I was polishing my account of the bridges' story and getting it typed up properly with copies made. While on a field firing exercise with Tod Sweeney at Imber, Colonel Roberts turned up to visit unexpectedly. I was pleased to see my old CO and took the opportunity of discussing my proposed move to the Paras with him. A night exercise followed, still in unrelenting rain, and I noted that the men were very enthusiastic and their spirits high. Absorbed once more into my Army life, I nevertheless made a quick visit back to my home in Oxford taking Phil Bordinat with me, who was lonely being so far from home and appreciated being welcomed into our home and seeing my family. I managed to be at home again for 28 October 1944, for our fifth wedding anniversary which we celebrated with friends.

In the first few days of November 1944, I was down in Dorset with 'D' Company on exercises. I commented that the 'Company Frontal Attack was a great success – bags of fire power', my experiences in Normandy having certainly not put me off explosions and the sound of battle. There was field firing the following day and I was very pleased with the company's artillery skills. We didn't get back to barracks until 20.00 but I noted with some frustration that Darrell-Brown wouldn't cancel the RSM's drill. The next day was Saturday and I did some administration work in the morning and managed to dodge off by 11.30 with four large brown eggs to take home to Joy; a treat indeed. But I was unable to have the Sunday at home and had to leave at 06.00 to be back in camp for a morning out on the ranges in a howling autumn gale, classifying the men's firing practice.

There was more field firing the next day and I was satisfied with my own performance and noted that in the regimental field firing, 'D' Company was singled out for praise. Of course, I had no way of knowing that I was experiencing my last days as their OC and when the company went out on night training on the Tuesday night, I remarked that neither Darrell-Brown nor Flaps Edmunds were ever seen on training sessions. My dissatisfaction with the battalion command had not waned. However, I had run into Digby Tatham-Warter in the officers' mess and had been delighted to see him back safe and sound again. My week continued in an unremarkable way with a chance to go up in a WACO glider – the American version of the Horsa – and I reflected ruefully that I had been sick as usual but still enjoyed the experience. I felt that it was the movement of the glider being tugged behind an aircraft that made me ill, not the actual flying. But fate had decreed that I was never able to put this theory to the test again.

I was off like a shot by 11.00 on the following Saturday, using an Army Jeep and travelling with my driver Stock and fellow officers, who also wanted to go to Oxford for the weekend to visit their families. I had a bad head cold that weekend but Joy was suitably attentive and her ministrations soothed me. We were supposed to return to Bulford on Sunday evening but there was no sign of fog on the weather forecast, so I telephoned my driver and decided to go back on the Monday morning instead. Back at Bulford for 07.15 I was immediately involved in a morning of explosives training and then in the afternoon there was a platoon run. Naturally, I competed myself and was none too pleased to come in seventeenth, complaining that I was becoming an old man. After rising so early and having such an active day, I was certainly very tired but was determined to return to Oxford to be with my family for the Monday night and got hold of a Jeep. My company 2 I/C, Dick Osborne, and Harry Styles decided to join me. It was commented upon later that Stock should have been driving the Jeep, but I insisted on taking the wheel because I felt I could drive faster than he could. Dick Osborne was in the front next to me, and Styles and Stock were at the back. We were driving towards Basingstoke when we met a convoy of American trucks. It was about 17.30 on a rainy night in mid-November and I admit that I was driving fast to get us all home as quickly as possible. But in the line of trucks forming the convoy, one of the American drivers decided to pull out to 'leap-frog' the others in the line, and our Jeep met the truck head-on. I was staring ahead in the gloom of the gathering night, half blinded by the headlights of the other trucks. I can only remember being aware of headlights dazzling us straight ahead, horns blaring and then the scream of brakes and sound of breaking glass and rending metalwork. At that moment, the war ended for me.

163

Chapter 13

13 November 1944 to April 1945: Recovery, Realization and Regret

The Oxford & Buckinghamshire Light Infantry *Quarterly Journal*, February 1945: [Footnote. We regret to report that Major R. J. Howard, after missing all the worst the Boche could do in France, came off second best in his jeep in a clash with an American convoy. He now lies with a fractured thigh, a broken pelvis, and a crack in his tibia in the Wingfield Morris Hospital. It was hard to believe this when the writer visited him, and his many friends will be glad to hear he is very cheerful and beginning to mend. Editor]

The editor was my good friend Graham Greenfield and the visit he referred to was probably around Christmas 1944. I had been through much by then and was, in fact, still a long way from any kind of recovery.

The diary entries for the period after 13 November 1944, although written with my usual fountain pen, are at times difficult even for me to read, the writing displaying my pain and frustration at that time. I had been taken to Tidworth Hospital at first as it was the nearest hospital to the accident. Dick Osborne came as well as his legs had also suffered in the crash, although my injuries were more serious. On the first day, I optimistically recorded that I was 'lucky enough to get away with a dislocated hip and possible fractured pelvis,' but it would emerge that it was much worse than that. Both Harry Styles and Stock were badly shaken but unhurt and I was grateful to Harry Styles who was a great help at the scene.

My first days and nights at Tidworth Hospital passed in a blur of excruciating pain and disorientation as the full extent of the injuries became apparent. But it would be many weeks before the shock of what had happened receded enough for me to realize the full implications of what had happened and the impact it would have on my future. The nights were to be particular agony for me, being a restless and active man, as the unending pain prevented me from sleeping without large doses of painkillers. I was left alone with only my discomfort and disquieting thoughts for company. Two days after the accident I commented in my scribbled diary that it was the left knee and leg that was giving me the worst pain, and that I was suffering what I called 'spasms of shock' shooting agonizingly through the leg at intervals. It was to be almost three weeks before it was realized that my left tibia was fractured as well. My pelvis was fractured and the right leg also injured. But on 16 November, Joy came in to see me, being driven down in their car by the obliging Colliers. My leg was in a splint and there must have been lines of weariness and pain etched into my face. But she swallowed her anxiety and smiled, reassuring me that arrangements would be made for me to be moved to the Wingfield Orthopaedic Hospital in Headington.

On Saturday 18 November I received a visit from my friend and fellow officer John Tillett, who had been Adjutant to the battalion. Tillett informed me that he would be taking command of 'D' Company in my absence and that another officer, Freddie Scott, would be his 2 I/C, taking Dick Osborne's place. I realized that this was inevitable but I wondered why Tod Sweeney had not been promoted to take over 'D' Company. The pain in my left knee, which had swollen up with fluid and had to be pierced and drained overnight, prevented me giving it much attention.

Next day the swelling in the knee had subsided and the nurse redid the splint for me. The doctor came round and explained that my kneecap had been fractured and there was nerve damage as well because the knee is a very complex joint. But that night the agonizing pain in the leg was worse than ever and I became, as I described at the time, 'frantic'. This was probably because the undiagnosed break in my left leg was tightly splinted and the resulting pain was terrible. I was grateful to be offered communion by a priest as I lay on my bed of pain. There had been no letter from Joy and I was downcast but was obliged to put on a good show for I was visited in the afternoon by John Tillet and Freddie Scott who, I felt, seemed settled commanding 'D' Company together.

The following morning I felt much better because I'd actually managed to have a reasonable night's sleep. It was a Tuesday and I was surprised and delighted when Joy walked into the ward with Superintendent Quelch of the Oxford City Police. He was man who seemed to have a lot of time for me and his help and advice were to prove invaluable. He had telephoned Joy at home and offered to drive her down to Tidworth and Joy had quickly arranged for the Wormalds to have Terry and Penny for the day. Joy let Superintendent Quelch have a private word with me as he had a reason for bringing Joy down to see me. He had realized straight away that my army career was probably at an end and was hoping to attract me back to the Police Force after demob. We had discussed the possibility of me serving overseas some months before, and now Quelch put it to me that there would most probably be opportunities, especially for men with a good military background, when the war was over. It would be necessary to keep not only a military presence in Germany but for their new police force to be overseen by the Allies as well, to ensure that there was no repetition of extreme right-wing groups taking over again. Quelch told me that he would certainly recommend me for such a job and it left me with a great deal to think about. But I noted in my diary that I would not know what to do about such an offer, because I had a feeling the job would almost certainly be unaccompanied, and I knew that Joy was not at all happy with me being away again and wanted me to live at home.

I had a better night and a lot of visitors the next day including Peter Young, Harry Styles and John Tillett. But I found that by being in bed all the time, kept in a cramped position with the leg injuries, splints and the broken pelvis, I was having increasing pain in my thighs. I had to have the painkiller 'APC' administered during the night. The following day I had stitches removed which was a fairly unpleasant procedure in those days. My daughter would recall that it became a legend in the family about me having 'ninety-nine' stitches in my leg wounds, but whether it had been at this time or later on, I cannot now recall. My diary recorded my frustration at not being moved quickly to the Wingfield Hospital in Oxford, which being me, I had expected to happen almost immediately.

On Saturday, 25 November, I noted that it was my friend Platoon Leader Sandy Smith's wedding day and that they had a brilliantly fine, cold day for it. I regretted bitterly that I could not be in Oxford attending the wedding with my fellow officers and their wives. That night it was very cold on the ward and I caught a chill and ran a temperature. The next afternoon, I received a visit from two American Army officers, which caused quite a stir amongst the nursing staff. The two men were very polite but I sensed their unease, for they were there to take a statement from me about my recollections of the crash. The truck had been driven by what the British Army had referred to as 'an American Negro GI'. The soldier had, for some reason, pulled out of the convoy in order to overtake on a bend in the road and this had meant that the truck was approaching on the wrong side of the road. But my Jeep had been probably travelling too fast to take evasive action even if it had been possible. I stuck firmly to my assertion that I rounded a bend in the road and found the American truck straight ahead of me and that the collision was therefore inevitable. Dick Osborne gave a statement as well.

If this accident had occurred today, effectively ending the careers of two young British Army officers by the negligent and dangerous driving of an American army vehicle, one can imagine that claims for massive financial compensation would result. But this was wartime and there was no provision for such an eventuality. The American Army officers were there simply to get the record straight to present to the official enquiry into the incident. All they had to worry about was that the officer in charge of the convoy would receive a reprimand and the errant driver would be fined, possibly invalided out of the army, and be sent home. I now faced a very uncertain future with a career in the British Army, that had been brimming with potential, snatched away from me overnight and a dependant family, whose lives had been changed forever. But at such a time when men were still laying down their lives for their country, and being maimed in battle, compensation claims were not even thought about or were, at least, shelved until after the war ended. However, it did occur to me in the dark reaches of the night, racked with pain from my injuries in the crash, that it was indeed ironic that I had been the only officer to come back alive and relatively unhurt from capturing those bridges and was then smashed up in a road crash on the road to Basingstoke, barely two months later.

The next day I wrote to Superintendent Quelch asking him to do whatever he could to get me moved to the Wingfield in Oxford. I had no visitors and ended the day writing in my diary that I was 'fearfully browned off'. Joy's letters had plainly been held up in the post, for two fat letters arrived the next morning. That afternoon I had plenty of visitors in the shape of some of the men of 'D' Company – Titch Rayner, Corporal Hunt and two others. I was very touched that they would use an afternoon off to visit me and there was much discussion on the new command of 'D' Company that the lads all agreed was 'Alright – but not the same as you, sir!' We also talked about the Court of Enquiry that was being held that day about the crash.

Joy actually came down on the train to see me two days later. I felt very guilty for the journey by train was difficult and time-consuming. My reaction to her visit was double-edged, for it was marvellous to see her and she cheered me up and made me promise to remain in good spirits, for she was sure I would soon be moved to Oxford. But I found myself plunging into gloom once more after she had gone. I knew any chance of a career change to the Paras was out of the question now my legs were smashed up. Perhaps I would never make A1 fit again and would have to leave the Army. My agitation made the pain worse somehow and I felt that I was becoming addicted to those ruddy APC painkillers, but just couldn't get through the nights without them. I sank into a trough of depression and not even a letter from Superintendent Quelch, saying he was pulling every string possible to get me moved to the Wingfield, could lift my spirits.

But the very next day, Friday, 1 December, I was at last moved after an early lunch and was taken by ambulance arriving at the Wingfield Morris Hospital in the afternoon. Joy came in during the evening to visit me and though the journey had been tiresome and painful, I felt that my recovery could really begin. The next morning I was seen by the surgeon who was a French–Canadian chap called Truett. He informed me that they had detected a fractured tibia from examining the X-rays done at Tidworth. Therefore they would be operating on the Monday to deal with that. Whether it was the move or a different bed, but I experienced very severe back pain that night and my groaning kept the others in the ward awake. The next day it was raining very hard and I was afraid it would prevent

Joy from visiting but, to my delight she turned up with our old friend Kingsley Belsten and they had brought both of the children in to see me. The Belstens' house, where Joy and I had once been billeted, was just down the road from the hospital in Headington.

On Monday, 4 December, I had my left shin-bone manipulated and set in plaster. They gave me an anaesthetic which made me high, and I went back to the ward rambling and singing, causing the chap in the next bed to burst his stitches laughing at me.

But when the drug wore off, I was in severe pain for the next two days as the heavy plaster stretched my leg and tendons. A week later my leg was manipulated again and re-plastered. It was a very complicated fracture and I noticed the surgeon Mr Truett, always referred to as 'JT', and the Sister having 'quite a pow-wow' discussing my treatment. Later on JT told me that I would be 'OK by March,' whatever that meant, but that it would be the tibia that held things up.

Now I was in Oxford, I received lots of visitors from old friends in the police force, neighbours, and Army friends who could make an excuse to call in at the Slade barracks nearby and drop in to see me. Graham Greenfield, the editor of the Ox & Bucks *Quarterly Journal* called often, bringing in red wine on one occasion and a bottle of Scotch on another. This was shared with friends I made on the ward and a merry time was had by all. Sister was gratified to note that we did not need the painkillers to go to sleep on such occasions. Joy tried to visit me on most evenings, and brought Penny and Terry in the afternoons as well, when she could get a lift in a friend's car. When the weather was good she would walk up from Cowley pushing the children in a double pram. My birthday was on 8 December and I was very amused by my son's chatter. It was his Daddy's 'buff-day' and he called my plaster cast 'Daddy's sugar-leg'. Joy was excited because her mother and sister Lorna were arriving the following week for a visit.

One afternoon, there was a Christmas sale of toys and other gifts made by the Occupational Therapy Unit and it occurred to me that I could use up some time sitting in bed to good effect. I soon picked it up from the lady who taught occupational therapy and was busy making toys in no time. Walt Disney's film *Dumbo* had just come out and I found my Dumbos in great demand. This kept me very busy up to Christmas. Betty Caine came in to see me with Lorna and made a great fuss of me. Later in life Lorna could remember visiting me in hospital, and particularly the Morrison shelter in the front room at our house on Garsington Road. Lorna recalled covering it with a blanket and having great games in it with Terry. Joy loved having their company at home and it broke the routine for her, but they were only able to stay a few days and, as they left, a very cold spell of weather began. This meant that it was too cold for Joy to walk the couple of miles up to Headington from Cowley with the children and I missed seeing them. But she still tried to get in to see me herself in the evenings when Harold Collier would run her up in the car and his wife Mary would sit with the children.

On 22 December, I telephoned Bulford camp to get one of my friends to bring me bottles of whisky and gin for Christmas, but I found no one there that I knew. I was told that they'd all left and realized that the Division must have been mobilized again. They were probably in transit camp somewhere. I reflected that they must have gone in a hurry and had another bad night thinking about them all going off again without me. I would learn in due course that the 6th Airborne had gone to Belgium to assist the Americans for what became known as the Ardennes Offensive. But Joy had a different viewpoint, which had rather surprised me for, when she heard that my battalion had been mobilized again, she told me that in her opinion 'everything that has happened is for the best'. She did not want me risking my life again in battle and if the price to pay for that was for me to be badly injured in hospital after a road accident, then so be it. I tried to tell myself that she was right and I should feel that way too but somehow I didn't, and my heart was still out there with my men ready for battle again.

Christmas in hospital was a lonely time even though Joy arrived in the afternoon with the children and all the Collier family. I selfishly wished that I could have had my family all to myself, and felt immensely homesick when they all left to go back to Garsington Road. Joy was providing Christmas tea and I would have given anything to be able to go with them. In the days after Christmas it was very cold indeed. The ward windows were iced up on the inside and I woke each night at 03.00 chilled to the bone. Terry and Penny both had colds. On 28 December Digby Tatham-Warter called in to see me looking as nonchalant and debonair as ever but could give me no news of the Airborne. I received a letter telling me that I was categorized 'D' in the 'Fitness for Battle' ratings with the army. This made me feel dreadful and I wondered if I would ever be A1 fit again. It also affected my army pay, removing various allowances only received when active. Despite the continuing bitter cold weather, all the patients were taken outside each day in our beds for a breath of fresh air. I realized just how much I had missed fresh air and felt I slept better for it. Then on New Year's Eve, Tod Sweeney called in with a bottle of Scotch for me, and welcome news of the battalion. It appeared they had all gone by sea to the Ardennes.

New Year's Day always made me reflective and I viewed 1945 ahead, hoping desperately that I would be at home with my family in a year's time. Joy came in to visit me in the evening but she was quiet and very tired from all the extra work of the Christmas season and having to come to the hospital almost every day. As ever, I only saw it from my own point of view and I expected Joy to be endlessly charming and delightful and we fell out and had a few sharp words. Later, writing in my diary I put, 'Joy's evening visit a flop – she as good as said it was too much trouble to come!' With the benefit of maturity and hindsight, I can see that poor Joy had a lot on her plate at that time, with providing for two small children with the restrictions of rationing, and making a great effort to turn out on a bitter cold night and walk all that way up to the hospital, or beg yet another lift in Collier's car. Looking back over my diary entries, I note with some shame that I didn't ever mention my wife's difficulties. I was a selfish bugger then and it probably never occurred to me how tired she got coping all on her own. I wrote a letter to give to her but she did not arrive at the visiting time that evening. In fact she kept away for the next two days and this left me very dejected indeed. On 4 January, her birthday, she arrived in the afternoon with Terry. She was looking radiant, wearing a sheepskin hat that suited her very well. She was delighted with her gift from me, which I had ordered by telephone, and returned in the evening, to see me alone.

On the radio I heard about the 6th Airborne in the Ardennes. I wrote, 'Good luck to them. I hope they do well.' Feeling very useless and bored, I began to make a handbag for Joy in Occupational Therapy while outside there was snow falling. On 17 January, the surgeon told me that I would be in bed for another month and then I would be on crutches. I was cheered by a visit from a police friend and it was interesting to note the kind of gifts that visitors brought in when coming to see me. Fresh eggs were considered a great treat, but usually only two or three could be spared. Friends Bill and Nina Gibbs turned up with two sausages and a couple of eggs. Another visitor offered to get hold of a pack of butter and someone else brought beer and some sugar! However by this time, I was very bored indeed.

After such an active and full life, the enforced bed-rest was indeed very tedious. I asked Kingsley Belsten to bring me some books and Joy brought an atlas and some geography books for me to study, but it was difficult to concentrate on the ward. Finally, I began to write notes about my experiences in the army, using plain ruled government issue exercise books. I started with the training of 'D' Company, planning for the bridge assault, and then my recollections about the attack itself. Unfortunately I was discharged from hospital before I'd finished, and despite there being nine exercise books in my archives, only three of them were ever written in. This detailed account therefore remained unfinished. Other accounts I wrote for Army records are more formal than those I wrote when in hospital. I had intended to turn these recollections into a book called *Go to it* (the Airborne motto) but somehow I never found the time in the years after the war and someone else got there first! In the end, I showed these notes to the American historian, Stephen Ambrose, in the early 1980s and he used them when writing his best selling book *Pegasus Bridge*.

Towards the end of January, I heard that my old 2 I/C Dick Osborne was back on his feet. I could not even imagine at that time how long it would be before I was at that stage myself. Fractures of the lower limbs then were usually treated by applying a Thomas Splint which was a complicated contraption consisting of metal bars forming a frame supported from a metal belt around the groin. The limb was then suspended in a series of slings and further held by bandaging. The idea was to produce immobilization without putting pressure on the injury. In my case my lower left leg was in plaster as well. While in a Thomas Splint, one was obliged to remain bedridden.

On 23 January 1945 I wrote in my diary that, 'both knees bending as far as Thomas Splint and bed allows'. The Sister changed the bandages and I was able to rub my legs and it gave me a lot of relief, although I observed that the skin was flaking off my legs rather alarmingly. The nickname for the splint seems to have been 'beams' and on 24 January I wrote, 'JT still won't let me off beams – Blast!' On that day my tibia was X-rayed again as well.

My morale was not improved by learning the following day that, despite the Court of Enquiry into the road crash having laid the blame for the accident on the American truck driver, he had only been fined $80. I can recall that this was intensely demoralizing just at that time when my own future was still so much in the balance. In fact, after the war ended a commission was set up to look into genuine compensation claims and, after a very lengthy process, I was awarded a reasonable sum from the American Army in 1947. This money meant that my family could move to a better house and helped us considerably. But in hospital in January 1945, I accepted the likelihood that I would probably never receive any kind of compensation for the accident, even though it had not been my fault.

The weather at the end of January was still intensely cold with my diary recording that a frost of 25 °F had been reported in Birmingham. The men on the ward were all shouting for hot water bottles and the pipes froze. But despite the arctic temperatures, it was the practice to wrap blankets around the men and wheel our beds out onto a kind of covered veranda that ran along the outside wall of the ward.

I was closely monitoring the progress of the war and noted that 'the Russians are only 100 miles from Berlin – a terrific effort! They will finish the Huns now.' By 1 February the Russians were just fifty miles from Berlin and there had been a thousand bomber air raid on Berlin. Although I was no longer a part of that war, I was busy chasing up the citation for my own battle honour, the DSO, which I had never received from the War Office. It arrived in early February 1945 and I said in my diary that it 'fills me with a queer sort of pride'. I wrote many letters while forced to remain in bed, and received many in return, being especially pleased to hear from the men of 'D' Company. I heard from Corporal Ted Tappenden, my old wireless officer, and also from my driver, Stock.

At the end of the first week of February, while JT was making his Wednesday visit, I was thrilled to be told that the Thomas Splint could be removed at last. 'Off beam!' I wrote in my diary, but went on ruefully to note that I was 'feeling too useless for words and can't get comfortable'. My legs were wasted and I felt as weak as a kitten. However, I was able to be wheeled down to the bathroom for my first bath in three months and said I 'could have soaked forever and it was heaven'. The following day I felt I was getting some power back into my legs but it was evidently going to be a very long job. To add to my concerns about my physical condition, my Army pay had been reduced and my friend, Graham Greenfield, offered to look into it for me, for which I was most grateful. I reflected that it was a good thing that Joy was such an excellent manager at home.

The weather had warmed up by mid-February but brought rain. I was still going outside onto the veranda for fresh air, but now could be pushed in a wheelchair by another patient on the ward. Around that time my brothers, Gin and Bill, came in and I was especially glad to see them after so long. They had brought little Terry with them. From then on, I seemed to make a rapid recovery and began to feel restricted and bored with the hospital regime. My impatience got me into trouble with the ward Sister. I tried out a fellow patient's crutches and this spurred me on to persuading Joy to wheel me out of the hospital on the following day, which was a Sunday. She managed to take me carefully down the road in the wheelchair to Chelwood, Jim and Kingsley Belsten's house, for a cup of tea. I was 'practising' with the crutches and commented that I was 'fairly steady already but awfully tired'. Next day my exhaustion was quickly picked up by Sister and also Miss Myers, the physical therapist. 'Hell to pay' I wrote. Miss Myers had reprimanded me fairly gently but Sister had been much more blunt and I was obliged to sit meekly in bed trying to read.

On the Wednesday JT made his rounds and the test results were good on both of my legs. To my delight I was officially told I could get up and put pressure onto both legs, with emphasis on the more badly injured left one. JT had been amused by me getting up onto crutches before I was supposed to and now I was able to use crutches to get about the hospital but with Sister ever watchful in case I overdid it. I found my feet muscles ached having to bear weight after so long.

On a brilliant early spring day in late February I decided to put on my battledress again – a great morale booster for me. I used the crutches to go all the way down to the gate to meet Joy at visiting time, which delighted us both. Late in the afternoon Brigadier Napier Crookenden called in on me, having come to the hospital to visit his brothers who were also there. He hadn't much time to spare but was able to tell me that the 6th Airborne were back in the UK from Belgium.

The Ardennes Offensive had taken place from 16 December 1944 to 28 January 1945. Hitler had decided to make one last stand, in an attempt to change the course of the Second World War. The Ardennes was chosen because he could build up his troops and armaments there, under cover of the thick forests, and the American forces in that area were very light. The German attack depended on speed and accuracy, Hitler being confident that the Allies would not be able to react in time. His commanders however, were far more doubtful that the plan would succeed and tried to get Hitler to change his mind, it being felt that he was unstable by this time in the war. But he was inflexible and the plan went ahead. The attack, at dawn on 16 December, was on five American divisions and at first the Germans advanced rapidly. This offensive became known as the Battle of the Bulge and was the largest land battle fought by the American forces in the Second World War. The British were brought in largely to plug the gap in the defences on the French border under the command of General Montgomery, who managed to offend all the American generals – Bradley, Patton and even Eisenhower – to such an extent that Churchill was obliged to stand up in the House of Commons and make a statement, praising the conduct of the American forces. They managed to halt the German advance by 17 December and the Allies launched their counter-offensive two days before the New Year. By 28 January, the Battle of the Bulge had been won. The Americans lost 19,000 troops killed to 200 British dead, which clearly illustrates to what extent it was an American victory. The Germans lost 100,000 men, killed, wounded or captured, and Hitler's final attempt to win the war had failed. It was reckoned that this famous American victory shortened the war by several months.

I was, of course, unaware of these historical events, my world having shrunk to the hospital in Oxford and my own recuperation and finally my boredom and impatience got the better of me. When someone offered me a lift into Oxford, I went to meet a chum in the bar of the Mitre Hotel. One drink became several and I admit to becoming 'quite squiffy'. We shot back to the Wingfield just in time for lunch but the merriment continued, and I recall that several off-colour jokes were made over the sausages that were on the menu that day! The Ward Sister glared at us and must have taken note of our 'barrack-room humour'. But I was not aware that I had been issued with a 'yellow card' because, the next day, I once again hitched a ride into town. I had been told I could begin using two sticks instead of the crutches and was in a celebratory mood. A few more drinks were consumed at The Mitre and my fellow conspirators and I committed the frightful sin of being back late for lunch at the hospital. That was the last straw for Sister. She stood in the middle of the ward as I tried to slip unobtrusively in, after leaving my two chums to go off to their own wards. But it is hard to be nonchalant and inconspicuous on two sticks and wearing a silly grin. Sister was at the end of her tether with me and she told me that since it was evident that I no longer needed to be in hospital, she intended to make arrangements for me to go home the next day! With that she walked straight past me and out of the ward, her starched uniform rustling alarmingly, leaving me feeling like a new conscript put on a charge.

Thus it was that on Thursday, 1 March 1945, I found myself back at home in the little house on Garsington Road, away from the camaraderie and security of the hospital ward. I wrote in my diary, 'I feel like a fish out of water'. My cavalier behaviour had meant that I was sent home from hospital very suddenly and, after almost four months, I was ill prepared for the transition. I sat in a chair in the dining room at the back of the house, beside the fire which Joy lit every morning. I suddenly became aware of the neglect of a winter without a man in the house, how badly it needed repainting and how overgrown and untidy the garden had become. I felt useless sitting there, my usual vigour having deserted me, and the two sticks I had to use to get about making me feel clumsy and awkward in the small house. Joy had her usual routine with the children keeping her busy, but was certainly pleased to have the extra time now that she no longer had to fit in lengthy visits to the hospital. She probably also felt strange about having me at home again after so long. Enforced separation causes great strain on a marriage. The children too would have had to get used to sharing their Mummy with this man whom they had never been used to having at home. The boisterous two-and-a-half year old Terry scampered excitedly around me and tried to scramble onto my knee prompting bellows of pain from me with my still-tender wounds. I tried to pull myself out of this depression and began to sort my kit out and help Joy by entertaining the children. This was, in truth, the first time I really got to know my children and, critical of my offsprings' performance as I inevitably would become, I commented in my diary, 'Pen not even crawling yet'.

My progress seemed far too slow for me but we managed to attend the Police dance on 6 March. The next day I was able to go out for the first time with only one stick but I felt like an old man, the sluggish pace I was obliged to adopt making me edgy and despondent. I was always extremely impatient all my life and at that time, in the spring of 1945, I was like a wounded bear, angry about my own inability to move easily and quickly again. I realize now that I must have been hell to live with.

On 8 March I went back to the Wingfield hospital to see JT, who told me that I should not expect to be able to return to the Army again before the war ended. I was appalled and determined to prove him wrong. I persuaded the consultant to see me again in a fortnight. At the same clinic I ran into my old 2 I/C Dick Osborne, who seemed much more accepting of the fact that he would never make 'A1 fit' again and I found that I did not admire his attitude. Osborne never did return to the Army, in fact, choosing to further his education by taking a course at Balliol College – an opportunity which I never considered probably because I needed an income. The following day, I was back at the Wingfield visiting the gym there for treatment. I committed myself to an exercise regime with the single-minded dedication that was typical of my nature. I ran into people there who were visiting other patients, such as Jill and John Heath-Smith who had a son, another John, serving with my battalion. My old friend Laurie 'Nick' Nicholson, still serving with the battalion, came for lunch with us at home, for his parents lived at a farm called Bucknell, near Bicester. Neither of us could possibly have known it, but it would be the last time I saw him.

I was beginning to settle into a routine with my recuperation, exercising at the Wingfield most days and enjoying quiet evenings at home with Joy. It was little Penny's first birthday on Sunday, 11 March. Joy made a special tea with a birthday cake and Penny's godparents, the Belstens, joined us. A few days later, I was up to doing a bit of gardening and was very pleased with my achievement, although I paid for it afterwards with aching limbs. The Colliers were letting me use their car for the hospital treatment each day and I started doing a few errands for them to repay them for their kindness. I commented in my diary that, 'I'm down to Captain now' reflecting my diminished pay-packet. It meant that we were on a serious economy drive.

Thus pleasantly rehabilitating myself, it came as a great shock for me to learn that once again the battalion was off to war without me, for on 24 March 1945 Operation VARSITY was launched, later to be known generally as the Rhine Crossing. Major General Ridgeway was in command of the Regiment, with General 'Windy' Gale as his deputy. In this assault, the tactic of surprise landings by glider was once again employed to take and hold two bridges, using men from the Royal Ulster Rifles and the Ox & Bucks Light Infantry. Both Brigadiers James Hill and Nigel Poett were once more in battle with the 3 and 5 Parachute Brigades. This operation went down in history as a victory, but inevitably was not without casualties.

I realized with foreboding that I had some serious nerve problems in my bad leg which resulted in the left foot going numb and then completely dead after I'd been on it for a while. This growing realization, which I kept to myself at first, seriously affected me for I knew only too well that lack of feeling could lead to lack of blood supply and thence possibly to gangrene and amputation. I had always been such an active man and my recuperation up until then was going so well. I was terrified of such a possibility.

A day or so later and the Rhine Crossing was announced on the wireless and all my feelings of guilt and inadequacy overwhelmed me. There I was living a cushy life at home with my family and worrying about a numb foot while my comrades were once more in the thick of battle with some of them being maimed and killed. At the end of March, I decided to tell the hospital about the nerve problem with my leg. Nevertheless we had made arrangements to spend Easter in Church Stretton using the Colliers' car once more and taking Mary Collier as far as Shrewsbury where she would catch a train up to Southport to see her family. We were back in Oxford after a few days, collecting Mary at Shrewsbury station and Tom Caine having generously helped out with some petrol, which was still strictly rationed. On 5 April I had an appointment at the Wingfield to see JT about the nerve problem in my leg and I was referred to another specialist. I went home to tell Joy and hadn't been home long when Pop Wormald from next-door knocked to say that Betty Caine was on the telephone for us. I went quickly next-door and received the sad news that Gram had died in Wallasey. Joy was terribly distressed to lose her grandmother and a few days later she made the journey up to New Brighton to comfort her Auntie Mollie and to bid her grandmother farewell.

I went to see the other specialist, Mr Zachery, at the hospital and was given what I referred to then as 'a sweat test'. This confirmed the nerve damage but did not reveal why it was happening, which depressed me even more. A few days later, I had to go to the Wingfield for an experimental X-ray on my pelvis to locate the nerve trouble.

I had been told about a job at the Morris Motor Works by the general manager, S. V. Smith, whom I had met when I had been asked to address the men at the factory after my return from Normandy the previous September. The job I'd applied for was on the welfare side of the business. I was not a regular soldier but had been called up from the Reserve List at the start of the war and unless I was offered a good position I would be demobbed when hostilities ceased. Now that it looked as if I would not be categorized as being 'A1 Fit' again, I could not be sure of the excellent career prospects in the Army that I had anticipated before the accident the previous November. So I'd paid much attention to S. V. Smith's advice and hoped that his patronage might help me to secure a good job. Strangely, Joy seemed to dislike him and to resent the influence he had over me, telling me not to hold out too much hope of a job at the Morris works. Joy could be very prejudiced at times, but in this case she turned out to be right.

She had just returned from her grandmother's funeral and I reported that the children had been no trouble at all. In fact, Mary Collier had been much in evidence; one thing the Army teaches its officers well is the art of delegation. But there was much sadness to come for I had been contacted by one of my battalion commanders with a request for me to deliver the news of their son's death to Jill and John Heath-Smith. I had also been a friend of the younger John Heath-Smith and was very upset by his death, but I carried out the mission as requested. He had died in the Rhine Crossing operation and under the circumstances, beyond knowing that it had been highly successful for the Allies, few details would have been released by that time. So I once more set off in Collier's car bound for the Heath-Smiths' home. It was an extremely difficult duty for me to have to break such dreadful news to a couple I knew and liked very much.

The next day brought more bad news when I learnt of the death of my good friend Laurie 'Nick' Nicholson. It was a grim time for both Joy and me. She was still mourning the loss of her grandmother and was very quiet and preoccupied. I was so full of pent-up emotion myself that I decided to get out of the house and walk up to Headington to see Kingsley Belsten. Pounding along the pavements, using the solid wooden walking stick that would become like another limb to me in the years to come, I found myself turning things over in my mind. I reflected bitterly that just about a year before, I had been full of enthusiasm and pride when I'd been informed by Mike Roberts that my company had been selected for a special job for the invasion. Looking back now, I realize how naive I had been then, filled with the glory of war and proud of our mission. Now I had tasted the bitter fruit of bereavement, seeing my friends cut down in their prime and knowing that, on this occasion I had not even been there to play my part. Later I would rationalize, see my experiences in perspective and accept that it had ever been thus. I'd been warned that I probably faced having to return to the hospital for more surgery and I was fearful of the future and being able to provide for my family. And now I had lost yet another of the best friends I ever had! I hit the hedge I was passing with my walking stick. Reaching Chelwood I rang the front doorbell and Kingsley answered it, recognizing at once from the expression on my face that I was in need of comfort. The obliging Jemima declared that she was going to make herself a cup of cocoa and have an early night with a good book, and left us to it in the sitting room. Kingsley went to the cupboard and produced a bottle of Scotch and poured us a large slug each. 'Right-oh, old man,' he'd said gently in his Oxfordshire burr, 'Let's hear all about it'.

Chapter 14

April 1945 to March 1946: Disillusion, Determination and Deliverance

T he consultants had reached the conclusion that the problem with my foot going dead was caused by the bony substance, which is formed as a bone fracture heals and which is known as callus, pressing onto the sciatic nerve running down the leg. I would have to go back into hospital again for exploratory surgery.

Although my foot went dead after I'd walked on it for a short time, I found that I could cycle and immediately began cycling everywhere for exercise. I took Collier's car again to go to the farm at Bucknell near Bicester to see Laurie Nicholson's parents. Nick's mother had taken his death very badly and I spent some time with her. The Nicholsons were very kind people and they sent me back home with some eggs, milk and flowers for Joy. I felt humbled by their good heartedness amidst their grief at losing their son. If my errands for the Colliers took me towards Boars Hill I would also call on the Heath-Smiths to see how they were and I saw S. V. Smith as well and he told me how sorry he was that I had missed the job at the Morris works. However, I was left with the distinct feeling that he was losing interest in me by that time.

By the end of April Berlin was surrounded, the Russians having advanced rapidly from the east. Then a few days later there was a ceasefire in Italy. Berlin had fallen to the Russians and it was alleged that Hitler had committed suicide. An announcement was made that there would be a nationwide celebration of VE Day – Victory in Europe Day on 8 May 1945. But I was filled with gloom over the realization that my leg was no better and that I would have to have another operation. The unseasonably chilly weather had prevented us going out in the Colliers' car for a picnic. It was considered a great treat for us to be able to do this and I'd been looking forward to this simple pleasure. As an Army officer, I had been given tokens for fourteen gallons of petrol, to last three months, and was able to collect my allowance of cigarettes and chocolate from the NAAFI at the Slade barracks. I did not smoke but Joy certainly did and the extras were useful as gifts. With the return to hospital hanging over me, I took Joy, the children and Mary Collier to Ellistons in Oxford for 'an ice cream tea', in celebration of the impending cessation of hostilities. I tried to do as many jobs around the house as I could, not knowing how long I would be laid up with my leg operation. The house needed painting on the outside but it was very difficult to get the paint then even if you found someone to carry out the work.

On 6 May I was once again admitted to the Wingfield Hospital and was operated on early the following day. I had complete confidence in the surgeon, JT, but Joy was very worried about it. VE Day found me coming round from the operation feeling nauseous and very groggy. There were to be celebrations in every town and village in the British Isles. Harold Collier brought Joy and the children in to hospital to visit me but they found me drowsy and unwell. They left to join a party with friends and I was left behind, almost alone, on the ward. It was glorious weather outside and it seemed as if the whole world was joyfully celebrating, but I can still recall how depressed I'd felt on that day, unable to forget all the dear friends I'd lost in the war who had not seen peace restored.

The day after VE Day, the wireless news said that Hitler's body had been found and burned by the Russians. Two days later, when I needed money for the first time since my operation to buy a newspaper, I made the unpleasant discovery that £4.10s. had been taken from my wallet, probably while I was unconscious. This was a large sum in those days and it caused a wave of tension and suspicion to go around the hospital. I thought that I knew who was responsible but had no proof. Joy arrived for afternoon visiting with the children, which took my mind off the matter somewhat. There was an official enquiry into the theft two days later but I never recovered the money.

The routine of hospital days and visits quickly fell into place again as did the squabbles with Joy unfortunately. Perhaps subconsciously, I resented the fact that my wife was a part of the world outside whilst I was confined in a hospital bed again. Both of us felt the strain of my hospitalization. I was uncomfortable now that the stitches in my wound were pulling, but was obliged to write her a conciliatory letter. I wrote also to Mark Darrell-Brown, my commanding officer, and to Tod Sweeney and to the Nicholsons. The next day I heard from Tod, our letters having crossed in the post, and also from my old friend Gilbert Rahr, bringing me welcome news of 'D' Company, which I was reluctantly having to accept was now part of my past life. But Joy had been in to see me with the children, which cheered me up.

Tod Sweeney and John Tillett visited me and they confirmed that some of the Regiment at least were rumoured to be going to China. I felt an immense wave of longing to be fit and able to go off with them all and was quite surprised by its intensity. Tod and John had looked so well and been full of tales of Germany and it had made me feel very sorry for myself. But I knew that Joy would be dead against me taking up a post with my old battalion again. The following day, JT came round the ward and ordered my dressings to be removed and, to my relief the long wound in my leg seemed to be healing marvellously. I felt very up-beat and was full of energy and confidence when I received a visit from Graham Greenfield and Colonel Bartlett later that day. It seemed evident that the possibility of my recovery was being discussed by the battalion command and they were attempting to include me in their future plans.

However, it came as a bolt out of the blue for me when, on 25 May, I received a letter from Mark Darrell-Brown, offering me the job of 2 I/C of the battalion. I commented in my diary that it was 'a job I've often wanted, and it puts me in a spot'. This was a huge understatement for this offer was one of the most pivotal moments in my military career. I recall that it was a thundery and overcast day and, despite the diversion of several visitors later in the afternoon, I was deep in thought about the promotion I had been offered by Darrell-Brown and the prospects for my future. I knew that I must reply within a few days and I was plainly very confused and under a good deal of pressure at this time, making such a vital decision which I knew would dictate the outcome of my whole army career and therefore, the future of my wife and family as well. I was also at an important time in my recovery, for I realized that it was probably my 'bull at a gate' attitude to recuperating that had contributed to the set-back in my condition. This time I resolved to curb my impatience and take things slower. I therefore remained obediently in bed, allowing the wound to heal. I had naturally shown Joy the letter from Mark Darrell-Brown and her reaction, predictably, was for me to turn it down and to seek a career where I could live at home.

A couple of days later Joy's uncle, Arthur Sagar from Church Stretton, was staying at home with Joy and the children. When JT made his round the following morning, I asked him if I could go home and, to my great surprise, the consultant said he did not see why not. I contacted Graham Greenfield immediately and was collected by him and was back at home by noon. I had been mentally struggling with the decision over the job offer from Mark Darrell-Brown. I tried logically to consider my position and to realistically assess my rate of recovery. It was the beginning of June and Darrell-Brown had said that I must take up the position of 2 I/C by 20 July, because the Regiment was being posted abroad. My commonsense told me that it was unlikely that I would be A1 Fit in a bare eight weeks and I did not want to let anyone down. All my life I would be a man who never promised anything that I could not deliver. Added to this I knew that Joy would be extremely distressed by me returning to take up a post with my old battalion. She took the view, and it was an understandable one, that I had already served my country well. I had answered the call of duty and carried out my assignment with courage and determination. The war was not yet over in the

Far East where the Regiment could well be posted, and Joy did not want to go through enforced separation from me again or the continual anxiety of me being further maimed or even killed in battle. She had expressed her views to me eloquently and passionately. She was a very pretty woman in her mid-twenties, still young enough to attract a good deal of attention from the opposite sex and frankly, I could not bear the thought of leaving her on her own again, possibly bitter at my decision to return to Army life. I knew only too well the strain it would place on our marriage. Then there were my two babes. Until I had my own children and had lived with them, enjoying a normal family life, I could not have imagined just how much I would feel for my son and daughter and want to be at home with them. And yet there was a strong part of my nature that missed military life so much and yearned to be out there with my men facing another challenge in a new environment. I felt completely pulled in two directions, and there were times when I put my head in my hands and mentally cried out in despair over what to do for the best. Upon this occasion, I made the decision to turn down Mark Darrell-Brown's offer. The entry in my diary on 1 June 1945 was, 'Wrote Mark Darrell-Brown saying I wouldn't be fit by July 20th, so couldn't accept 2 I/C – in my heart I feel I've done the wrong thing, only Joy has stopped me'. This was slightly unfair of me blaming Joy, for the question of my fitness certainly played a large part in this decision. Also in the mix of my emotions was doubt over my personal attitude to Mark Darrell-Brown. Thus the deed was done but I would face this dilemma of military versus home life again later in the year.

Putting my decision behind me, next day I took Joy and the children into Oxford in Collier's car. We splashed out on a bottle of champagne and drank it at home that evening. Joy was visibly more relaxed, plainly feeling we had passed a watershed in our life together. But when, on Monday 4 June, Oxford celebrated its third VE Day, I was able to enjoy it and participate in the celebrations, being asked to attend a street party held on the barracks field by an Army colleague. I went along with Joy and the children. It was a sunny day and Terry and Penny were very excited. Terry had been bought a second hand toy pedal-car which he pedalled with enormous enthusiasm, beginning what would be a lifetime obsession with cars. I took him out on the pavements around our home in Cowley, my walking-stick hooked into the back of the little car behind Terry's seat to stop him going too fast for my pace. I idolized my little son at that time and thought him intelligent and lively – cast in my own image of course. This fixation with Terry's development would be a double-edged aspect in my relationship with my son as he grew up, for he was destined to be a very different character from myself with other qualities, and I would find this difficult to accept.

It came as a shock to me to realize, on 5 June 1945, that it was a year since we had landed by glider in Normandy. Somehow it seemed much longer. Once more I was returning to the gym at the Wingfield Hospital for exercise on my bad leg. There I learned that the Airborne had contacted the Wingfield for their opinion on my fitness. On 8 June, I was informed that the hospital had assessed that I would never be A1 Fit again. This came as a slap in the face, and I reflected sadly that I had made the right decision when I had turned down the job offer from Darrell-Brown.

There was to be a General Election in mid-June and I declared in my diary 'I don't think Labour has a chance!' This shows how much I knew about politics at the time, for Labour won a famous victory. I was filled with apprehension about my future, for the likelihood of me never being A1 Fit again had made the prospects of a career in the Army seem even more remote. On Kingsley Belsten's recommendation, I'd joined a club for businessmen in Oxford. It was called the Frewen Club and was on St Aldgates in the town centre. Eventually, it was to be my network of friends in Oxford who would come to my aid at this difficult time in my life.

Mrs Nicholson was still very depressed about Nick's death and her daughter suggested a holiday by the sea in Swanage. I was asked to help Mr Nicholson on the farm in her absence and to take Joy and the children to stay over there. I jumped at the chance for I loved being on the farm at Bucknell. It was only twenty-five miles or so away from Oxford but was in the heart of the countryside. Thus, on Saturday, 23 June, I collected one of the Nicholsons' cars, referred to as 'the tourer' and drove my family up there. I was obliged to return most days to the Wingfield Hospital for my orthopaedic therapy, which made it at times a great rush. Helping out on the farm kept me very busy while Joy was happily cooking and spring-cleaning the farmhouse for Mrs Nicholson. The weather was fine and the children had a wonderful time.

News reached me that the 6th Airborne had arranged an investiture but I had evidently not been invited. I was deeply hurt by this omission. A letter from the War Office at the beginning of July stated baldly that my rank was reduced to captain. This left me feeling disillusioned and I began to have a distinct feeling that, having served my purpose in the assault on Pegasus Bridge, the officers now left were closing ranks and jostling for position, with the prospect of a pared-down peacetime Army. Because I lacked the right connections and was also now categorized as being too disabled for an active life, I would not be considered favourably for any jobs, even in administration. I tried not to think about it and enjoy our break in the countryside.

The Nicholsons had said we could use the tourer for a trip to Church Stretton and I was dismayed when it broke down somewhat terminally – cars were liable to do that in those days. However, I brightened considerably when Mr Nicholson declared that he would have to now get the 1½ litre MG off the blocks where it had been stored since the beginning of the war. Mrs Nicholson returned home on 5 July and was delighted with her spotlessly clean house. It was agreed that now the Nicholsons could use their saloon car at home, we could take the MG if I could get the vehicle taxed and roadworthy. You bet I could! I rushed off to get it taxed in Oxford and the car was cleaned and oiled in no time. Our little family returned home that evening and the next day I used the MG to drive myself and Terry up to London to visit my parents while Joy packed again ready to go up to Shropshire. We set off by 09.00 next morning and I was having the time of my life driving my family in the MG and delighting in its performance. Betty Caine had killed a goose in readiness for the family dinner and we found that Lorna was growing into a nice girl and was very good at keeping Terry entertained. While we were there, it was Terry's third birthday and I wrote in my diary, 'Terry extremely intelligent – very interested in books'. In fact there was a tricycle waiting at home for him, but time would show that anything on wheels would always interest Terry far more than books of any kind! Tom Caine was on good form and helped us out with more petrol so that we could drive on to visit Joy's Aunt Mollie in New Brighton, for Joy was concerned about her, now living alone after her mother's death. After a couple of days seeing Mollie and another night in Church Stretton, we returned home. I was obliged to drive the MG regretfully back to Bucknell and return it safely to the Nicholsons.

But we found ourselves glad to be back in our home again after a month away from it. Terry was thrilled at being able to play with his new tricycle and I set to in the garden to harvest our crop of vegetables and to restore order. The house painting had been completed and the bill for it was £34, which was a large amount for those days. My leg was improving all the time, and I planted out Brussels sprouts and managed to run about half a mile one evening. On 2 August I had my final appointment with JT at the Wingfield. I wrote 'Passed fit! He says I've made an amazing recovery, it's good to know. My Joy is sceptical'. My wife still didn't want me to return to military life but she knew that I had, in fact, made a trip to Bulford just the day before, in order to talk to Colonel Guy Rowley about the possibility of a staff job with the battalion of an old acquaintance, Lieutenant Colonel Alistair Pearson. Pearson had a sound military background having been in the Sicily landings and Normandy with the Paras and had earned three DSOs. He was known as a fine officer but was notoriously plain-spoken and the Sandhurst types were rather wary of him. This reputation rather endeared him to me. There were of course, other considerations for me to take into account. I had been advised that I needed to do some more time in order to adjust my Army pension so that I could be demobbed with as much financial benefit as possible. Always a careful man, I made a point of finding out my exact position in this matter. As well as this, I felt that I wanted the opportunity to give my Army career one last chance before letting it go forever. Certainly, I missed the discipline and camaraderie of military life, and also the status of being in command; so hard won in my case. However I decided that it was wisest to impress on Joy that it was my pension rights that I was protecting, for she was always intuitive of my motives. At that time, she was on Red Alert for any signs that I might disappear again on a foreign posting, leaving her at home with the children.

I wrote to Colonel Alistair Pearson on 7 August about the prospects of joining his battalion, both of us knowing it would be a temporary assignment. A couple of days later, Colonel Rowley wrote to me confirming these arrangements and also that I would need to go before a formal Board in order to officially leave my old battalion and 'D' Company. I felt a great pang of sadness to think that my ties would thus be finally severed with my old company.

An atomic bomb had been dropped on the Japanese city of Hiroshima, forcing the Japanese to end the war in the Pacific. Japan finally capitulated on 10 August, agreeing to peace only if Emperor Hirohito was allowed to remain as their leader. The 15 August 1945 was declared VJ Day. It was an occasion to celebrate and Joy and I had dinner at the Mitre Hotel in Oxford with the Colliers. I had been told to report for duty to Beverley in East Yorkshire, on the following Monday, to join Alistair Pearson's battalion. I found myself looking round at my friends and family and dreading having to leave home again, but I was obliged to complete my Army career in a proper manner.

Early in the morning on Sunday, 19 August, I left my home and family again for the Army. I travelled via London and went to Buck Lane to take my father to the Chelsea studio of the artist Norman Hepple, who had been commissioned to paint a picture of the midnight assault on Pegasus Bridge. It made me feel immensely proud to see the picture in progress and even more so, to take my father along with me. Pop was almost dumbstruck while we were there but apparently didn't stop talking about it for weeks after. Norman Hepple presented the 'cartoon' sketch he made of this painting to me, and it adorned the walls of my various homes thereafter.

I took the 08.55 train up to Beverley on the Monday morning and arrived mid-afternoon at the barracks. I was given a warm welcome from Alistair Pearson, shaking me by the hand heartily. But I knew no one else there and, after so many years of friendship and familiarity in my Army life, I found it a very bleak experience. I commented in my diary that 'the messing not bad', but I felt strangely out of place there. I was put onto general duties, dealing with farmers who had grievances about something the Army had done to their property and I noted wryly that the complaints were louder and more various now that hostilities had ceased. I was also trying to get an appointment for an Army Board to confirm my medical grading. On 24 August I was overseeing field firing training and I noted that Colonel Pearson was 'a sick man, he should be on sick leave'. Three days later I went out onto the moors for Alistair Pearson because he 'had a bad chest' and from then on for the next month took over many of the Colonel's duties. Alistair Pearson was commuting down south to Piddlehinton in Dorset where there was a military camp, originally occupied by an American Infantry Division. By August 1945, this small camp was being used by the British Army, and Alistair Pearson's work took him there frequently. He found it convenient to hand over to me his more active duties on training, and I found myself certainly relishing the role of battalion commander, albeit so briefly. I wrote in my diary 'Am liking this commanding the Battalion, it's a lot easier than Company Commander!' A week later I wrote, 'I like this Big White Chief stunt'.

Despite an overnight visit to Church Stretton to visit Joy, who had decided to take the opportunity of visiting her mother again, my dissatisfaction intensified. I was bored and listless back at the barracks and annoyed not to have heard anything about my Board. Alistair Pearson departed for a ten-day stint down in Dorset and I was pleased to have a letter from Brigadier Hugh Kindersley giving me 'a grand testimonial'. But I was not active enough to take my mind off worrying about the future. I decided I must write to S. V. Smith again to clarify the possibility of there being any prospect of a job at the Morris Motor works in Oxford. I had been strongly assured, if not actually promised, several positions by a variety of people whom I felt I could trust, and I had been so convinced that at least one of them would come up trumps. There had been my good friend Superintendent Quelch and the Chief Constable at the Oxford City Police, who had seemed so sure that I would be able to return to the Force again. But it had been made clear that I would be obliged to start from the bottom up, pounding the beat as a regular 'bobby' for a time at least. I did not relish that prospect at all for I felt I'd come too far in the past five years, and there was the question about whether or not my legs would cope with so much walking and physical activity. I could see that the possibility of securing a cushy desk job higher up in the Police Force was not a realistic proposition. It looked as if Joy had been right about S. V. Smith not being reliable. He had been so effusive when we'd first met, anxious to encourage me to consider a career at the Morris works and I had envisaged being offered a sound middle-management position there with a good salary, pension and car thrown in. But nothing had come of it.

As for the Army – I feared that I was now looked upon as 'damaged goods' with my gammy leg.

I had always been known for my physical fitness, and remembered bitterly that I had been planning to transfer to the Paras just before the accident last November. Deep within myself, I did not believe that I had the background and connections to push myself forward to find a staff job with some battalion, and certainly not without doing some overseas service, which would cause dreadful repercussions in my marriage. I didn't really see myself doing a desk job in the Army anyway, not having been such an active, hands-on commanding officer. It would probably have driven me barmy! As I turned all these things over in my mind, I could only see all the difficulties I faced and no resolutions.

But the next day I brightened up when finally told that I had a Board at 14.00 hours on Wednesday, 12 September. With something positive to aim for at last, I rushed around making arrangements to travel south. On the Tuesday I left Beverley at 08.30 and arrived back home by 17.00. I was at Slade barracks by 14.00 on the Wednesday for the Board. To my horror, I found my medical category was very nearly put back to 'D'. Only by emphasizing my activities up in Yorkshire, was I granted 'Category C' for another three months, which I felt would certainly help my pension. However, in the opinion of the Board, based on the medical evidence, they did not feel that I would ever be fit for active service again and must therefore seriously consider myself only suitable for an office orientated career. It came as a shock to me to be told this so directly. The doctors at the Wingfield had been so encouraging about my recovery that I had ventured to hope that I would gradually be upgraded medically again. But one of the officers on the Board, who knew me well, looked up from my medical report and told me, 'John, it says here that there's a strong likelihood that you will end up in a wheelchair and not be able to even walk'. This came as a slap in the face and left me seriously reconsidering my options.

I had to leave home next day to return to Beverley but commented 'maybe for the last time'. Back in Yorkshire I rang both Colonel Rowley and Alistair Pearson to try to get my gratuity increased because of the 'Category C' grading, but was told that I would only receive a 'regular gratuity'. I was stung by this and commented sourly 'wish I'd never left home'. Alistair Pearson returned from Dorset on the Saturday evening and on the Sunday, I had a chance to speak informally with him and tell him what the Board had said. He considered this and having seen me in action he said that if I could stay until March, he could promise me a job somewhere. I wrote to Joy about this and she was appalled to think I could be away from home for so long. I'd also received a letter from S. V. Smith, which was very disappointing. I tossed and turned all night thinking about what to do for the best, but there was not enough to do up in Beverley to keep me occupied and I decided to tell Alistair Pearson that I would stay on only until Christmas. I also telephoned a contact at the CAE (Command Airborne Establishment) to find out whether they knew of any jobs coming up there, for I had realized that a desk job was the only sensible option open to me now that I was disabled. A couple of weeks back in the Army, and acceptance of what the Board had told me, had forced me to digest this unpalatable fact. My recovery from the surgery on my left leg, the one worst affected, was complete and my mobility was therefore unlikely to improve beyond my current condition. But I was determined to prove the Army doctors wrong and not to end up in a wheelchair. 'Damn them all!' I thought.

It was at this time that I made the decision that the battalion at Beverley was definitely not for me, and informed Alistair Pearson, who left once more for Dorset promising that he would put in a good word at CAE for me and use his influence to place me in a desk job there. Another weekend loomed with little to do, and I found the lonely mess depressing in the extreme. My mood was not helped by another call from Joy, laying down the law. She must have been afraid that I was weakening and allowing the charismatic Pearson to talk me into staying on in the army. The only cheerful sight in the mess was a crackling fire, and I stared into the flames gloomily. 'This uncertainty regarding my future is slowly sending me crackers!' I wrote. My last day at Beverley was 24 September and I packed my things and left the following morning to travel back to Oxford by train. I sent a telegram to my holding battalion in Plymouth to ask for instructions. Thus it was, in the following three days my fate was sealed. For some reason, the Gods were against me at that time, and all the irons that I had so carefully placed in the fire in the hope that at least one of them would lead to my future career, were to fizzle out and fall to the floor in ashes.

On Wednesday 26 September, I left the house on Garsington Road at 11.00 and went first to the Police station to find out once and for all, what the chances of a job being offered to me there, really were. I was told that 'the Police outlook was terrible', and therefore I tried to accept that there was no hope of being able to return to the Force. I told myself that door was closed to me, and took the train to Bulford, lunching at Newbury on the way. I arrived in time for tea with my old regiment. They were full of their imminent posting to Palestine and I wished keenly that I was able to go with them. I was still being pulled in both directions, but knew in my heart that my physical disability would make it impossible for me to carry out my duties, to say nothing of Joy's implacable attitude to an overseas posting. I learned that my old friend Harry Styles had been made 2 I/C of the battalion and was glad for him. I travelled on to Piddlehinton by army transport for a meeting at 19.00 with Alistair Pearson. I had dinner there and Pearson was obliged to give me the bad news, that despite making enquiries on my behalf, there was no prospect of a job in the near future as far as he could see at CAE. He was genuinely sorry that he could be of no help at all in finding me a home posting. After the day I had had and all the discouraging news I'd received, I was profoundly depressed and extremely worried.

The next day, I left Piddlehinton to travel to my holding battalion in Plymouth. I truly felt I had no options left but to accept demobilization from the Army with as good a grace as I could muster. I felt very low and defeated. You can struggle and strive in life, but without that little dash of good fortune at the right time, all is in vain.

I reached 16 Holding Battalion at 17.00 hours and made myself known to a Colonel McMartrie, who greeted me informally and took me into the bar for a drink. After dinner I went to my room, too tired and depressed to think. The following morning I had an interview with McMartrie who, unless he was very insensitive, must have realized that he was looking at a man who had reached the end of his rope. A brief look at my file and the knowledge that I had been awarded the DSO would have told McMartrie what kind of man I really was, and he must have wondered why I had lost my zeal for Army life. He probably put it down to my disability. However, he was very helpful to me with advice on how to proceed. To tell the truth, I recall very little of that meeting, for I left the office a free man with no future planned for the first time in my adult life. I agreed to take a month's leave pending my demob. My financial obligations were settled and my gratuity agreed. That was it. My life in the Army was over. I took the train from Plymouth and arrived back in Oxford by 20.00. I had managed to telephone Joy and she was at the station to meet me, having been given a lift by Superintendent Quelch. She would have realized from my voice on the phone just how desolate I was feeling and, recognizing immediately that this day represented a significant moment in my life, she had ensured that I was met from the train by a good friend and that she was right there to support me.

Licking my wounds, I took comfort in my home life with my family, surprisingly comforted by my little son's delight at having his father home again. But I wrote in my diary that I was 'feeling sore over CAE letting me down'. I had harboured high hopes that with my record, the Airborne would have found a job for me in their administration. I might have suspected that it was what they called 'jobs for the boys'. I can see now that some people might think that I had a chip on my shoulder at times but, in this instance, there was probably some justification. Feeling in need of companionship, I took myself off on my bicycle to Headington to call on Kingsley Belsten. It was a Sunday and I found Kingsley in the long and pretty garden at his house, making the most of a fine autumn day. I told him all that had happened and asked for advice. Kingsley lit a pipe and was drawing on it thoughtfully, his eyes wrinkled as he considered what I had told him. 'Well John', he said, 'Your first move is to get your name down at the Ministry of Labour in Oxford and ask them to make suggestions. Look, let me turn it over in my mind and I'll let you know if I have any ideas. I just never imagined that you'd be left in this position!'

'Neither did I, Kingsley' I replied, grimacing, 'Neither did I ...'.

First thing Monday morning, I went into Oxford to the Ministry of Labour and organized the appropriate forms to fill in and then Kingsley called in at our home on the Tuesday and made the suggestion to me that would set the course for my civilian life, although at the time, it did not strike me as a very exciting proposition. Kingsley had put feelers out to his many connections in the business community of Oxford and discovered that there was a need for a responsible and able man to assist the head of the National Savings Office in Oxford. The job was a civil service post, which carried a good salary and the usual pension prospects and also had the possibility of a permit for a new car. It was this last consideration that carried the most weight with me, for in 1945 it was impossible to get a new car without an official permit from an occupation that required one. The National Savings position was such a job. Second hand cars were much sought after as a result of this law, and consequently very expensive. I decided that it was worth trying for the National Savings job and telephoned immediately.

Such was the need for people with mathematical ability and the personality to promote National Savings, which were considered to be a vital part of this country's recovery from the depredations of the war, that my application was acted on with amazing haste and two days later I was on my way to London for an interview. It all happened almost too fast for me and I found myself offered the job and then accepting it on the spot. On the way home on the train, I wondered if I had been too hasty. I felt perplexed by the suddenness of it all, the ease with which all the anxieties and difficulties of the past weeks had been resolved. I felt almost panicked by this turn of events, as if I was consigning myself to a dreary desk job when there must be something else out there that would suit an active chap like me much better. I could not conceive that I would ever find an office job challenging enough or the possibility that I could be content with such a life. It took me some time to accept that I had changed, matured, and my priorities had shifted from constantly needing to prove myself.

The following day, I called by the Police Station and saw the Chief Constable who told me that he was very willing to help me find another job with the Force. I was so undecided about taking the civil service job that I had my hopes once again raised by this, as it turned out, empty encouragement. I had a complete mind-set at that time about being part of a recognized uniformed force with all that went with it. It was all I had ever known of course, and perhaps I had a mental block about becoming a civilian again, wearing an ordinary suit of clothes and becoming an anonymous member of the public doing an office job. It was a huge transition for me and I was confused by my conflicting emotions and the loss of self-image and esteem I feared would result from becoming just another civil servant. I grasped at this last straw and went home to tell Joy all about it. She had been so pleased by the prospect of me taking the National Savings job with a peaceful and settled future, living at home and earning a good salary. My news about the prospect of a police job again upset and bewildered her. But next day I received good news about the Army gratuity being more generous than expected and Joy consoled herself by going out to spend some of it.

Against my wife's advice, I had called in at the Morris Motor works to see S. V. Smith and had been advised by him to take the Savings job. For once, Joy could say that she agreed with him. I'd heard from the National Savings office that I must have an interview at local level with a Mr Dunhill, but wouldn't be able to see him until the following week. This gave me more time for reflection. I cycled round to talk to Kingsley Belsten again, anxious to be reassured that I was making the right decision. Normally a decisive man, I found myself at a loss to know what I should do for the best. But I was looking out for a car and saw a Standard Flying Nine advertised for £230, which I considered an outrageous price. This swung me towards the Savings job, which might send a permit for a new car. I had been talking to many old friends and had come to realize that the chance of the job with the National Savings was my best option and I wrote off somewhat prematurely for a permit for a new car on the strength of it. But the permits were hard to come by and it would be some time before my application bore fruit. My only concerns were whether the job would be permanent or if I would be able to

189

move into another civil service position once the push for National Savings had passed.

Kingsley Belsten was still smoothing my path and had invited Ted Dunhill, the Commissioner for National Savings who would be my boss, to his house for me to meet informally. I liked him immediately and we became very good friends. I had to make another trip to my holding battalion on 1 November for a medical, as part of my demobilization process. I only had one more formality to go through before I was officially out of the Army. The following Saturday I went back to Plymouth for my formal demobilization which went through very efficiently, but I missed the train back and didn't get home until 04.00 the next day, 11 November. It was fortunate indeed that my old friends at the Oxford City Police Station had told me to ring them from the station any time I needed a lift home. I would have had to walk back from town otherwise, but there was always a car around to pick me up and I was very grateful for this and never forgot those kindnesses.

As I listened to the service held at the Cenotaph in London on the wireless that morning, I found the tears coursing down my cheeks and remarked that it was, 'just as well that I didn't attend a public show'. I never missed hearing this event, and later watching it on the television as the years and then the decades passed by, and I was always unable to prevent the tears welling up in my eyes for I could never forget my fallen comrades. Later that day, I wrote two letters; one was the official letter of acceptance of the job as Assistant Commissioner for National Savings in Oxford, and the other was to the Chief Constable, for I had to formally resign from the Police Force as well. Thus I was ready to begin my new life the next day, commenting 'back to civilian life'.

So began my career in the civil service, which would take me through my life right up to retirement as a Chief Executive Officer, head of the Ministry of Agriculture and Fisheries for Cornwall and the Scilly Isles in 1974. I tried to put into my office work the same conscientious attention to detail and leadership qualities that I had applied in the Army. On one of my first days at National Savings I commented in my diary that '. . . the decline of saving apparent, I'm starting at a difficult time'. That suited me fine for I liked a challenge more than anything. It was the sheer idleness of that posting in Beverley that had finished me off. Better by far to be back in civilian life, living at home with my family and doing a useful job in society boosting national savings. That is how I came to look at it.

I settled into the routine of a five and a half day week, having what was called a 'short day' on Saturdays, finishing at lunchtime. Then I was sent on a two-week course in London in early December. Back in the office on the Cornmarket in Oxford, I was disappointed that there was still no permit for a car. I had to go out visiting the various sub-offices in Banbury, Bicester, Thame and even Aylesbury – I damn well needed a car! I made a telephone call to MOWT – the Ministry of Wartime Transport, but was told that my application was still under consideration. As Christmas approached, the search for a way to obtain a car practically eclipsed everything else in our lives for I was very single-minded once I had the bit between my teeth. I got onto the Headquarters for National Savings and they gave me priority for an official car on 20 December. On the 21st I collected poultry from the train that Betty Caine had sent from Shropshire for our Christmas meals. Then on Saturday 22 December we finished for Christmas at the office and I took my colleague Ted Dunhill back home for a Scotch while Joy was out having her hair done. I recorded that, 'the children have a terrific pile of toys' for Christmas and that Joy had decorated the lounge wonderfully – 'she's very clever that way'. I wrote in my diary for 25 December, 'My first Christmas with my precious family, too wonderful for words!' We held a party for the Colliers and Wormalds in the evening and had a very enjoyable time. More friends came in for a drink on Boxing Day, but I was back to work on 27 December, for Christmas was a two-day affair in those days.

On New Year's Day, 1946, I wrote in the diary 'Yes, I'm home', replying to my hope written the previous year, that New Year 1946 would find me living at home. I added, 'Fairly settled but still get pangs for khaki'. I had a real stab of nostalgia at that time for I noted that my friend, another 'officer from the ranks', Harry Styles was now commanding the battalion. Also, I was very glad to hear that Tod Sweeney had 'got his majority'. But I did not dwell on what might have been for long, because on 2 January, I finally took delivery of an official car of my own – a Hillman 10, which I said was 'a nice looking car. Needs a good wash'. I gave it a run over to Witney to visit the office there the following day. After that journey, bowling along at the wheel of my very own car for the first time, I announced the car was 'super!' and managed to get £8 for my bicycle, deciding that my cycling days were over.

Later in that first week of January, there was a Ladies' Night at the Frewen Club; the club Kingsley had encouraged me to join the previous year. I now felt for the first time, the glow of being an accepted part of the business world in Oxford. Joy was beside me, looking lovely as usual with her grandmother's pearls at her throat. Jemima Belsten sat on my other side with Kingsley next to her, pointing out people who he would introduce me to later. I felt satisfied that I was just beginning to make my mark at the National Savings, taking on new staff and enlisting voluntary helpers. It was a cold night outside, but I knew that my Hillman car was parked ready to take us all home warm and safe. It had been so gratifying to tell Kingsley, 'We can give you and Jim a lift in our car, old man!' My thoughts took me back briefly to the year before when I had been lying broken in a hospital bed, and to the years of training my men and the dazzling success of the assault on the two bridges in Normandy. Such thoughts were immediately followed by a nightmare flashback to the carnage in Escoville, and of how many of my men had not come back to make new lives for themselves in post-war England. Joy had glanced at me and evidently noticed the far-away, intensely sad expression on my face. She put her gloved hand on mine and said, 'Is everything all right, John?' I squeezed her hand and said, 'Of course it is, darling. Never better!' And I knew that I really meant it.

Two months later, we were at Buckingham Palace for me to receive my Distinguished Service Order from His Majesty King George VI. Joy was sitting with the other relatives, resplendent in a new fur coat with a little hat to match, Terry wriggling on her knee. Two year old Penny had stayed at home in Oxford, looked after by Mary Collier.

I was standing smartly to attention out at the front, and the King was just pinning the medal onto my chest when I heard Terry's voice clearly saying, 'Mummy, what's that man doing to my Daddy?' Terry was known for his big voice and I heard Joy hushing him. She said later that several people nearby smiled and others turned round as she whispered, 'That's the King, and he's giving Daddy a medal for being brave'. If the King heard the childish voice he never wavered but nodded to me, and the next man stood forward as I moved back. But I stole a glance at where the royal party were sitting and saw Queen Elizabeth smiling.

Epilogue

John Howard transferred from National Savings to the Ministry of Agriculture & Fisheries, moving to Nottingham in 1951 where Terry and Penny grew up. That year he received the *Croix de Guerre avec Palme*, France's highest award for bravery, from the French president. Through the 1950s and 1960s Howard returned to Normandy each June and lectured to the Sandhurst Staff College on the landing zone by Pegasus Bridge. In 1961 he was a technical advisor for the making of the film *The Longest Day* in which his role was played by Richard Todd, himself a veteran of the D-Day landings. In 1964 Howard was promoted to head of the Ministry of Agriculture for Cornwall and the Scillies and moved, with his wife Joy, to Truro in Cornwall where eventually Terry settled as well.

Joy Howard suffered a major stroke in 1969 when she was only forty-nine years old and was an invalid for the rest of her life. Howard took early retirement to care for her in 1972 and they moved to Burcot near Abingdon in Oxfordshire, where Joy died in January 1986. John Howard then moved to the Mansion at Albury near Guildford (a Country House Association property) where he had the 'battlement' apartment.

Freed from the responsibilities of a house, and with Joy gone, John Howard enjoyed some contented years making several trips to Normandy annually. The Staff College trips falling victim to defence cuts in the early seventies, the Swedish Navy were quick to seize Howard's lecturing abilities and unique experience to lecture their own cadets during the Cold War years, when there was a distinct possibility of a Soviet attack on their coastline. Howard continued to lecture to the Swedish cadets almost to the end of his life.

In 1984, he assisted the American historian Stephen Ambrose with his own notes and editing for the book *Pegasus Bridge*. It was reissued as a paperback in 2001, following Ambrose's death, and became a UK best seller. Howard had made several trips to the USA both lecturing for Stephen Ambrose's group and visiting the many friends he made, especially in Texas. He suffered from the injuries he received in the car crash in November 1944 for the rest of his life, using a stick and eventually elbow-crutches, but very seldom succumbing to a wheelchair. He lived near to his daughter Penny in his last years and died on 5 May 1999.

Tom and Betty Caine left Hill Crest to move a short distance to Hazler Hill Farm, Church Stretton in the late 1940s. Betty died in 1965 but Tom lived well into his eighties in Shropshire. Their daughter Lorna married Brian Kelly, a Sandhurst graduate, in 1958. They had two children and Lorna lived in Germany for several years when her husband's tours of duty took him there. Major Brian Kelly and Lorna retired to Frimley in Surrey. She has continued to be very close to her nephew and niece, Terry and Penny.

Both of John Howard's parents lived to a good age near their family in London, celebrating their Diamond Wedding in 1972.

David Wood remained in the Army serving abroad in a variety of postings, before retiring as colonel after thirty-six years' service in 1978. He now lives in retirement with his wife Alice in Cullompton, Devon.

Tod Sweeney also stayed on for a full career in the Army retiring as colonel. He died in June 2000.

Brian Priday received a shrapnel wound to his mouth and left the Army at the end of the war. His family emigrated to Australia.

John Tillett also served his working life in the Army and retired, as colonel, to Micheldever in Hampshire. In retirement he continues to work with the Ox & Bucks museums, the Royal Green Jackets Regiment and organizes pilgrimages to Normandy.

Jim Wallwork and his family emigrated to Canada in 1957. After an amicable divorce in 1977, he married Genevieve. His work took him to many parts of Canada and the USA, but their favourite trip has always been 'meeting old friends at their favourite bridge'. Jim retired in 1984 and joined John Howard and Wally Parr occasionally as guest lecturers on tours organized by Stephen Ambrose (dubbed 'Ambrose's Performing Sea Lions' by the irrepressible Jim). Jim and Gen are now happily retired in British Columbia.

Tony Hooper, Sandy Smith and Dennis Fox all left the Army at the end of the war.

Den Brotheridge left a daughter, Margaret, who finally returned to Normandy in June 1994 to visit her father's grave and meet what she movingly called her 'Normandy family' of the *coup de main* group. Den's grave is in the churchyard at Ranville, and there is a memorial to him close by the original Pegasus Bridge, which is in the grounds of the Pegasus Memorial Museum on the Ranville side of the new bridge at Bénouville. This new museum was opened by HRH Prince

Charles in June 2000. John Howard's helmet with the bullet hole through it can be seen in the display there.

Terry Howard has two sons, Nicholas and Simon and a grandson, Sunny. He has retired and lives in Newquay, Cornwall. Penny married George Bates in 1965 and has lived in Bradford-on-Avon, Bristol and Surrey. She has two daughters, Suzanne and Kerry Joy. She was a civil servant in Bath before leaving work for some years to bring up her family. Penny returned to work to train as a chef in the late 1970s and then as a cookery tutor in adult education. George left his job in the audit department of an American oil company and in 1986 both he and Penny decided to enter the licensed trade together. They retired to Farnham in Surrey in 2001 after running two pubs, The Barley Mow and The Hankley in nearby Tilford.

Index